2740

Daylighting for Sustainable Design

Daylighting for Sustainable Design

MARY GUZOWSKI

McGraw-Hill

New York   San Francisco   Washington, D.C.   Auckland   Bogotá
Caracas   Lisbon   London   Madrid   Mexico City   Milan
Montreal   New Delhi   San Juan   Singapore
Sydney   Tokyo   Toronto

Library of Congress Cataloging-in-Publication Data

Guzowski, Mary.
    Daylighting for sustainable design / Mary Guzowski.
       p.   cm.
    Includes bibliographical references and index.
    ISBN 0-07-025439-7
    1. Daylighting. 2. Light in architecture. 3. Architectural design—
History—20th century. I. Title.
    NA2542.3.G89 1999
    720'.47—dc21   99-32791
                                                          CIP

McGraw-Hill

*A Division of The **McGraw·Hill** Companies*

1 2 3 4 5 6 7 8 9 0 DOC/DOC 9 0 9 8 7 6 5 4 3 2 1 0 9

ISBN 0-07-025439-7

The sponsoring editor for this book was Wendy Lochner, the editing supervisor was Christine Furry, and the production supervisor was Sherri Souffrance. This book was set in Matt Antique by North Market Street Graphics.

Printed and bound by R.R. Donnelley & Sons Company.

McGraw-Hill books are available at special quantity discounts to use as premiums and sales promotions, or for use in corporate training programs. For more information, please write to the Director of Special Sales, McGraw-Hill, 11 West 19th Street, New York, NY 10011. Or contact your local bookstore.

With love and appreciation to
James Lindbeck
and all things wild

In wildness is the preservation of the world.
—HENRY DAVID THOREAU

Contents

List of Projects

Alberts & von Huut
    ING Bank, Amsterdam, the Netherlands

Alvar Aalto
    Mount Angel Library, Mount Angel, Oregon
    Seinäjoki Library, Seinäjoki, Finland

Arthur Erickson
    Anthropology Museum, University of British Columbia,
      Vancouver, British Columbia

Behnisch & Partner
    German Bundestag, Bonn, Germany

Bennetts Associates
    PowerGen Headquarters, Coventry, England

Cannon & Associates
    Center for Environmental Sciences and Technology
      Management (CESTM), Albany, New York

Carlos Scarpa
    Brion Family Chapel, near Treviso, Italy
    Passagno Plaster Cast Gallery, Passagno, Italy

Clare Design
    Clare House, Buderim, Australia
    Rainbow Shores Housing, near the Sunshine Coast, Australia

Doug Pollard Architects
    Boyne River Ecology Centre (The Grange), Shelbourne,
      Ontario

Emilio Ambasz
    Lucille Halsell Conservatory, San Antonio, Texas

Kaija and Heikki Sirens
Chapel at Otaniemi, Espoo, Finland

Kaira-Lahdelma-Mahlamäki Partnership Company
The Finnish Forest Museum, Punkaharju, Finland

Kiss Cathcart Anders
Advanced Photovoltaic Systems Pilot Plant, Trenton, New Jersey

Kurt Ackermann and Partner
Office for Josef Gartner & Sons, Gundelfingen, Germany

Le Corbusier
Notre Dame du Haut, Ronchamp, France
Chapel at La Tourette, Eveux-sur-l'Arbresle, France

Louis I. Kahn
Center for the British Arts and Studies, New Haven, Connecticut
Kimbell Art Museum, Houston, Texas
Phillips Exeter Library, Exeter, New Hampshire

Luis Barragan
Capuchinas Sacramentarias del Purismo Corazon de Maria Chapel, Tlalpán, Mexico

Maki and Associates
Tokyo Church of Christ, Tokyo, Japan

Matsuzaki Wright Architects
C. K. Choi Building for the Institute of Asian Research, University of British Columbia, Vancouver, British Columbia

McDonough + Partners
Oberlin College Environmental Studies Center, Oberlin, Ohio

Meyer, Scherer & Rockcastle
MS&R Office, Minneapolis, Minnesota
Sahara West Library and Fine Arts Museum, Las Vegas, Nevada
SEI Headquarters, Oaks, Pennsylvania

Michael Maltzan Architecture and Marmol & Radziner Architecture
Mark Taper Center, Los Angeles, California

Foreword

In a few pages you're going to read that a 1981 book of mine played a part in shaping Mary Guzowski's environmental thinking. If it did, I now have reason to consider myself a success, for she has assembled in this book an array of information that can only be called vast.

Her vision is worldwide and her palette is rich: Light. Architecture. Color. Health. Design. Plants. Energy. Time. Reflection. Shading. Comfort. Form. Economy. Weather. Nature. Heat. Seasons. . . . Here we find all the ways that art and technology are learning to acknowledge, respect, and echo what the natural world long since perfected.

As I read *Daylighting for Sustainable Design* it struck me as appropriate that much of what the book is based upon is one of the earth's most common materials: sand . . . silicon. We learned to cook sand in order to get glass, and through that crystal we opened up for ourselves the hugely varied world of daylighting.

Still we go ahead, most of us, merrily trashing the planet, cheered on by all who stand to profit from our consumerism and waste. The world today presents a terribly depressing picture. But it's only half the picture. The other half can be seen in the book you now hold in your hands. Mary Guzowski is showing us the way back to an appropriate, balanced, and beautiful world.

She brings light into our lives.

Malcolm Wells

Acknowledgments

I would like to extend my sincere thanks and appreciation to the many colleagues, professional associates, friends, and family members who have helped, contributed, and supported in various ways the realization of this project. I want to thank the Department of Architecture and the College of Architecture and Landscape Architecture at the University of Minnesota for their support during the past several years. My special thanks to Michelle Juneau, whose thoughtful and thorough research assistance was invaluable. Although too numerous to list, I greatly appreciate the kindness and generosity of those individuals, firms, and photographers who made accessible their beautiful photographs and drawings—on which this book is so dependent. For their support and encouragement, I especially thank James, Bert, and my dear family and friends. Finally, I want to thank my editor, Wendy Lochner, and her associates at McGraw-Hill, and Christine Furry and the designers at North Market Street Graphics.

Introduction

In the early 1980s, I came across a small but significant book called *Gentle Architecture* by Malcolm Wells. Wells had no idea that the juxtaposition of those two words—*gentle* and *architecture*—would open for me (and undoubtedly for others) a new way of envisioning the built environment. What was significant about this modest book? Many other environmental and ecological writings and projects preceded its publication. The 1960s and 1970s were known for experimentation and explorations in passive solar, earth-sheltered, and energy-efficient architecture. It was Wells's distinction between the means and the end that was eye-opening for me. The book suggested to me that these approaches to design (passive solar, earth-sheltered, energy-efficient design, and other environmental concepts) are only ways of achieving larger architectural goals, which Malcolm Wells characterizes as "gentle architecture."

The term *gentle* added a new dimension—a new intention—to architectural design. What is an architecture that is gentle, and why is it desirable? By definition gentle is considerate, kind, patient, graceful, and even noble (from the Latin *gentilis,* "of noble birth"). The suggestion that architecture could embody these characteristics—gentleness, kindness, and grace—endows architecture with a life and spirit, and maybe even a soul. It is not enough to save energy, conserve resources, and minimize environmental impacts; it is equally important to create environments that are meaningful, humane, and worth living in. This intriguing juxtaposition of the words *gentle* and *architecture* has stayed with me through the years and is a quiet reminder that the end is about more than saving energy and important natural resources. Gentle architecture also expresses a point of view, a perspective, and an ethical way of thinking and acting in relation to the environment.

Though we may use the terms *environmental design, ecological design, sustainable design,* or even *green design* instead of "gentle architecture," all of these approaches strive to define and create more respectful relationships between humans and all of life—to create ecological relationships. Perhaps the term *ecological design* most clearly embodies the spirit of recent design efforts; however, I also find the term *sustainable design* useful because it adds the dimension of time. Although I will use both terms in this book, I suggest that the role of time and the promise of the future are explicit in the term *sustainable design* and implicit in the term *ecological design.* Sustainable design is ecological design with our responsibility to the future made apparent. The definition of the word *sustainable* is to "keep in existence, prolong, and maintain." When the word *sustainable* is combined with the word *design,* a dimension of time and its future implications are overlaid on the making of the built environment. We can no longer view architecture as disposable or something that can be thrown away as though it has little material, cultural, or emotional value. We have a responsibility to keep, maintain, and nurture environments through time. Yet the use of the term *sustainable design* upsets some people because they know full well that today it is impossible to achieve sustainability and that the term is perhaps even an oxymoron. Despite its complexities and ambiguities, I still appreciate the term *sustainable design* because of its promise for a new future.

Although we could spend significant effort exploring definitions of sustainable design (and their distinctions from environmental and ecological design), it is helpful to consider a definition found in *From One Earth to One World,* an overview of sustainable development by the World Commission on Environmental Development. Although the commission is speaking of sustainable development, I find their definition relevant and compelling because it is simple and open-ended. The commission suggests that sustainable development involves ". . . meeting the needs of the present without compromising the ability of future generations to meet their own needs."* Here the element of time is made explicit. Surely we need to make things better for today, but we also have to address tomorrow, and the next day, and on into the

---

* World Commission on Environmental Development, *From One Earth to One World* (Oxford, England: Oxford University Press, 1987), 8.

future. Yet, even in this simple definition, the use of the words "without compromising" lets us off too easily. We certainly should not compromise the future, but are we not responsible for more than that? Are we not responsible for meeting the needs of the present while also *enriching and enhancing* the ability for future generations to meet their own needs? Should we prepare a path that helps those in the future go beyond where we are today or even tomorrow? I use the term *sustainable design* despite these unanswered questions and despite its inherent complexities and contradictions; I'm also fully aware that we are nowhere near its realization—that it will probably be generations before we approach such a dream. Despite these conditions, the term is useful because it embodies a desire to go beyond where we are today. The term *sustainable design* holds a vision of the future, a hope of where we might go. As a result, the term itself becomes a reminder that we have important work to do today and tomorrow.

While there is some debate about what types of issues are included under the topic of sustainable design, a discussion by the American Institute of Architects (AIA) and the International Union of Architects (IUA) is helpful in suggesting its scope and breadth: ". . . sustainable design integrates considerations of resource and energy efficiency, healthy buildings and materials, ecologically and socially sensitive land-use, and an aesthetic sensitivity that inspires, affirms, and ennobles. . . ."* I find it encouraging that the AIA and IUA include the phrase "aesthetic sensitivity that inspires, affirms, and ennobles" in their discussion. This clearly distinguishes sustainable design from the emphasis on energy and natural resources in the 1960s and 1970s. It is this distinction that I find so compelling and so promising. It suggests to me that we need to create environments that sustain all of life—including humans and their seemingly unique aesthetic, physiological, psychological, and spiritual needs. Aesthetics, beauty, health, well-being, and quality of life are as important to sustainable design as are reducing waste, energy consumption, and environmental impacts. Yet some people are apprehensive about these nonquantifiable aspects of sustainable design. When pressed, a surprising number of people

---

* Susan Maxman and Olufemi Majekodunmi, "Declaration of Interdependence for a Sustainable Future," in *A Primer on Sustainable Building* (Snowmass, Colo.: Rocky Mountain Institute, 1995), 119.

view sustainable design as just another incarnation of energy-efficient and resource-efficient design.

Daylighting is an intriguing aspect of design in which these environmental, aesthetic, and human factors come together. Daylighting design (which can be viewed as just one topic under sustainable design) can be explored from various perspectives. It is not uncommon for different aspects of the daylighting design to be addressed by different people during the design process. In extreme cases, "building scientists" study the energy and environmental impacts of daylighting, "designers" explore its formal and aesthetic implications, and "behaviorists" address the human implications of daylighting. The problem is to synthesize and integrate seemingly disparate daylighting issues when so many considerations (and perhaps people) may be involved. Most would agree that daylighting design includes environmental, architectonic, and human factors. Yet, the emphasis on daylighting within the context of sustainable design still tends to focus on a particular set of environmental issues related to energy and natural resources. This book suggests that this triad—environmental, architectonic, and human considerations—need to be woven together in an ecological or sustainable approach to design. The inclusion of environmental factors, energy, and natural resources is critical; however, without architectonic and human considerations the vision of sustainable design is incomplete. We are well aware of the pragmatic aspects of sustainable design, but what are its poetic and experiential implications?

This book is organized into three parts: environmental, architectonic, and human considerations. Each part includes several chapters that are presented as design principles. Each chapter in turn explores related design concepts, strategies, and precedents.

Part I, Environmental Considerations, includes three chapters that focus on how external environmental factors influence an ecological approach to daylighting design. External factors include environmental forces such as sun and wind as well as environmental resources such as energy, materials, and the related issue of waste. *Chapter 1, Take a Bioregional Approach,* considers how the environmental forces of sun and wind shape daylighting and how these forces interact with climate and site. *Chapter 2, Do More with Less,* addresses how daylighting can be coupled with other design issues to reduce the consumption of energy and natural resources. *Chapter 3, Design for Evolution,* explores how daylighting design can provide adaptability and flexibility, thereby encouraging building reuse and recycling and waste reduction.

Part II, Architectonic Considerations, includes two chapters that explore the daylighting and ecological potentials of architectural form and technology. *Chapter 4, Shape Form to Guide Flow,* addresses how formal and aesthetic daylighting considerations are related to ecological design. *Chapter 5, Use Appropriate Technology,* investigates new ecological approaches to daylighting technology and the building envelope. Both of these chapters consider the role of daylight aesthetics in ecological design.

Part III, Human Considerations, includes three chapters that address how the internal environment, and its influences on human well-being, are as important to sustainable design as the external environment. *Chapter 6, Address Health and Well-Being,* considers the ecological links between light, health, and our physiological and psychological well-being. *Chapter 7, Consider Quality of Life,* addresses the relationships between daylighting and environmental, social, and spiritual connections. Finally, *Chapter 8, Learn from Nature,* explores how daylighting can be used to enhance our ecological literacy. It considers the educational opportunities of the built and natural luminous environments.

As we move through the chapters of the book we shift our attention from the world outside of architecture to the architecture itself and, finally, to the inner world inhabited by humans. Ultimately, all three layers need to be integrated into a comprehensive whole that is ecologically appropriate and meaningful for the place, program, and users. As these three layers are integrated we move toward the realization of a "living architecture," one that more fully supports and engages life. Architecture becomes a part of the ecological system rather than a filter or mediator of the environment. Through ecological architecture, a relationship can be established—connections can be made—that weave together people, environment, and design into an ecological whole.

Although this book is intended as a framework for an ecological or sustainable approach to daylighting design, it is just one way of understanding how complex layers of issues can foster and contribute to an ecological (and ultimately a sustainable) approach to daylighting. As a result, the framework should be viewed as something that is flexible, adaptable, and capable of change and growth. It is my hope that it will provide a point of departure for designers, architects, and students to reconsider the potential of daylighting in a sustainable future. The book is inherently broad in scope and suggestive in its nature. Building precedents are used to explore how designers have approached related ecological issues. The lessons of these precedents should be interpreted for the possibilities they suggest rather than their particular answers. The precedents are not always explicitly ecologically responsive. Some even blatantly ignore ecological concerns; however, all of the projects reveal—in some way—various concepts that support a sustainable approach to daylighting.

It is my hope that through this book, design professionals, students, clients, and users might better understand the *aesthetic and human implications* of a sustainable approach to daylighting as well as its more widely accepted environmental implications. Some have asked me, "Which buildings best represent a sustainable approach to daylighting?" My response is that perhaps there is no building that yet does it all—that this is a dream for tomorrow, a dream of a more sustainable future. Yet I suspect that the wisdom and clarity of architects such as Glenn Murcutt and the late Eric Asmussen well represent a vision of daylighting that weaves together environmental, architectonic, and human considerations. Their works respect the land, wildlife, and environmental forces while creating meaningful, healthy, healing, and aesthetically beautiful environments. While daylighting design is just one small piece of a much larger ecological picture, it represents an intriguing point of intersection between external and internal environmental forces that are ultimately shaped by and given meaning through architectural form. As a result, a sustainable approach to daylighting embodies not only environmental, but also rich aesthetic and human opportunities. It is my hope that the balancing of this triad (environmental, architectonic, and human considerations) will lead to a greater realization of daylighting design and will perhaps even make the built environment a little more gentle.

ENVIRONMENTAL CONSIDERATIONS

Take a Bioregional Approach

It is my feeling that living things and non-living things are dichotomous. . . . But I feel that if all living plants and creatures were to disappear, the sun would still shine and the rain still fall. We need Nature, but Nature doesn't need us.[1]

—LOUIS I. KAHN

A bioregional approach to daylighting concerns the ways that design can grow from, respond to, engage in, and benefit from the life forces of a specific region. The track of the sun, the conditions of the sky, the climate, and the nature of the site are significant bioregional forces that influence daylighting. The effects and experiences of each force are made to be place-specific through the interactions of each with the particular geology, geography, latitude, and longitude of the place. Throughout history, architectural forms and building technologies have responded to bioregional forces in ingenious and resourceful ways. The sun, the climate, and the site have all shaped architecture as much as have the materials from which our structures have been built. Survival and comfort depend on responses to the cycles of night and day, to the moods of the seasons, and to complex climatic patterns.

The sun has always provided more than light and heat; it has long held symbolic and cultural positions that have informed and guided daily life. Whether found in an Egyptian tomb, an Anasazi kiva, or a Maya temple, architecture has honored the influences of the sun and nature through forms, construction techniques, and daylighting strategies. Ancient, often-sacred structures in-

3

crease our awareness of and our respect for natural phenomena. Throughout history, stories, myths, and rituals have also reflected our relationships with the sun and with bioregional forces. Even today, there are people who still celebrate the power of the sun. A contemporary solar ritual, held by the Tewa of the desert Southwest, is described by zoologist David Suzuki and biologist Peter Knudtsun:

> During the four perilous days of solar transition, each household in San Juan Pueblo shares in a period of rest and spiritual retreat within their home as an expression of collective awe and respect for the Sun. . . . Through this and other ritual observances during the Days of the Sun, the Tewa people pay tribute to the pivotal role of the Sun's warm, nurturing presence in their lives and in the lives of all species. They have collectively remembered to honor the generous spiritual and ecological gifts of the Sun.[2]

For many people the sun is an abstraction, something to which we pay little attention. The concept that the sun is a force, which regulates and guides our lives, is often distant from our daily thinking.

What ecological, experiential, cultural, and aesthetic benefits could we gain if architecture would help reveal to us the cycles of day and night, the rhythms of the seasons, and the climates of places? The following discussion will focus on the implications of four important bioregional forces: the apparent movement of the sun (the recurring patterns of the sun), sky conditions (the moods and qualities of overcast and clear skies), climate, and site (two inseparable microclimatic influences).

APPARENT MOVEMENT OF THE SUN

Nothing influences the earth's biological systems more profoundly than does the seasonal migration of the earth around the sun, or as it appears from our point of view, the sun's migration through the sky. Transcribing days, seasons, and years, the earth cycles through the heavens. These cyclical rhythms orient us in time by marking diurnal cycles of night and day. They orient our seasons as the moods of light shift from month to month. The rhythms orient us geographically with changing altitudes and azimuths as the sun crosses longitudes and latitudes. They orient us spatially by distinguishing the cardinal directions, the movement of the sun, and the shifting colors of light. Daylighting designs that reveal the apparent movement of the sun can enhance human awareness of at least three bioregional phenomena: time of day, seasons, and geographic and spatial location.

Time of Day

The marking of time is perhaps the most obvious phenomenon that results from the apparent movement of the sun. Despite our many ways of keeping track of time (clocks, calendars, seasons, holidays, birthdays, anniversaries, etc.) time is often intangible and elusive. We have all experienced the deception of time. Depending on the activity or task, minutes can seem like hours and hours can seem like minutes. Robert Grudin, Professor of English at the University of Oregon, questions the usefulness of our methods of timekeeping in *Time and the Art of Living:* "Our units of temporal measurement, from seconds on up to months, are so complicated, asymmetrical and disjunctive as to make coherent mental reckoning in time all but impossible. . . ."[3] Many of the reasons we pay such close attention to time have to do with our increasingly busy schedules. As a result, we use time in many different ways: we have to be "on time" for a meeting, we "make time" for the children, we "give time" to a cause, and we "take time off." There is a pragmatic aspect of time that keeps our lives organized and structured.

   Yet what have we gained and what have we lost as we have become dependent on mechanical rather than biological means of tracking time? In *A Sense of Place, a Sense of Time,* J. B. Jackson suggests that we are tampering with our human biologic rhythms and our relationship to nature: "Much of our social life is temporally structured in accordance with 'mechanical time,' which is quite independent of 'the rhythm of man's organic impulses and needs.' In other words, we are increasingly detaching ourselves from 'organic and functional periodicity' which is dictated by nature, and replacing it by 'mechanical periodicity' which is dictated by the schedule, the calendar, and the clock."[4] Daylight may be one of the most important means of maintaining our biologic rhythms and connection to rhythms of nature. The experience of light is a vivid means of marking important diurnal events (sunrise, morning, midday, afternoon, sunset, and evening). The occurrence of these luminous events may seem idiosyncratic since they expand and contract with the seasons. Sunrise might occur at 5:45 A.M. in June and at 7:45 A.M. in December. Yet if we are aware of these diurnal and seasonal patterns of light we have a very accurate means of orienting ourselves in time. We usually think of clocks and calendars as our most important means of ordering time; yet the color, angle, and intensity of the daylight are also significant. After several days without a wristwatch many people would be surprised to learn how quickly their bodies become synchronized with the rhythms and changing qualities of light.

Throughout history, sacred aspects of light and time have been marked in the built environment. Today we speculate on the implications of the stone monoliths at Stonehenge, the possible celestial observatories in Chaco Canyon, and the temples at Chichén Itzá and Machu Picchu. There is also much we can learn about the sacredness of time from rituals, prayers, and myths, as Ruth Gendler explains in *Changing Light:*

> Throughout the world people have prayed at the border between sleep and waking, turned their faces east to greet the sun, chanted and taken purifying baths at dawn, offered sun salutations in the morning and sun dances on special days. . . . The traditional Catholic prayer cycle includes prayers for the eight canonical hours. Traditional Moslems pray five times a day; Jews gather in groups of ten for morning, late afternoon, and evening prayers.[5]

In *The Soul of the World,* Phil Cousineau discusses the significance of the medieval *Book of Hours:* ". . . [it] helped laypeople focus on what was sacred about the hours of their everyday life. . . . Secular time was sanctified for ordinary people as it had long been for the privileged few in the cloistered monasteries."[6] There is something inherently sacred about telling time by the quality and characteristics of light. It is less precise; we know sunrise not by a particular hour, minute, or second, but rather through an experience that results from the position of the sun in the east, its appearance over the horizon, the color of the sky, and the light reflected from surfaces. The experience of time through light is a physical and emotional sensation rather than a phenomenon that can be quantified and measured. Light tells a different story about time than does a clock or a calendar. Light is an experience of time that is about place, nature, and even the sacred.

How does architecture reveal time? Our ability to read time through light is dependent first on our awareness and knowledge of the natural cycles of daylight and secondly on whether time is realized in the built form. Ralph Knowles, in his essay "For Those Who Spend Time in a Place," suggests that room orientation is an important consideration:

> Any space that is oriented from east to west strengthens our experience of the seasons. One main wall is nearly always dark; on the other side of the space, a shadow line moves gradually up the wall then down again. To experience the complete cycle takes one year. . . . Any space that is oriented from north to south sharpens our experience of a day. Both main walls are lighted, but at different hours. Every morning, light from the east will cast a shadow that moves quickly down the opposite wall and across the floor. Every afternoon, light from the west will cast a shadow that crosses the floor and climbs the opposing wall.[7]

In order to express time through daylighting design, we must first ask, "What aspects of time are we trying to reveal?" What luminous phenomena occur over time, and how can they be captured? What moods and qualities of light in time correspond with programs, activities, and users? The room and window orientation, forms, configurations, and detailing can be shaped to realize the desired luminous effects over time. Herzog & de Meuron's Residential and Commercial Building in Basel, Switzerland, illustrates simple yet elegant ways in which the building envelope can tell time. Located on a thin parcel within the boundaries of the old medieval city, the building ingeniously captures daylight within a dense urban fabric. The thin linear floor plan opens to the south, gathering daylight and a view of the adjacent garden. Patio terraces are offset on each floor to provide access to the outside while creating a degree of privacy. In contrast to the private inner spaces, the west facade creates a public show of light in time. The glass facade is screened with a series of operable iron grilles (or shutters), which can be opened and closed by occupants on each floor. During the daytime, vertical slots within the grilles create dramatic patterns of light on the interior. Different patterns of light and shadow are created on the facade depending on which grilles are open or closed. During the night, the curving slots in the iron grilles create a shimmering effect as electric light is projected through to the street outside. The grilles of the facade can be completely closed, completely opened, or positioned in an infinite variety of patterns that create distinct luminous effects. The changing moods of the facade are as dramatic during the day as they are at night. (See Figures 1.1 and 1.2.)

The experience of time is brought to life in the Chapel at Mount Rokko through attention to window form and orientation and the dynamic movement of light in space. Located in Japan and designed by Tadao Ando, this plain rectilinear box is sited on

Figure 1.1
Daytime view of the Residential and Commercial Building in Basel.

(Margherita Spiluttini)

Figure 1.2 Nighttime view of the Residential and Commercial Building in Basel.

(Margherita Spiluttini)

a northwest-to-southeast alignment. The chapel is entered through a long tunnel of diffusing glass that opens at the end to reveal expansive views of the landscape. After passing through the tunnel, a 90° turn is required before entering the stark concrete and glass chapel. Three types of daylighting apertures in the chapel play distinct roles in the experience of time. A large expanse of glass near the center of the southwest wall admits sidelighting and provides views to an adjacent grass court. Two tall, thin vertical windows are positioned in opposite corners (on the south edge of the east wall and the north edge of the west wall). In addition, two narrow linear skylights run the length of east and west walls.

A stunning diurnal choreography of light results from the window forms, positions, and orientations in the chapel at Mount Rokko. Distinct sequences of luminous events occur over the course of a day. Under clear-sky conditions, a sliver of light enters the eastern window in the morning and washes across the surface of the south wall. As the sun moves southward at midmorning it slips through the skylights to illuminate the eastern and western walls. Daylight floods through the large south window during midday to illuminate the center of the chapel. Finally, by late afternoon, a sliver of light enters the west window to wash the northern wall. Sunlight spirals around the perimeter of the room in the morning and afternoon and fills the center of the space at midday. The experience of time and the cardinal directions are made vivid as light progresses through the space on an east-to-west journey. The simplicity of the daylighting strategies and the starkness of the space combine to create a striking experience of time. The movement of the sun is captured on the large expanses of uninterrupted walls that are washed in light.

To fully understand the diurnal and seasonal cycles it would be necessary to spend days if not months within the chapel. As a wedding chapel, visitors rarely spend more than a brief period within the space; however, even these visits capture a particular moment of light in time. Ando's Chapel at Mount Rokko is but one example of capturing time through light. There are other compelling works from architects such as Le Corbusier, Kahn, and Aalto that illustrate how we can experience time in ways vastly different from our clocks and calendars. (See Figure 1.3.)

Seasons

The daily and seasonal paths of the sun have their own rhythms and characteristics that are specific to geographic location. The different seasonal patterns in the Arctic, Temperate, and Equatorial Zones illustrate that location strongly influences our experience of light. Those of us living in the Temperate Zone often forget that not all places on earth have four distinct seasons. We

Figure 1.3 Lightscape renderings of the Chapel on Mount Rokko from morning to midafternoon during the winter solstice.

(Lars Peterssen and Tim Guyette)

take for granted the different moods and feelings that are created from changing qualities of light over the course of the year: the long, brilliant days of summer, the bittersweet return of night in the fall, the brief withdrawn days of winter, and the exhilaration of spring as light returns. Although individuals react differently to passage of time through the year, there are palpable qualities associated with the seasonal migrations of the sun. We all make our adjustments, however minor, to accommodate the changing qualities of light in time. Even the most mundane acts are affected by light—from what we eat to the way we dress to how we feel. In the summer we wake up early with the return of the sun and birds; we shield ourselves with shades and sunscreen; we spend more time outside—gardening, barbecuing, canoeing; and we savor the lingering twilight. As the sun moves southward in the fall, we grudgingly set our clocks back an hour; we prepare our gardens, homes, and ourselves for the advent of winter; we unpack our winter clothes and bedding; and we lament the loss of evening light—for our days have begun to disappear. Finally, as winter arrives, we wake in darkness and we return home in darkness; the day seems to disappear in a moment while night relentlessly lingers; we escape—if we can—on tropical vacations; we sleep more; and we wait for the return of spring.

The ancient Egyptians noted our synchronicity with the sun in *The Hymn to Ra:* "The truth of what we call our knowing is both light and dark. Men are always dying and waking. . . . A creature of light am I."[8] The sun's migration creates distinct seasonal phenomena that have long been celebrated on the summer and winter solstices and the fall and spring equinoxes. In the Northern Hemisphere, the summer and winter solstices mark the transitions of the sun's extreme northern and southern migrations. The word *solstice,* from the Latin *solstitium,* or "sun standing still," is an apt description for the time of the year when the sun terminates its journey to the north or south. The summer solstice on June 21, the longest day of the year, is traditionally a time of celebration that honors the beginning of summer. As phototropic beings, it is odd that we celebrate (often unknowingly) the return of darkness, with days becoming progressively shorter until the winter solstice on December 21. Conversely, the first day of winter is the shortest day of the year and marks the return of light,

with each day progressively lengthening until the cycle is repeated. The equinox, from the Latin *aequinoctium,* or "equal night," marks the two times of the year when the length of day and night are approximately equal. The autumnal or fall equinox is on or near September 21, while the vernal or spring equinox is on March 21. The inversion of these seasons in the Southern Hemisphere reminds us that the rhythm of the sun is an amazingly choreographed global phenomenon.

As we study the changing movement of the sun over the day and seasons it becomes increasingly apparent that architecture which responds to the rhythms of the sun must be equally dynamic. A shutter, a simple canvas awning, or drapes and curtains are not decorative elements or historic remnants, but instead, means to respond to changes in light and heat through time. The orientation, position, and detailing of a window can respond to the particular luminous and thermal needs during summer, winter, spring, or fall. Space planning and the zoning of activities can be synchronized with the moods of the seasons.

Figure 1.4 Exterior view of the Chapel at Otaniemi. (CALA Visual Resources Collection)

Figure 1.5 View of the south clerestory in the Chapel at Otaniemi.

(CALA Visual Resources Collection)

The Chapel at Otaniemi, in Otaniemi, Finland, by Kaija and Heikki Sirens captures the qualities and characteristics of the seasons through several simple daylighting strategies. The chapel is located on a remote and quiet wooded site at the University of Otaniemi. Entry to the building is through an enclosed forecourt on the south. The sanctuary is rectilinear in plan and oriented to the cardinal directions. Masonry walls enclose the sanctuary on the east and west, while delicate wood and cable trusses frame the ceiling overhead. Bilateral daylighting is admitted to the chapel through a large south clerestory and a floor-to-ceiling window on the north. All seats in the chapel are oriented to the large north window that overlooks a clearing in the evergreen forest. A single white cross is located in the center of this outdoor room. The pulpit is positioned in front of the window, which backlights the speaker. Although the voice of the speaker can be heard, he or she is cast in shadow to become of secondary visual importance to the illuminated landscape.

The detailing, scale, and placement of the north window unify the inside and outside of the chapel. The visual focus is on the landscape and its changing qualities of light. Each day and season brings a unique luminous experience as violet and blue shadows on a field of snow gradually give way to dappled green light in spring and summer. The diffuse light from the north window contrasts with the direct sunlight from the south clerestory. Changing angles, colors, and patterns of light are projected from the clerestory onto the surfaces of the chapel. The source of this light is not visible to visitors because the clerestory is located behind them at the back of the sanctuary. During the winter months, the low sunlight casts shadows from the trusses onto the ceiling plane. The dynamic pattern of light overhead during the winter shifts slowly down the walls during the year. As the sun angles increase toward summer, light grazes the east and west sides of the chapel to reveal the texture and color of the masonry walls. A translucent fabric curtain can be drawn across the clerestory to diffuse the sunlight, control glare, and reduce contrast during the summer months. The north window literally frames a visual image of the seasonal variations in the landscape, while the south clerestory marks the seasons through the play of light against the interior of the chapel.

The Sirens use views of the landscape, dynamic shading, and the color, pattern, and texture of sunlight to enhance awareness of the seasons. The lessons of the Chapel at Otaniemi illustrate that a design need not be complex to capture the joy of the seasons. The simplicity of the building form and the daylighting strategies enable visitors to focus their attention on the seasonal variations, while the plain masonry walls and wood ceiling provide surfaces on which seasonal sun patterns can be projected. (See Figures 1.4 to 1.7.)

Figure 1.6 View of the forest clearing from the sanctuary of the Chapel at Otaniemi. (Simon Beeson)

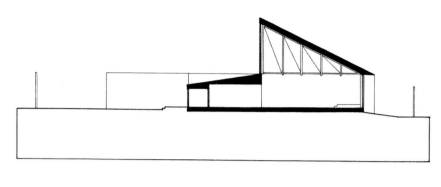

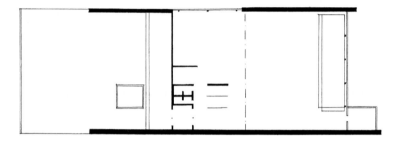

Geographic and Spatial Location

The position of the sun in the sky, the length of a shadow that is cast from an overhang onto a facade, or the shape of a patch of sunlight projected from a window are all unique to a specific geographic location in space and time. No other place on earth experiences the same luminous phenomena that you experience at this moment. We all understand that the movement of the sun tells a story about the seasons; however, less apparent is the way that it also reveals a story about where we live. We become so familiar with our own seasonal patterns of light that we have difficulty imagining the experience of the sun in different parts of the world. What would the sun tell us about our location if it were to rise and set in virtually the same place all year (as at the equator)? Would we know our location if the sun never appeared over the horizon in winter and circled overhead in the summer (as in the Arctic)? Could the brilliant robust light and high sun angles of the southern latitudes be mistaken for the low translucent light of the northern latitudes?

Although we are increasingly mobile, moving from state to state and even country to country, many of us have little awareness of the dramatic solar variations that occur on a north-south axis as we move from the Northern Hemisphere past the equator to the Southern Hemisphere. Yet daylighting design is dependent on our knowledge of how latitude and longitude affect the movement of the sun. Barry Lopez vividly describes this north-south journey and the subsequent experience of the sun in his book *Arctic Dreams:*

> Imagine standing precisely at the North Pole on June 21, the summer solstice . . . On this day the sun is making a flat 360° orbit exactly 23½° above the horizon. . . . If we could stay within the limits of this twenty-four-hour day and if you could walk down the 100th meridian, toward Mexico City, you would notice at first very little change in the sun's path around the sky. . . . When you reached the vicinity of Gary Lake . . . at 66°33′N (the Arctic Circle), the sun would have dropped low enough to touch the northern horizon behind you for the first time. . . . You would say, now, that the sun seemed more to move across the sky than around in it . . . you would start to experience "night." Short nights, only prolonged periods of twilight really, at first. . . . If you carried on, as you could if we held June 21 in suspension like this, you would begin to notice three things: the nights would get noticeably longer; the sun would stand higher and higher in the southern sky at noon (and more clearly seem to "rise in the east" and "set in the west"); and periods of twilight at dawn and dusk would shorten, until twilight would be only a passing phenomenon. The sun rises and sets sharply in Mexico City. Sunshine is a daily, not a seasonal, phenomenon, as it is in the North.[9]

Suspending time in this manner enables us to visualize the markedly different diurnal patterns of the sun on a global scale. This same north-south journey on December 21 would illustrate the sun's seasonal shifts. A dramatic winter reversal occurs which is distinguished by unending nights in the Arctic. As Lopez suggests, most of us assume that light is a diurnal phenomenon; yet the sun does not rise everyday at all places on earth.

The position of the sun not only informs us about our latitude on the north-south axis, but it also informs us about our orientation relative to the cardinal directions. If one has knowledge of the patterns of the sun it is always possible to orient oneself relative to north, south, east, and west. In *A Natural History of the Senses,* Diane Ackerman describes how as a child she used the sun for orientation: ". . . we found our direction during the day by putting a straight stick in the ground. Then we'd go about our

business for a few hours and return when the stick cast a shadow about six inches long. The sun would have moved west, and the shadow would be pointing east."[10] Each of us, whether consciously or unconsciously, uses the position of the sun to orient ourselves and to move through space. We are all aware that the migration of birds is signaled by the changing light of seasons; however, few of us note that people migrate with the sun. Ruth Gendler describes her solar migrations in *Changing Light:* "Often as I work, I follow the light around the house from writing in the morning at the desk with a window facing the eastern light to the drawing table in a studio which faces west to San Francisco Bay—in the late afternoon the sycamore trees seem to move inside the room to dance their leafy sunset dance across white walls. What shade is the shadow of green leaf and branch in July, of gray branch in late January?"[11] While this experience may mark time—morning, midday, afternoon—it also differentiates east, south, west, and north by the position and the color of light. The progression of the day is marked by different qualities of light that orient us spatially: warm yellow light from the east, crisp white light from the south, golden hues from the west, and the cool indirect light from the north. Daylight, thermal energy, and rich experiential opportunities can be captured if designers are able to tune a building to the rhythms of the sun. The sun is not only a resource but also a force that can create meaningful architectural experiences.

The Seinäjoki Library in Finland and the Mount Angel Library in Oregon by Alvar Aalto are two classic daylighting examples that illustrate how buildings can respond to a particular geographic location. Although the libraries are vastly different in many ways, the building plans and daylighting strategies are similar, yet both are responsive to place. The basic plan of each project comprises a long rectilinear bar that is oriented on an east-west axis and a protruding fan-shaped space. Both projects use a skylight monitor with an adjacent reflective surface to capture and redistribute daylight. At Seinäjoki, the fan and monitor are oriented to the south, while at Mount Angel both are rotated 180° to face north. The roles of the monitor and reflective surface are distinct in each geographic location. At Seinäjoki, which is

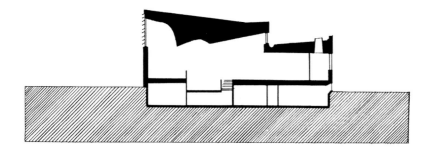

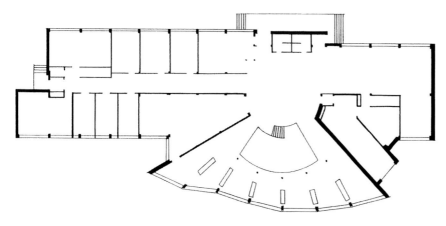

Figure 1.9 Plan and section of the Seinäjoki Library.

(Donovan Nelson)

located at 63° north latitude, the length of day during the winter is extremely short, and the sun barely rises over the horizon. In summer, days are extremely long, dusk occurs for only a brief period, and there is no night as we commonly know it. The south-facing monitor contains a series of white horizontal louvers mounted on the exterior of the glass. Louvers are positioned at a 45° profile angle to prevent the high summer sunlight from entering the library while admitting the low winter sun to be reflected off of the ceiling to the space below. A similar effect is achieved in the summer; however, sunlight is first reflected off the small exterior louvers and redirected to the ceiling surface where it is reflected for a second time to the stacks below. Additional views of the sky and a small amount of indirect daylighting are provided by the north clerestory window over the circulation desk. The section and form of the monitor as well as the reflective ceiling and louvers directly respond to the seasonal sun angles for the northern latitude at Seinäjoki. (See Figures 1.8 and 1.9.)

Even though the section and form of the monitor at Mount Angel is similar to Seinäjoki, it plays a very different daylighting role. Since the monitor is rotated 180° to the north, no louvers are needed to control direct sunlight. Only indirect light reflects off of the ceiling to the spaces below. Given the predominantly overcast skies in Oregon, it is peculiar that Aalto was so cautious about controlling sunlight, which is rare from fall through spring. Aalto could have oriented the monitor to the south and controlled the summer sun; however, given the plan configuration, this would have wreaked havoc on the section. The north-sloping topography and views that overlook agricultural lands were undoubtedly factors in rotating the fan and monitor 180° to the north. Given the pre-

Figure 1.10 Interior view of the north clerestory at the Mount Angel Library.

(Steve Weeks)

dominantly overcast skies, some play of sunlight (if held within the monitor) would have provided visual relief and delight during the occasionally sunny days in winter. Yet the daylight monitor at Mount Angel turns its back to the sun and captures the naturally diffuse light from the north. In contrast, Seinäjoki use the louvers and reflective ceiling to create diffuse illumination. Aalto modifies the window orientation, detailing, and shading to respond to sky conditions, climate, and site in these distinct geographic locations. (See Figures 1.10 and 1.11.)

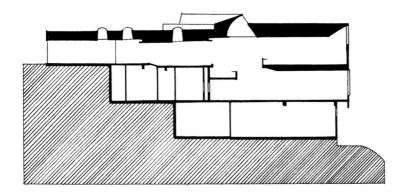

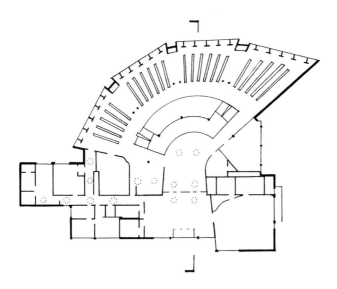

Figure 1.11 Plan and section of the Mount Angel Library.

(Donovan Nelson)

SKY CONDITIONS

In *Genius Loci,* Christian Norberg-Schulz describes the condition of the sky as a way of distinguishing one place from another: "Although the sky is distant and intangible, it has concrete 'properties,' and a very important characterizing function. In daily life we take the sky for granted: we notice that it changes with the weather, but hardly recognize its importance for the general 'atmosphere.' It is only when we visit other places that we experience the difference."[12]

To understand the impact of sky conditions on the experience of daylight, a designer must study its changing colors, qualities, and quantities. What are the specific characteristics of the sky conditions on a daily and seasonal basis? Do they change from moment to moment, day to day, or season to season? Are the skies predominantly overcast, clear, or partly cloudy? Do variations occur from morning to midday to afternoon? These questions encourage us to explore the unique qualities and characteristics of light in a particular place. The experience of the sky is one way in which we begin to inhabit and truly know the region in which we live.[13] The following discussion will address three ways that sky conditions strengthen our understanding of the bioregions in which we live: *cosmic order* (our relationship to the universe through diurnal cycles of day and night), *place* (connections to the particular qualities and experiences of a region), and *color and form* (the ways architecture is revealed or concealed by the light and colors of place).

Cosmic Order

Today we have fewer reasons to look to the skies than did our ancestors. Through time and across cultures, agricultural and ceremonial events were marked not only by the passage of the sun, but also by the changing sky conditions. Even today each season evokes particular experiences and activities related to sky conditions. The gray sky of fall signals a time for harvesting and preparation for the pending cold. The crisp blue sky after a winter snow signals a drop in temperatures. The soft misty sky of spring announces the rain and welcomes the return of plants and growth. The heavy humid sky of summer draws us to the lakes and rivers. We also look to the skies to plan our day; to prepare for a Fourth of July weekend, to check whether to take an umbrella to work, or to decide if the garden needs to be watered.

In the past, the sky also played cultural and symbolic roles. In *Topophilia,* geographer Yi-Fu Tuan explains that the sky was considered a symbol of life and death in ancient Egypt: "The sun, brilliant in the cloudless sky, is another fact of overwhelming importance to the Egyptian. He hates darkness and the cold. An ancient prayer called for the triumph of the sun over cloud and storm. Cloud may yield rain but Egypt does not depend on rain. Cloud hides the sun and, in winter, causes a sensible drop in temperature. . . . The scantily clad Egyptian feels the cold which, together with darkness, is a premonition of death."[14] Yi-Fu Tuan later explains the mythological powers of the sky in many ancient cultures:

> Among objects the sun, the sky, the earth, and corn play prominent roles in pueblo Indian mythology. . . . The sky is another important spiritual being. . . . To the Mesopotamians, *An* symbolized the majesty, authority, and power of the overarching sky, but it was a power at rest. *Enlil,* as air— the turbulent element between heaven and earth—embodied active power. He was the executor of the will of the gods. . . . The Turko-Tartars imagine the sky as a tent or roof, protecting the earth and life on earth. . . .[15]

Although the sky may no longer hold the mythological power of the past, it still plays an important yet often unconscious role in our daily lives. Architecture that celebrates the moods of the skies and its qualities over time can help us to better observe and experience local, regional, global, and even, as Tuan suggests, ancient cosmological patterns and relationships.

Architecture that considers the light of day must also consider the light of night. We might think of daylighting design as concerning those hours between sunrise and sunset when all is visible; however, daylighting design is also about the transitions from day into night and night into day. Sunrise and sunset are two luminous moments that are frequently noted and celebrated. The glorious moments when the sun first disappears at night or first appears in the morning are difficult to overlook. Robert Grudin argues in *Time and the Art of Living* that despite our attention to sunrise and sunset we miss the more subtle and compelling experiences that either precede or follow these two luminous events:

We are not great connoisseurs of the two twilights. We miss the dawning, excusably enough, by sleeping through it, and are as much strangers to the shadowless welling-up of day as to the hesitant return of consciousness in our slowly waking selves. But our obliviousness to evening twilight is less understandable. Why do we almost daily ignore a spectacle (and I do not mean sunset but rather the hour, more or less, afterward) that has a thousand tonalities, that alters and extends reality, that offers, more beautifully than anything man-made, a visual metaphor of peace? To say that it catches us at busy or tired moments won't do; for in temperate latitudes it varies by hours from solstice to solstice. Instead I suspect that we shun evening twilight because it offers two things which, as insecurely rational beings, we would rather not appreciate: the vision of irrevocable cosmic change (indeed, change into darkness), and a sense of deep ambiguity—of objects seeming more, less, other than we think them to be.[16]

While the threshold between day and night might be celebrated, the night itself is often associated with mystery, the unknown, and sometimes fear. We can even, if we choose, ignore the night by slipping from the light of day to the electric light of night. Yet the transitions of the sky from day to night and back to day are fundamental ecological phenomena that orient us in time and place. We generally think that the light of day reveals the sky and that the darkness of night "falls" to cover the sky. Justin Toms describes a more accurate perception of this diurnal transition in his essay "Night into Day into Night":

The light, in fortifying its hold on the day, put all of its energy on the horizons and left itself thin at the top of the dome. At last the day could hold out no longer and, opening up to the night sky with a great yawn, it fell back, yielding to the greater presence of night. . . . Night is always there, always surrounding us, like a mother's gentle arms. Day comes and goes for us, but the stars are always there no matter what is going on in our earthly neighborhood. The veil is the light of day. Day veils the true sky.[17]

Daylighting design can enhance our awareness of the qualities and characteristics of the sky's transitions between dawn, day, dusk, twilight, and night and can encourage us to pause and to note ecological and cosmological phenomena.

The Chapel of St. Ignatius at Seattle University in Washington by Steven Holl explores the sacred and cosmological implications of daylighting as well as the transitions from day to night. Holl describes the Jesuit chapel as a gathering of different lights:

The metaphor of light is shaped in different volumes emerging from the roof whose irregularities aim at different qualities of light: East facing, South facing, West and North facing, all gathered together for one united ceremony. Just as in the Jesuits "spiritual exercises," no single method is prescribed—"different methods helped different people . . . ," here is a unity of differences gathered into one. Each of the light volumes corresponds to a part of the program of Jesuit Catholic worship. . . . At night, which is the particular time of gatherings for mass in this university chapel, the light volumes are like beacons shining in all directions out across the campus.[18]

Different types and qualities of light are used throughout the chapel. These include direct sunlight (when available), indirect daylight, colored light (through colored lenses over the windows), and reflected and projected daylight and electric light. Holl used different types of light in the following spaces: processional ramp (natural sunlight), narthex (natural sunlight), nave (a yellow field with a blue lens on the east and a blue field with a yellow lens on the west), Blessed Sacrament Chapel (an orange field with a purple lens), choir space (a green field with a red lens), Reconciliation Chapel (a purple field with an orange lens), and the bell tower and pond (projecting and reflecting night light).

The rectilinear plan of the chapel is divided into a variety of distinct luminous experiences. Daylighting strategies can be grouped into three general categories: skylight monitors, indirect sidelighting, and direct sidelighting. Each of these strategies is modified to create varied luminous qualities based on program and activities. The overall pattern of daylighting includes indirect sidelighting (or reflected daylight) on the east and west, direct sidelighting on the south, and a combination of direct and indirect toplighting from seven skylight monitors oriented in varying directions. The entry is located at the southwest corner of the building adjacent to a shallow reflecting pool. Small oval windows of different sizes and configurations slice through the wooden doors to cast pools of light on the walls and floor of the entry foyer. The effect is reversed at night when the small oval windows emit light to the outside and provide glimpses of the interior. A monitor with diffusing glass is also recessed over the entry to mark the transition between the foyer and the processional ramp that leads to the baptismal font and the entry of the chapel. At night this monitor becomes a beacon illuminated with

Figure 1.12   Exterior view of the Chapel of St. Ignatius at midday.
(Nicholas McDaniel)

colored light which is reflected from the inside out. Small vertical and horizontal windows of cast glass are located along the west wall of the ramp. Backlit from the outside during the day and from the inside at night, the diffuse light and absence of color in this area contrast in stark simplicity to the colored light of the chapel.

The narthex (located to the east of the entry) is the only area in the chapel where visitors have direct views of the site. A large three-dimensional window, composed of south and west glazing, is located in the southwest corner of the narthex. The glazing of the window is sandblasted at the top, bottom, and sides to create a clear opening that frames the landscape. A thin adjacent window provides a vertical counterpoint. In contrast to the sidelighting on the south, a skylight monitor washes the north wall of the narthex. The otherwise diffuse glazing of the monitor has one small pane of green glass that casts a playful and changing patch of colored light on the wall. At night, the windows and monitors

Figure 1.13 Exterior view of the Chapel of St. Ignatius at night.

(Nicholas McDaniel)

project beautiful patterns of color and light to the sky and the surface of the reflecting pool.

The sanctuary has very different qualities of light that are essentially created with sidelighting. One of the main strategies is the use of reflective surfaces placed inside windows and colored on the back (so that the painted surface is not visible from the interior). These surfaces capture light from the window and mysteriously reflect colored light into the space. For example, a large, high window is placed above the altar on the east. Two solid planes with thin slots of various sizes and forms are suspended in front of the window. The slots, which are backlit, appear to either recede or advance depending on the position of the viewer and the daylighting conditions. The backs of the planes are painted with a high-chroma yellow paint that reflects colored light to the adjacent walls and floor. A single blue window behind one of the open slots creates a contrasting wash of blue light. The layered windows and planes create a three-dimensional quality of light that results from the illumination of the void between the two surfaces. The source of light is shielded from the visitor on both the east and west sides of the chapel, creating a mysterious luminous effect.

The final public space in the Chapel of St. Ignatius is the small Blessed Sacrament Chapel to the north of the main sanctuary. In many ways, the chapel is a sampler of daylighting strategies. Hidden light sources, light from above, reflected color, wallwashing, diffused light, and transitions from day to night all contribute to the luminous qualities of the space. A skylight monitor with a purple lens is combined with an orange-painted surface below the skylight to reflect warm light along the north wall. Depending on the sky conditions and time of day, changing patterns of light and

Figure 1.14 Plan of the Chapel of St. Ignatius.

(Stephen Holl Architects)

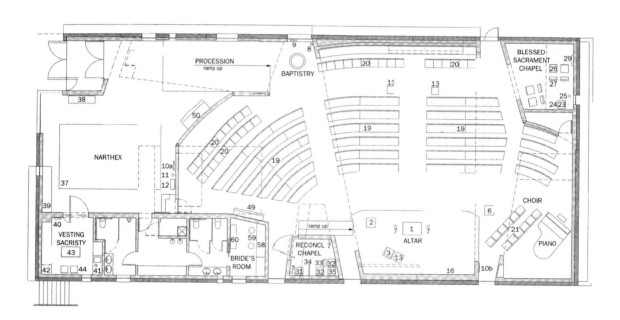

LITURGICAL FURNITURE LEGEND

1. Altar	12. Stand for Book	26. Chairs for Meditation	40. Clock
2. Ambo	13. Ancillary Tables	27. Prie-dieu	41. Sacrarium
3. Presider's Chair	14. Vessels for Mass	28. Candle Offering	42. Censer cabinet
4. Deacon/Minister Chair	15. Vessels for Holy Oils	31. Confessor's Chair	43. Vesting Table
5. Acolyte Seating	16. Fixed Cross (above)	32. Penitent's Chair	44. Chairs49. Marian Shrine
6. Cantor's Stand	19. Pews	33. Penitent's Prie-dieu	50. Patron Shrine
7. Candle Stand	20. Movable Chairs	34. Moveable Privacy Screen	58. Vanity Table
8. Pascal Candle Stand	21. Choir Chairs	35. Table/Book Stand	59. Vanity Stool
9. Ambry for Holy Oils	23. Tabernacle	37. 14' x 21' Carpet	60. Bench
10. Processional Cross	24. Tabernacle Stand	38. Brochure Rack	
11. Candle for Book	25. Tabernacle Lamp	39. Bench	

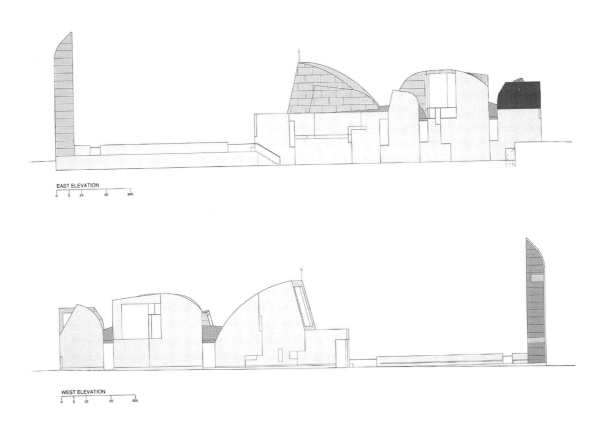

EAST ELEVATION

WEST ELEVATION

color animate the space. In the evening, apertures in both chapels are illuminated with electric lighting to project the color and light of the interior to the night sky. The exuberant daylighting design in the Chapel of St. Ignatius may lack the refinement and simplicity of strategies found in chapels by Le Corbusier, Scarpa, and Aalto, but Holl successfully captures transcendent qualities of light that speak to our inner spirituality as well as to our relationship to the outer cosmos. (See Figures 1.12 to 1.20.)

Figure 1.15 Elevations of the Chapel of St. Ignatius. (Stephen Holl Architects)

Place

Daylighting, perhaps more than any other phenomenon in architecture, is place-specific. The color, angle, and quality of light are dependent on the particular latitude, sky conditions, and climate of a given locale. To understand this relationship, we must begin by asking, what is the light of a particular place? How is "Seattle light" distinct from "Minneapolis, Phoenix, or Miami light"?

Figure 1.16   Detail of the
front door to the Chapel
of St. Ignatius.
(Nicholas McDaniel)

Figure 1.17   Processional
ramp leading to the
sanctuary.
(Nicholas McDaniel)

Figure 1.18 View to the south from the narthex of the Chapel of St. Ignatius.

(Nicholas McDaniel)

Figure 1.19 View of the altar in the Chapel of St. Ignatius.
(Nicholas McDaniel)

Figure 1.20 View of the Blessed Sacrament Chapel.

(Nicholas McDaniel)

Although Seattle and Minneapolis have a similar number of overcast days each year, the distribution of these days varies dramatically over the course of the year. Seattle light has seasonal patterns with overcast skies from fall to spring and predominantly clear skies in the summer. In contrast, Minneapolis sky conditions vary dynamically from day to day, and even hour to hour, creating volatile diurnal change. We must come to understand and experience the luminous qualities of a region before we can use daylighting to enhance these qualities.

The Seabird Island School in Agassiz, British Columbia, designed by Patkau Architects of Vancouver, skillfully uses daylighting to reveal the characters and qualities of place. The school is located on the Salish Indian Reservation at the delta of the Fraser River and the coastal mountain range. The long linear school is sited on the north edge of a clearing to complete and unify a circular grouping of community buildings. The region has a temperate climate, with cool, overcast winters and clear, mild

Figure 1.21 South facade of Seabird Island School.

(James Dow)

summers. During the winter, cold winds are funneled into the valley from the mountains to the north, temperatures are moderate, and low levels of illumination are available due to the prevailing overcast skies. In response, the building is oriented on an east-west axis, with the north and south facades differentiated to address the particulars of climate and site. A massive roof wraps the north side of the building to form a protective barrier to cold winter winds, while the south side celebrates a connection to the site and community buildings through extensive glazing and a colonnade.

The south facade of the school plays a critical role in creating an interaction between the students and the site. Operable windows and glass doors create an undulating rhythm that allows alternating views of the landscape, adjacent gardens, and community spaces. Daylight, wind, and the sounds and smells of the site are emitted through this permeable skin. All visitors must

Figure 1.22 Aerial view of roof and surrounding mountains.

(James Dow)

1. community buildings
2. village common space
3. bridge
4. dry creek bed
5. fire pit
6. Seabird Island School
7. outdoor play areas
8. traditional pit house
9. teaching gardens
10. salmon drying racks
11. bus & passenger drop-off
12. parking

Figure 1.23   Site plan of Seabird Island School.

(Patkau Architects)

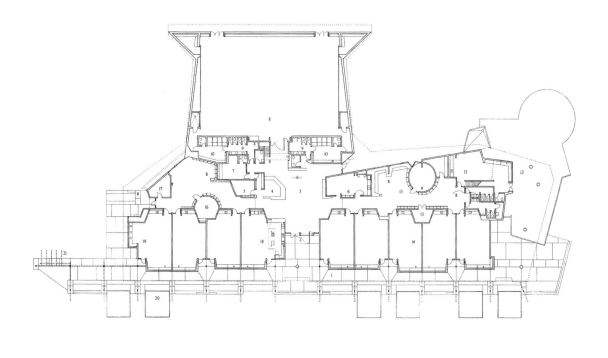

Figure 1.24 Plan of Seabird Island School.

(Patkau Architects)

1 covered porch	12 covered play area
2 entrance	13 storage
3 common area	14 classroom
4 reception	15 library/resource area
5 principal	16 reading room
6 staff room	17 workroom
7 health/counselling	18 home economics room
8 gym/community hall	19 science room
9 washrooms	20 teaching gardens
10 showers/change rooms	21 drying racks
11 kindergarten	

0 1 3 6m

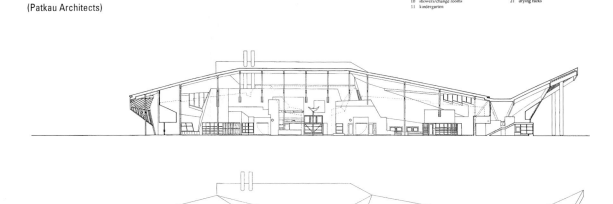

Figure 1.25 Sections of Seabird Island School.

(Patkau Architects)

Figure 1.26   View of the west library reading area in the circulation spine.

(James Dow)

pass under or along a colonnade on the south, which acts as a transitional space between the inside and outside. Physical and visual interactions between the community and students are encouraged by the openness of the facade and the layers between the inside and outside. The deep overhang of the colonnade controls direct sunlight.

On the south side of the school a large clerestory reaches to the sky, gathering daylight for the inner reaches of the building and marking the centrally located entry. A north-south circulation spine links the classrooms and accommodates open libraries on the east and west. High clerestory windows provide indirect illumination, while low irregularly shaped windows provide views of the agricultural fields and mountains to the north. The east facade has a huge second-story window that slopes upward and outward in gesture to the mountains. This second-story space is discovered only after passing through the kindergarten room and up a narrow flight of stairs. It is a place of reflection that visually and literally projects one into the surrounding landscape. Directly below this soaring space is a classroom with a series of smaller windows and a glass door which allows one to move directly outside to the adjacent play area. The distinct forms and sizes of the windows on each facade mark the cardinal directions and orient one to the land.

Each window in the Seabird Island School creates a different opportunity to engage the site and community. The building appears to have been pushed and pulled by a series of dynamic forces that move the occupant inward and outward to both reveal and conceal the relationship to place. The design of the building envelope plays a decisive role in expressing the forces of the site and in defining the interaction between inside and outside. Even the cladding expresses the different forces acting on the site. The north side of the building is enclosed with cedar shingles, while the frame on the south side is infilled with white-stained plywood, windows, and glass doors. The protective wrapping of the north is opened on the south to connect the interior to the site and community.

The shading devices used on the building are simple fixed overhangs that vary in scale and depth depending on the orientation. Although the overhangs control heat and light, they also define intermediate rooms. On the east, a large overhang blocks direct sunlight in the summer months and creates a sheltered outdoor space which mediates between the inside and the outside play area. This is also true of the shading device on the south facade, where the colonnade can be used as an outside classroom that connects to the teaching gardens. The roof is removed at the outer edge of the overhang on the south to provide a gentle transition from the site to the building and to increase the opportunity for daylighting to reach the classrooms. Alternating rhythms of light and shadow are created while still providing protection from the rain and sun.

Figure 1.27 View of a classroom at the Seabird Island School.

(James Dow)

The Seabird Island School illustrates many simple yet elegant ways of using daylighting to enhance the relationship to place. There are no new technologies and no sophisticated control systems at Seabird. Its innovation results from the inseparable links between the daylighting, occupants, and place. According to Patkau Architects: "Our approach to design is conditioned by an emphasis on the 'particular.' We have adopted this emphasis in an attempt to balance the tendency towards generalization, which is becoming an increasingly dominant characteristic of Western culture. We begin with a search for the 'found potential' of a project—a search for those aspects of the site, climate, building context, program, or local culture, etc., that will facilitate the development of an architectural order which is specific to circumstance."[19] (See Figures 1.21 to 1.27.)

Color and Form

Sky conditions also influence the color and quality of daylight, which in turn affect the rendering of architecture and its expression of place. Imagine the color of light in Tucson, Charleston, or Portland. Each city has a tangible palette of daylight colors that are particular to the sky conditions of its region. Sky conditions also affect our understanding of form. On a clear day colors are vivid and saturated; light and shadow emphasize depth and three-dimensional qualities. Facades are animated as sunlight reveals materials, texture, and detail. On an overcast day, daylight is subdued and soft, with only subtle distinctions in light and shadow. As a result, texture and detail are de-emphasized, forms seem two-dimensional, and colors appear monochromatic and dull.

The moods and qualities of the architecture change with the sky conditions. A building can be transformed from a somber, monolithic, and monochromatic structure under overcast conditions to an exuberant, articulated, and polychromatic structure under clear skies. Our perceptions of color change depending on the sky conditions, illuminance levels, and time of day. A red surface might shift from scarlet to vermilion to maroon as skies vary from clear to overcast and illuminance levels increase or decrease. The west facade of the Weisman Art Museum, designed by Frank Gehry, is like a stainless steel canvas on which the changing colors of light and time are painted. The dramatic sky conditions in Minnesota—which often vary from moment to moment—create a constantly changing field of color and light. The facade is particularly stunning as it reflects the setting sun across the Mississippi River. All of us have experienced shifts in our moods as the quality of light and our perceptions of color change with the sky conditions. Alexandra Tyng captures some of these color associations in *Louis I. Kahn's Philosophy of Architecture:*

> The different aspects of light are usually perceived as colors. The bluish light of a cloudy day might represent sobriety and depression. The build-up of tension before the drama of an approaching storm is symbolized in the angry and threatening qualities of purple light. The sun breaking through the clouds afterward has the subtle luminosity of silver. Colors encourage the play of the imagination. As they occur in nature, they are the sources of inspiration for the architect who composes a variety of spaces, each with its own mood and purpose. . . . Light's ability to give life to architecture is dependent on its own life, its changeability.[20]

Louis I. Kahn allowed daylight to color his spaces: "I have no color applied on the walls in my home. I wouldn't want to disturb the wonder of natural light. The light really does make the room. The changing light according to the time of day and the seasons of the year gives color. Then there are reflections from the floors, the furniture, the materials, all contributing to make my space made by the light, mine. Light is mood."[21] (See Figures 1.28 and 1.29.)

Different sky conditions also provide different illuminance levels and daylight distributions. In a predominantly overcast region, daylight is fairly evenly distributed throughout the sky vault, with the greatest illumination levels at the zenith. Conversely, under clear-sky conditions, the maximum amount of daylight is at the location of the sun, which moves throughout the sky over the course of the day. In addition, much greater quantities of daylight are available under clear-sky conditions. To achieve the same quantity of daylight, the size of a window could be smaller in regions with predominantly clear rather than overcast skies (although the quality of light would be different). Window orientation can also influence the color and quality of light. Under clear skies, the color of light is cooler at midday and warmer in the morning and afternoon, while little distinction in color is experienced in different orientations under overcast skies. Sky conditions may also influence whether toplighting or sidelighting is used. For example, under overcast skies, toplighting is the most

Figure 1.28 West facade of the Weisman Art Museum during midday.
(Rosemary D. Dolata)

Figure 1.29　West facade of the Weisman Art Museum at sunset.

(Rosemary D. Dolata)

Figure 1.30   Exterior view
of the Kimbell Art
Museum.
(Leon Satkowski)

appropriate strategy if maximum illumination is desired. In contrast, under clear skies, the maximum illumination is gathered from windows that track the movement of the sun. Daylighting can respond to sky conditions only if seasonal and diurnal patterns are studied and understood over the course of a year. These patterns can be used to develop appropriate design strategies that respond not only to seasonal variations, but also to programmatic activities and human comfort.

Louis Kahn's designs of the Kimbell Art Museum in Texas and the Center for British Art and Studies in Connecticut respond to sky conditions in distinctly regional ways. The thin linear skylight and reflector at the Kimbell Art Museum elegantly redirects the harsh Texas sunlight to the ceiling vault, which in turn redistributes a soft indirect illumination to the space below. A series of linear galleries and repetitive skylights are oriented on a north-south axis. Exterior sculpture galleries, which frame the intense blue sky, are periodically carved out of the interior of the building. A simple wire grid for vegetation is suspended over the sculpture courts to provide seasonal shading. Kahn explains that he contrasts the "silver light" of the gallery with the "green light" of the outdoor sculpture garden:

This light will give a glow of silver to the room without touching the objects directly, yet give the comforting feeling of knowing the time of day. Added to the sky light from the slit over the exhibit rooms, I cut across the vaults, at a right angle, a counterpoint of courts, open to the sky, of calculated dimensions and character, marking them Green Court, Yellow Court, Blue Court, named for the kind of light that I anticipate their proportions, their foliation, or their sky reflections on surfaces, or on water will give.[22]

Colors are not applied to the interior of the spaces; instead Kahn uses reflected or filtered daylight to create varied color experiences. The deeply recessed entry, thin linear skylights with reflectors, and small courtyards protect the artwork and visitors from the intense sunlight that results from the clear sky conditions of Texas. (See Figures 1.30 to 1.32.)

Figure 1.31 View of a gallery at the Kimbell Art Museum.

(Craig Johnson/CALA Visual Resources Collection)

Figure 1.32 View of a courtyard at the Kimbell Art Museum.
(Terri Meyer Boake)

At the Center for British Art and Studies in New Haven, Connecticut, we find very different daylighting strategies that respond to a cooler climate with more frequently overcast skies. The section and plan of the building reveal a series of nested spaces with galleries along the perimeter and interior courts. The sizes of the apertures at the Center for British Art are significantly larger than at the Kimbell due to lower levels of illumination. Skylights that have external louvers, diffusing glass, and deep wells illuminate the galleries. Two rows of galleries encircle the inner courtyards. On the perimeter of the building, some of the galleries have windows that provide views of the site, with wooden shutters providing solar control. Galleries on the inside have large interior windows that borrow daylight from the courtyard, allow visitors to observe the public gathering spaces, and provide visual relief. Direct sunlight is permitted in the courtyards, which provides an animated counterpoint to the diffuse illumination in the galleries.

The exterior of the Center for British Art is brushed stainless steel and glass. This provides a soft, diffuse, two-dimensional quality, in contrast to the dramatic play of light and shadow on the exterior and in the colonnade at the Kimbell Art Museum. The Center for British Art requires strategies that respond to both clear and overcast conditions. The exterior louvers, diffusing glass, and deep skylights control the sun, while the large apertures still admit significant levels of illumination under overcast skies. Sunlight in the galleries is controlled and filtered by the tiny apertures and reflectors at the Kimbell, while light and shadow are celebrated in the colonnade and sculpture courts. Although the programs are similar, the daylighting strategies for each project respond to the prevailing sky conditions of its region. (See Figures 1.33 and 1.34.)

Figure 1.33   Exterior view of the Center for British Art and Studies.
(Dale Mulfinger/CALA Visual Resources Collection)

CLIMATE AND SITE

Finally, a bioregional approach to daylighting considers climatic and site forces. The recurring weather patterns that constitute the climate of a region are altered by the features of a site to create a microclimate. It is the microclimate (or site-specific experience of climate) which most concerns designers, as Kevin Lynch explains in *Site Design:* ". . . the designer is particularly interested in the micro-climate—that detailed modification of the general climate which is brought about by topography, cover, ground surface, and structural form. This is the climate with which people are in contact, and it is the one that the designer can actually modify."[23] Climate and site are inseparably linked and most easily studied in tandem. A good working knowledge of the microclimate is needed before daylighting design, which requires both climatic and site analyses, can begin. Climatic factors to consider might include annual temperatures, precipitation, relative humidity, sky conditions, and prevailing winds. Site factors might include topogra-

Figure 1.34 View of a gallery at the Center for British Art and Studies.

(Dale Mulfinger/CALA Visual Resources Collection)

phy, structures, vegetation, water features, sources of sound or noise, and views. This information can be used to determine seasonal patterns that influence lighting, heating, and cooling as well as the integration of daylighting with contextual issues such as view, acoustics, or other amenities. Larger climate and site issues concern how daylighting can be used to establish a relationship between the site, architecture, and occupants. Subsequently, there are three microclimatic factors we will consider: the relationship between the building and the environment, solar access, and human comfort.

Relationship to the Environment

Daylighting is a critical factor in determining the quality of the relationship between people and the environment. The following depend primarily on the design of windows: the degree of connection or separation between inside and outside; physical or visual contacts with the site; and access to the sun, wind, sound, and smells. Advances in glazing technologies and mechanical systems during the early twentieth century have enabled designers to open buildings to the site in ways that were not feasible in the past. Frank Lloyd Wright describes this new relationship between inside and outside in *The Natural House:* "This dawning sense of the *Within* as *reality* when it is clearly seen as *Nature* will by way of glass make the garden be the building as much as the building will be the garden: the sky as treasured a feature of daily indoor life as the ground itself. . . . Walls themselves because of glass will become windows and windows as we used to know them as holes in walls will be seen no more."[24] The barriers between inside and outside are even more refined today than in Wright's time with the development of superwindows and new glazing systems. Yet just because technology has made it easier to minimize the distinction between inside and outside does not mean this is always appropriate or desirable. The degree of environmental separation or connection depends on conceptual, experiential, and functional concerns. An expansive window that minimizes the boundaries between inside and outside may be appropriate in one area of a building, while a tiny, deeply recessed window that emphasizes enclosure and differentiates the inside and outside might be appropriate in a different area. The challenge is to develop a correlation between the window form, the desired degree of connection to the environment, and the thermal and luminous considerations for the microclimate.

The Atlantic Center for the Arts in New Smyrna Beach by Thompson & Rose Architects illustrates daylighting strategies that create different types of relationships between inside and outside, at the same time responding to program and microclimate. The compound of buildings is gently inserted into the dense Florida jungle of scrub oaks, pines, and palmetto trees. Five of the buildings are clustered together: the gallery/theater and the dance studio are sited to the east; the sculpture and painting studios are centrally located; and the music studio is to the west. Boardwalks

Figure 1.35 Entry view of boardwalk and art facilities at the Atlantic Center for the Arts. (Chuck Choi)

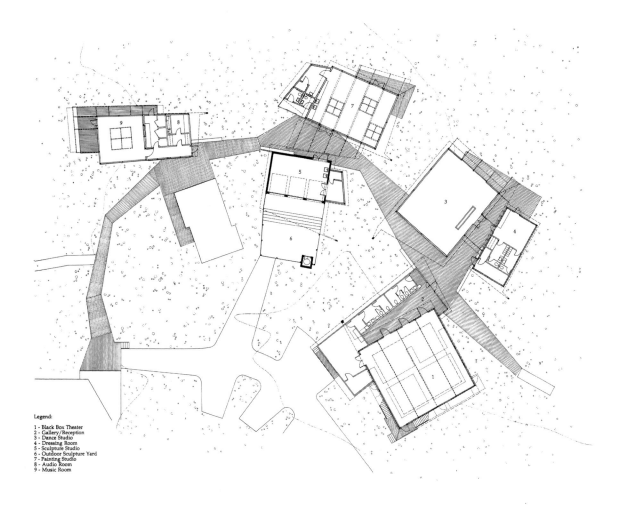

Legend:

1 - Black Box Theater
2 - Gallery/Reception
3 - Dance Studio
4 - Dressing Room
5 - Sculpture Studio
6 - Outdoor Sculpture Yard
7 - Painting Studio
8 - Audio Room
9 - Music Room

and outdoor rooms link the buildings. The library is sited alone to the southeast of the building compound.

Each structure uses the same materials (mahogany, glass, lead-coated copper roofs, and steel cable ties); however, the window forms and configurations vary depending on the luminous program and the desired connection to the site. The black-box theater and music room are internally focused spaces with few daylighting apertures. A single skylight punctures the cedar-lined music room to provide diffuse illumination and a view of the sky. Entry to this space is through a corridor with south sidelighting. The

Figure 1.36 Building plans at the Atlantic Center for the Arts.

(Thompson & Rose)

Figure 1.37 View of the
music room at the
Atlantic Center
for the Arts.
(Chuck Choi)

dance studio is more connected to the site. High clerestory windows with diffusing glass are contrasted by low horizontal windows on the west framing views of the dancers' feet from outside.
The north wall of the dance studio has large glass doors that open
onto a small terrace within the dense jungle. Painting and sculpture studios are sited adjacent to each other and linked by an
outdoor room. A high clerestory admits light on all sides of the

painting studio (sited to the north of the sculpture studio). Horizontal wooden louvers on the east, south, and west create a dappled quality of light in the upper volume of the space. Clear glazing on the north admits indirect light and provides an uninterrupted view of the treetops in the jungle. Three large roof monitors face north to gather additional indirect light and connect the painters to the sky. Since the lower portion of the room is enclosed by solid walls, the light from above draws the eyes upward to create a vertical emphasis within the space (doors facing the sculpture studio can be left open to provide views and sidelighting). Given the large expanse of clerestory windows and the scale of the room, the monitors seem redundant; however,

Figure 1.38 View of the dance studio and surrounding landscape at the Atlantic Center for the Arts.

(Chuck Choi)

they do frame and bring the sky inside the room in a very different way than the clerestory windows that overlook the trees.

Concrete walls that contrast with the wood-frame construction of the other buildings enclose the sculpture room. Clerestory windows and a wooden roof rest on top of the concrete walls. Several small windows are cut through the concrete to frame views of the

Figure 1.39   View of the painting studio at the Atlantic Center for the Arts.

(Chuck Choi)

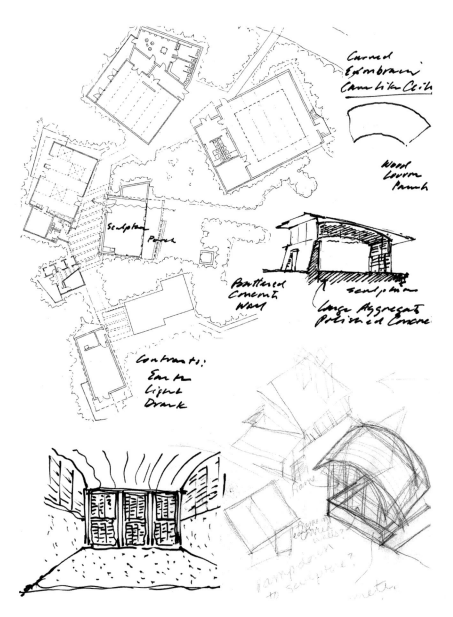

Figure 1.40 Conceptual sketches of the sculpture studio at the Atlantic Center for the Arts.

(Thompson & Rose)

vegetation and to emphasize the massiveness of the wall. The roof extends graciously beyond the south facade to provide shading, create an outdoor room, and provide a transition between inside and outside work areas. Clerestory windows on the south and north admit indirect daylight. Large garage doors can be rolled up on the south to extend the studio to the outside. The varied luminous experiences of the music room, dance studio, and painting and sculpture rooms are woven together by outdoor spaces created as the boardwalk expands, contracts, and moves through the landscape.

The library in the southwest of the compound is sited for privacy and personal reflection. A sloping roof reaches upward on

Figure 1.41 Exterior view of the north and west facades of the library at the Atlantic Center for the Arts.

(Chuck Choi)

the west to open the building to the landscape and distant views. A glass box protrudes from the northwest corner of the building to frame the sky and upper portions of the foliage. In contrast, the southwest corner is wrapped with large clerestory windows and wooden louvers that are similar to those found in the painting studio. Glazed doors open to a small deck that over-looks views of the water to the west. The windows on the west facade frame views at different levels within the landscape: sky, vegetation, earth, and water. Although many different daylight-ing strategies are used in the buildings, similar forms, details, and materials unify the parts into a whole. Skylight monitors, clerestory windows, external louvers, and sidelighting are brought together in various combinations to create daylighting solutions that are appropriate for the climate and program. The relation-ship between the inside and outside, the degree of connection with the environment, and an emphasis on the sky, land, and vegetation support the pragmatic requirements and enhance the poetic experience of each activity. An amazing variety of lumi-nous, site, and climatic experiences are created from a small palette of thoughtfully conceived daylighting strategies. (See Fig-ures 1.35 to 1.41.)

Solar Access

Daylighting must be available on the site before it can be effective in the interior of the building. If daylight is not accessible on the site, nothing can be done to the design of the building, rooms, or windows to overcome this challenge. For all but the hottest of cli-mates, solar access should be ensured on the site scale and con-trolled, as needed, at the building scale. We must first begin by defining the concept of *site*. Property lines that enclose a horizon-tal plane bound by the earth at the bottom and bound at the top by the outer edges of buildings and vegetation usually define the perimeter of the site. Yet environmental forces that are not lim-ited by property lines affect daylighting. We need to extend the site boundaries horizontally and vertically in order to consider views, the apparent movement of the sun, the sky conditions, and microclimatic effects of the surrounding landscape. With day-lighting design, the site must be considered three-dimensionally since the perimeters of the site extend downward into the earth and upward to embrace the sky and the sun. In *Topophilia,* Yi-Fu Tuan explains that we have lost this important third dimension in contemporary concepts of the landscape: "In Europe, some time between 1500 and 1700 A.D., the medieval conception of a vertical cosmos yielded slowly to a new and increasingly secular way of representing the world. The vertical dimension was being displaced by the horizontal; cosmos was giving way to a flat nonrotary segment of nature called landscape."[25] In *A Natural History of the Senses,* Diane Ackerman explains the relationship between the site and the sky in a slightly different way: "Look at your feet. You are standing in the sky. When we think of the sky, we tend to look up, but the sky actually begins at the earth. We walk through it, yell into it, rake leaves, wash the dog, and drive cars in it. We breathe it deep within us."[26] This expanded concept of the site enables designers to consider important solar and climatic forces that influence daylighting design.

Access to *sunlight* (direct beam radiation from the sun) or *daylight* (indirect light from the sky) raises different site issues. The designer must first define which activities require direct sunlight and which require indirect daylight. In order to ensure solar access during the appropriate times of day and year, the designer must develop design criteria that clarify when and where sunlight or indirect daylight are needed. This information can then be used to evaluate existing conditions on the site and to develop design strategies for solar access. If direct sunlight is desired for illumination, passive heating, or quality of light, the designer needs to define a "solar window" on the site. The solar window refers to a three-dimensional boundary that is defined by the altitude and azimuth of the sun during the times of day and year in which direct sunlight is desired in the building. For example, if direct sunlight is needed for illumination and passive heating during the underheated period of the year (i.e., from September 21 to March 21 and from 9:00 A.M. to 3:00 P.M.— the period of day in which the intensity of the sun is greatest), then the boundary of the solar window would correspond to the altitude and azimuth of the sun during this period of time. Vegetation, topography, and site structures would need to be located outside of this geometric boundary to ensure solar access to the building for light and heat. In this example, solar access would be provided at the site scale during the underheated period and controlled at the building scale with shading devices or vegetation during the overheated period. The size and shape of the solar window will depend on the times of day and year that sunlight is needed.

Solar access is also an important issue when indirect daylight is desired for uniform or controlled illumination. We often assume that light from the north will be used to provide indirect illumination. In fact, it is often appropriate to gather direct sunlight at the site scale and reflect or diffuse it at the building scale to create indirect illumination inside. Fuller Moore, professor of architecture at Miami University, discusses strategies for converting sunlight into indirect light in *Concepts and Practice of Architectural Daylighting:*

> . . . For contemporary architects designing in an environment of clearer skies and much higher relative energy costs, perhaps the single most valuable principle to be gleaned from Aalto is the use of white surfaces as diffuse, secondary illumination sources. This principle must now be adapted to the preferred use of sunlight (instead of diffuse sky light) to allow smaller glazing areas. The south-facing roof monitor (with suitable reflective baffles) for top lighting, and the light shelf for side lighting are two feasible adaptations of secondary-source reflective diffusers to the relatively high sun angles and present energy costs in the U.S.[27]

Although the most constant source of indirect light is available on the north side of a building, indirect light can be achieved by modifying or reflecting sunlight that is gathered from other orientations. It is also important to remember that even the north side of the building will receive sunlight in the summer. Indirect light can be created in any orientation if reflectors, shading systems, blinds, or other means are used to modify the sunlight. The roof can also provide indirect light as long as the depth and form of the skylight are designed to control direct sunlight. We often assume that windows or skylights should be oriented to the north to provide indirect daylight; however, given seasonal and diurnal variations in the position of the sun, there are many times of day when indirect light is available in other orientations. For example, the east facade has indirect light during all but the morning hours, when blinds can be used to control the sun. The challenge for the designer is to determine whether it is more appropriate to

Figure 1.42 Exterior view
of the Brunsell Residence
and Pacific Ocean.

(Obie G. Bowman)

gather indirect light from the north or to create diffuse light by
reflection or diffusion. In either case, a solar window must be
defined to ensure that vegetation, topography, and site structures
do not block either daylight or sunlight access to the building.

The Brunsell Residence by Obie G. Bowman at Sea Ranch in
California was shaped by the sun, climate, and site. Even though
this coastal region is frequently overcast, the clients were interested in combining daylighting and passive heating. The site is
located in an expansive and gently rolling meadow overlooking
the Pacific Ocean. The low, earth-sheltered structure is bermed to
the north and has a sod roof. Two bedroom wings extend to the
north and east from a central living area on the south. Skylights
in each earth-bermed wing provide illumination and views of the
sky. In contrast to the sheltered toplit wings, the living room has
extensive windows on the south, which gather views of the site,
passive gains, and daylighting. A brick floor over a concrete slab

provides thermal mass for passive heating. Solar panels on the south side of the deck heat hot water for general use and radiant heating in the floor, while a gas-fired radiant heating system supplements passive systems in overcast weather. Interior blinds can be adjusted to admit or block sunlight depending on luminous and thermal needs. The southern portion of the building appears to emerge from the site since the sod roof wraps up and over the building. An outdoor deck is recessed into the earth in front of the living room to create a sunny, private, and protected outdoor space. Natural ventilation in the summer is admitted through louvers on the north side of the building and exhausted through operable windows on the south. The building form and massing were carefully designed to respond to solar access, views, and prevailing winds. Bowman illustrates that it is possible to gracefully respond to solar access for daylighting and passive heating without compromising desired views or ventilation requirements. (See Figures 1.42 to 1.44.)

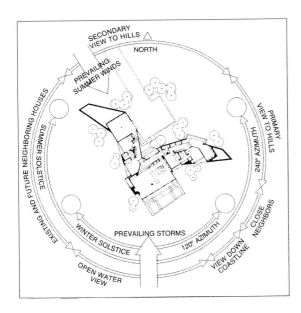

Figure 1.43 Plan with seasonal solar and wind conditions.

(Obie G. Bowman)

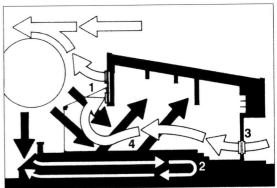

HEATING SECTION

1   CONTINUOUS DISCHARGE MANIFOLD
2   SOLAR-HOT-WATER COLLECTOR
3   AIR INTAKE LOUVERS
4   BRICK OVER FLOOR MASS

Figure 1.44 Section of the Brunsell Residence.

(Obie G. Bowman)

Comfort

The human experiences of climate and site are also related to our sense of luminous and thermal comfort. In *The Architecture of the Well-Tempered Environment,* Reyner Banham suggests that we could exist in most parts of the world, though there is a distinction between existing and truly living. He believes that in order to flourish we need to have some degree of ease and leisure that allows us to get beyond mere survival.[28] In architectural design, comfort usually implies shelter, warmth, and light. Comfort should also address our quality of life and sense of well-being. Our sense of comfort is affected by many factors, including personal preference, culture, and the traditions of our bioregion. There is a relative quality to climate that depends on our level of tolerance and past experiences. Yet humans are amazingly adaptable. Although a new place may not feel like home, we are usually able to adjust our behaviors, dress, and activities to respond to new climatic conditions. In *The Natural House,* Frank Lloyd Wright suggests that climatic adaptation is part of human experience: "Climate means something to man. It means something in relation to one's life in it. Nature makes the body flexible and so the life of the individual invariably becomes adapted to environment and circumstance."[29]

Despite our personal preferences and differences, distinct luminous and thermal approaches to comfort are found in each of the major climatic regions (hot-arid, hot-humid, temperate, and cold). As a result, we find recurring daylighting strategies and concepts for similar climates throughout the world. The delicate tracery of the Islamic screen, louvered shutters in southern Italy, and overhangs and jalousie windows in Australia are variations on a technique that filters the hot sun but admits the wind. Each climate has predominant concerns that lead to these recurring themes. Hot-arid climates encourage daylighting strategies that minimize heat gain, control glare, and provide relief and protection from the intense sunlight. Hot-humid climates require maximum ventilation and control of heat and direct sunlight. In contrast, temperate climates have greater flexibility due to the modest temperatures and seasonal changes that often lead to a greater connection between inside and outside. Finally, cold climates have the challenge of addressing tremendous seasonal changes in temperature, precipitation, and sky conditions. A comparison of daylighting strategies in the four major climatic regions will illustrate their predominant luminous concerns.

Distinct climatic and site responses to daylighting for cold versus hot-arid regions are evident in a comparison of Frank Lloyd Wright's Jacobs House II in Madison, Wisconsin, and William Bruder's Theuer House in Phoenix, Arizona. Although the hemicycle plans are similar, the architects respond to site and climate in very different ways. Wright's Jacobs House II, also known as the Solar Hemicycle, uses the building form and section to address concerns characteristic of a cold climate. The gently curving plan and extensive south glazing gather sunlight for illumination and heat during the winter months, while large roof overhangs control direct solar gains in the summer. An extensive thermal mass is located on the floor and north walls. In winter, direct sunlight warms the thermal mass during the day for release at night. The north side of the building is bermed into the hillside for additional thermal protection. In summer, cross ventilation is admitted through operable windows on the south and exhausted on the north side of the second floor. A number of upgrades were done in the 1980s (the building was constructed in 1944). These modifications included the addition of double glazing, installation of a thermal curtain on the interior of the south glazing, replacement of the radiant floor, installation of a gas-fired air furnace,

Figure 1.45 South facade of the Jacobs House II.

(CALA Visual Resources Collection)

Figure 1.46   View of the lower level of the Jacobs House II.

(CALA Visual Resources Collection)

and caulking and sealing of joints.[30] Based on a recent thermal analysis of the house, Donald Aitken from the Union of Concerned Scientists concluded that: ". . . the house performs to the highest standards of today's passive solar architects. Its design is a 49-year-old testament to the inherent truth in Frank Lloyd Wright's intuitive approach to 'organic' architecture."[31] Although alterations were needed to maximize the building performance, the basic architectural strategies that included the two-story section, narrow plan, south glazing, roof overhang, and cross ventilation successfully respond to luminous and thermal concerns for cold climates during different times of the year. (See Figures 1.45 to 1.47.)

A similar building form is used in a different way at the Theuer House in Phoenix, designed by William Bruder. The hemicycle plan was rotated 180° to orient the large expanse of glazing away from the sun and toward views of distant mountains. Control of direct sunlight is a primary concern in a hot-arid climate. Glazing (which is oriented north to gather indirect light) is further protected by operable vertical louvers mounted outside of the glazing. As the sun moves around to the north side of the house during the summer, the louvers can be positioned to block direct sunlight. During the rest of the year the louvers can be opened to admit indirect light. Bruder places the thermal mass on the south rather than the north side of the building. The mass acts as a heat sink that prevents the interior from overheating. Jacobs II is concerned with admitting, controlling, or storing sunlight. In contrast, the Theuer House makes every effort to prevent direct sunlight from entering the building. Although passive solar design is feasible in a hot-arid climate, Bruder chose to have the building turn its back to the sun and instead to open itself to the mountain vistas and privacy of a north garden. Because the glazing is on the north side of the Theuer House, Bruder cannot integrate daylighting and passive solar design; yet his approach is appropriate given the extensive overheated period and brief underheated period in Phoenix. In contrast, the cold climate in Madison has a long underheated period and only a brief overheated period. The length of time during the year when sunlight can be welcomed into the building is significantly different in each climate. Similar building forms are transformed to reveal daylighting and thermal responses that are tailored to the climate, program, and design concept. (See Figures 1.48 to 1.50.)

A hot-humid climate presents still different daylighting opportunities. At the Jersey Devil's Palmetto House in southern Florida, the hot-humid climate suggests an integration of daylighting and natural ventilation. The Palmetto House, like the Theuer House, avoids direct sunlight at all costs. The windows are sized and positioned to admit indirect daylight while maximizing airflow. Extensive roof overhangs prevent direct sun penetration throughout the year, and windows are oriented to maximize cross ventilation from

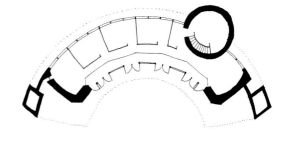

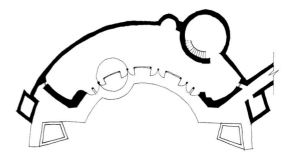

Figure 1.47 Plans of the Jacobs House II.

(Donovan Nelson)

Figure 1.48 View of the north facade of the Theuer House.

(Tim Hursley)

the prevailing winds. Jalousie windows allow occupants to adjust the direction and flow of air within the interior. Although the original owners no longer live in the house, and it has suffered through a hurricane, its form and zoning are instructive. It was designed with a lower-level workshop, living areas on the second floor, and an upper-level study. The house is perched above the site to maximize wind flow, and it is nestled under the canopy of the palmetto trees to minimize solar access. Steel grates are inserted between the second and third floor to allow air from the living area to be exhausted through the windows on the upper level. Conversely, indirect daylight from the study filters through the grate to the living area below. A large screened porch is located on the east to extend the living space and provide ventilation on the north-south axis. The building is shaped to control sunlight, provide indirect illumination, and admit the wind. (See Figures 1.51 to 1.53.)

The Jaech House (also known as House Two) in Kirkland, Washington, by Jim Olson of Olson-Sundberg challenges our preconceptions about daylighting design in a temperate climate. Buildings located in this predominantly mild, overcast climate are rarely considered candidates for passive solar design or for extensive shading systems. Yet, similar to Wright's Jacobs II, Olson's Jaech House opens itself to the site and sun with extensive south

Figure 1.49 View to the north from inside the Theuer House.

(Tim Hursley)

Figure 1.50
Plan of the
Theuer House.
(William Bruder Architect)

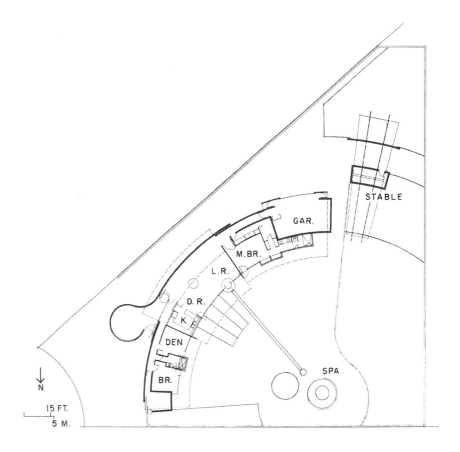

glazing. Floor-to-ceiling windows extend the interior into the land-scape. On the occasional clear winter day, direct sunlight pene-trates deeply into the living area. The summer sun, which is surprisingly abundant in Seattle, is controlled by a series of hori-zontal louvers that reflect daylight to the ceiling plane and softly down to the room below. A low, flat roof and mass walls on the north contrast with a soaring roof and glazing on the south side of the house. Although there are similarities in the window form, relationship to the site, and building orientation between the Jaech House and Jacobs II, the two projects have distinctly differ-ent climatic intentions. The climate in Washington is too mild and overcast to fully benefit from passive solar strategies. Since pas-sive gains are not maximized, the expansive south windows are

Figure 1.52 Interior of the living area in the Palmetto House.

(© Bill Sanders)

Figure 1.51 Exterior of the Palmetto House.

(© Bill Sanders)

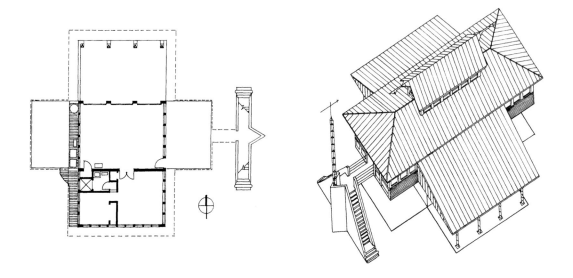

Figure 1.53 Plan and axonometric drawing of the Palmetto House.

(Joe Ford)

feasible only because of the mild climate. In any other climate, either thermal gains or heat loss would compromise the design. Large glazing areas are provided for illumination, view, and ventilation without the consequence of extensive heat loss during the winter months (when temperatures rarely dip below freezing).

Figure 1.54 View of the south facade at the Jaech Residence.

(Michael Shopenn)

The shading devices are a reminder that sun control is needed in the summer. It is the connection to the site and landscape that are of greatest importance. The south glazing extends the inside to the outside and provides expansive vistas of the water and landscape. Daylighting design in this temperate climate involves gathering sufficient illumination from the predominantly overcast skies in the winter and providing control of sunlight in the mild, but often sunny summer. The moderate climate provides great freedom to open the building to the site and environmental forces. (See Figures 1.54 to 1.57.)

Though the strategies used in these four houses share similar elements, the daylighting designs are adapted to respond to the prevailing conditions of the particular climate. Extreme temperature changes in the cold climate encourage the coupling of daylighting and passive solar design. High temperatures and predominantly clear skies encourage strategies that control sunlight in hot-arid climates. Humidity, glare, and high tempera-

Figure 1.55 View of the interior of the Jaech Residence.

(Michael Shopenn)

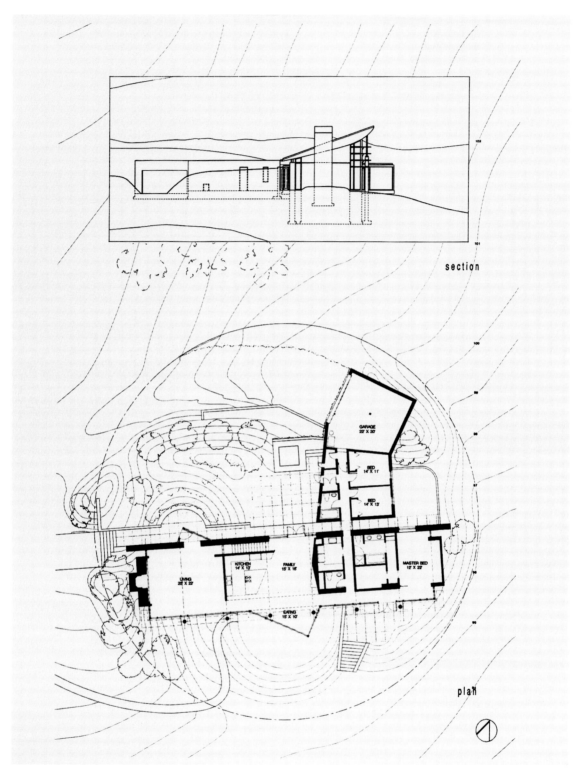

Figure 1.56 Plan and section of the Jaech Residence.

(Olson Sundberg Architects)

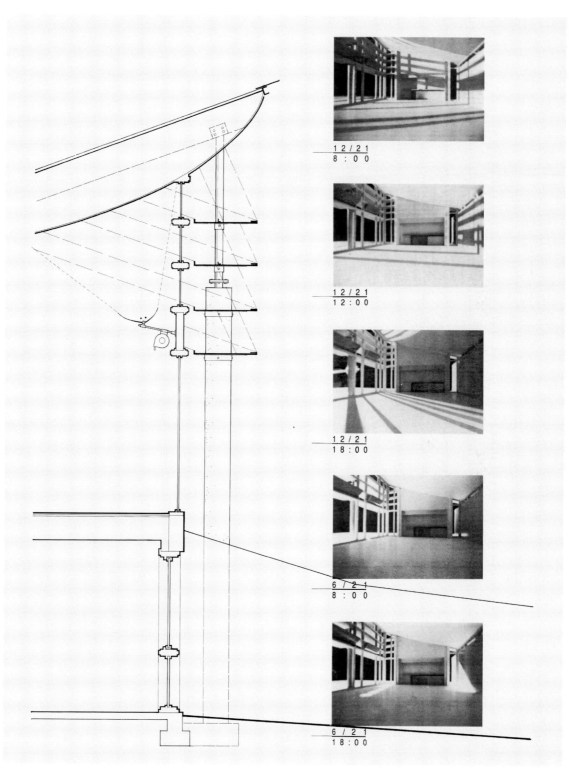

12 / 21
8 : 0 0

12 / 21
12 : 0 0

12 / 21
18 : 0 0

6 / 2 1
8 : 0 0

6 / 2 1
18 : 0 0

Figure 1.57   Detail of south facade and daylighting studies.
(Olson Sundberg Architects)

tures bring together daylighting and ventilation in hot-humid climates. Finally, the mildness of temperate climates presents greater opportunities to connect the inside and outside and to use larger glazing areas with less thermal consequence. Each climate provides opportunities and constraints that can inform the development of daylighting strategies. Human comfort and human experiences are the ultimate tests of whether strategies are appropriate or inappropriate. One might argue that we no longer need to respond to the bioregional forces of sun, sky conditions, climate, and site. We have the technology to create environments that provide shelter, light, and heat without the sun. Yet a bioregional approach to daylighting goes beyond these basic physiological requirements to also help us to know "where we are" and "who we are" by rooting us in the ecological phenomena of a particular place, for a particular climate, and on a particular site. A bioregional approach to daylighting weaves together diverse layers of ecological, physiological, and experiential issues to enhance our understanding of the unique bioregions in which we live.

ENDNOTES

1. Alexandra Tyng, *Beginnings: Louis I. Kahn's Philosophy of Architecture* (New York: John Wiley & Sons, 1984), 169–170.
2. David Suzuki and Peter Knudtsun, *Wisdom of the Elders: Sacred Native Stories of Nature* (New York: Bantam Books, 1993), 61. This compelling collection of stories and myths captures ecological traditions from all corners of the world.
3. Robert Grudin, *Time and the Art of Living* (New York: Ticknor & Fields, 1982), 149.
4. John Brinckerhoff Jackson, *A Sense of Place, a Sense of Time* (New Haven: Yale University Press, 1994), 160–161.
5. Ruth Gendler, *Changing Light: The Eternal Cycle of Night and Day* (New York: HarperCollins Publishers, 1991), xii. This outstanding collection of myths, poems, and prayers captures experiences of light through time and across cultures. It should be required reading for all teachers and students of daylighting design.
6. Phil Cousineau, ed., introduction to *The Soul of the World* (New York: HarperCollins Publishers, 1993).

7. Ralph Knowles, "For those who spend time in a place," *Places* 8, no. 2 (1992): 42.

8. Ruth Gendler, 84–85.

9. Barry Lopez, *Arctic Dreams: Imagination and Desire in a Northern Landscape* (Toronto: Bantam Books, 1986), 17–19. Lopez's keen observations of the natural environment and its qualities of light are not only beautifully described but they also provide valuable lessons that can inform daylighting design in different geographic locations. Chapter 1, "Arktikós," provides a particularly rich description of luminous phenomena on a global scale.

10. Diane Ackerman, *A Natural History of the Senses* (New York: Vintage Books, 1990), 246.

11. Ruth Gendler, xv.

12. Christian Norberg-Schulz, *Genius Loci* (New York: Rizzoli, 1980), 39.

13. David Orr explains a critical difference between being a "resident" and an "inhabitant" in *Ecological Literacy*: "A resident is a temporary occupant, putting down few roots and investing little, knowing little, and perhaps caring little for the immediate locale beyond its ability to gratify. . . . The inhabitant, in contrast, 'dwells,' as Illich puts it, in an intimate, organic, and mutually nurturing relationship with a place. Good inhabitance is an art requiring detailed knowledge of a place, the capacity for observation, and a sense of care and rootedness." David Orr, *Ecological Literacy* (New York: State University of New York Press, 1992), 130–131.

14. Yi-Fu Tuan, *Topophilia* (New York: Columbia University Press, 1974), 85–86. Yi-Fu Tuan's descriptions of the cultural and historical roles of the sun in different cultures are vivid reminders of how detached contemporary life has become from fundamental natural phenomena. Not only are solar rituals lost or threatened, but more important, so are our physical and spiritual relationships with nature.

15. Yi-Fu Tuan, 82–90, 131.

16. Robert Grudin, 166.

17. Ruth Gendler, 75–76.

18. Stephen Holl Architects, firm literature on the Chapel of St. Ignatius, 1.

19. "Seabird Island School, Patkau Architects," *The Governor General's Awards for Architecture,* Royal Architectural Insti-

tute of Canada (1992): 60. The rich ecological and human experiences at Seabird Island School are unforgettable. It is obvious from the moment of arriving at the school that the Salish community takes great pride and joy in the facility. It is more than a school, for it brings people of all ages together to form a community that is part of the stunning environment of mountains, fields, water, and sky.

20. Alexandra Tyng, 130–131.
21. Richard Saul Wurman, *What Will Be Has Always Been: The Words of Louis I. Kahn* (New York: Rizzoli, 1986), 175.
22. Alexandra Tyng, 170.
23. Kevin Lynch, *Site Design* (Cambridge, Mass: MIT Press, 1984), 49.
24. Frank Lloyd Wright, *The Natural House* (New York: Horizon Press, 1954), 53.
25. Yi-Fu Tuan, 129.
26. Diane Ackerman, 236.
27. Fuller Moore, *Concepts and Practice of Architectural Daylighting* (New York: Van Nostrand Reinhold Company, 1985), 49.
28. Reyner Banham, *The Architecture of the Well-Tempered Environment* (Chicago: University of Chicago Press, 1969), 18.
29. Frank Lloyd Wright, 178.
30. Donald Aitken, "Frank Lloyd Wright's Solar Hemicycle Revisited: Measured Performance Following Thermal Upgrading," *Proceedings of the 17th National Passive Solar Conference* (Boulder, Colo.: American Solar Energy Society), 1992, 52. Donald Aitken's analysis of the solar hemicycle confirms the success of straightforward passive solar strategies even in such cold corners of the country as Madison, Wisconsin. Yet it is surprising how few designers are interested in or willing to use passive solar systems despite their advantages (when properly designed).
31. Ibid., 57.

Do More with Less

Doing as little as possible, or economy of means,
involves the idea that from minimum resources and
energy, maximum environmental and social benefits are
available.[1]

—MICHAEL HOUGH

We most commonly think of daylighting as a means of providing energy-efficient illumination; however, it has far greater ecological potential if we explore ways that it can be coupled with other solar design strategies for heating, cooling, hot water, electricity generation, waste processing, and even food production. As Michael Hough explains in *Out of Place,* "doing more with less" implies achieving maximum benefits through minimum efforts. And, as developer Michael Corbett suggests, ". . . you are on the right track when your solution for one problem accidentally solves several others."[2] Yet we should go beyond "accidental" solutions. Daylighting design needs explicitly and actively to seek connections and integration between different types and layers of concern. If designers are to do more with less, they need to intentionally weave together seemingly disparate issues.

Doing more with less encourages designers to reconsider the social, cultural, and ecological roles of daylighting in architectural design. At the 1995 conference of the American Solar Energy Society, John Reynolds, professor of architecture at the University of Oregon, described windows as the eyes, ears, and nose of a building.[3] This metaphor invites us to explore the experiential and sensuous aspects of windows and to consider how they welcome not only the light, but also the sounds and smells of a particular place. Windows will always serve multiple purposes. A large café window can be a stage for human interactions, a place to see and be seen, and an area for display. A small cabin window can be a beacon at night, a foil against the cold, and a frame for a special view. A residential window can be a filter for privately observing life on the street, a greenhouse for winter herbs, and a sunny nook for a cat. These images, which surround us every day, are reminders that we already (and with little effort) use windows and daylighting to achieve multiple goals. Think of the additional ecological, cultural, and sociological benefits we would gain if we purposely used daylighting to "do more with less." To this end, what role can daylighting play, and how can it be coupled with other tasks and issues? As a beginning (or a point of departure for the imagination), this discussion will explore the relationship between daylighting and illumination, passive heating and cooling, water and waste processing, electric energy generation, and plant growth for food, health, and pleasure.

ILLUMINATION

It seems almost unnecessary to explain that daylighting can be used to provide illumination and to reduce electric lighting loads. Yet, although many buildings admit daylight to their interiors, surprisingly few actually use it for illumination. A quick tour of typical office buildings in any city will show how infrequently electric lights are shut off, dimmed, or in any way correlated with the available daylight. Hundreds of thousands of electric lamps needlessly burn throughout the country as daylight streams through the windows. Until recently, Alvar Aalto's Mount Angel Library was one of the few buildings in the United States in which occupants actually shut off the electric lights during the day (which results in a delightfully rich architectural experience and increased awareness of the luminous environment). Fortunately, more designers, building owners, and occupants are beginning to realize that illumination is a fundamental benefit of daylighting. In some cases, its use may simply be a question of altering our routine of turning on electric lights during the day (or encouraging us to use only those lights that are needed). However, poor design is more often the reason we do not use daylighting for illumination. Thick buildings, excessively large or small windows, inadequate solar access, and lack of control all contribute to inappropriate illuminance levels, glare, excessive heat gain or heat loss, and poor visual comfort (which can also give daylighting a bad reputation and discourage its use for illumination).

The first way of using daylighting to do more with less is to use it for illumination. This is a deceptively simple statement. It requires thoughtful planning and significant effort to achieve design goals (reduce electric lighting loads, energy consumption, and related ecological impacts) and alleviate typical problems (too much or too little light, glare, heat loss and heat gain, privacy, noise, visual comfort). While there are many human and aesthetic benefits of using daylighting for illumination, its most evident ecological benefit is to reduce peak energy demand and subsequent environmental impacts. Although research studies have proven time and again that daylighting is a successful strategy for reducing electric lighting loads (as well as heating and cooling loads), too few designers approach architectural design with this explicit goal. Fortunately, recent innovations in electric lighting controls provide a variety of design options, from simple switching and dimming to photocells and even sophisticated computerized environmental control systems, which make it easier to choreograph the available daylight with illuminance requirements and human comfort.[4] Over the past decade, the reliability and durability of these systems have significantly improved, which enables designers to more easily and confidently use available daylighting for illumination.

The Ionica Building in Cambridge, England, by the RH Partnership elegantly uses daylighting to reduce electric lighting loads, energy consumption, and related environmental impacts while also fostering human comfort, health, and well-being. In addition to the predicted 20 to 35 percent energy savings from lighting, a building survey by Adam Jackaway and David Greene (which compared the Ionica and PowerGen Buildings by Bennetts Associates), found that the occupants overwhelmingly appreciate the quality and experience of the luminous environment: "The vast majority of occupants surveyed feel the daylighting in these buildings contributes substantially to their productivity and well-being during the working day. Additionally, there is unanimous agreement that the buildings successfully establish a connection between the internal and external environments, keeping occupants in contact with the world outside."[5]

Figure 2.1   View of the south and east facades of the Ionica Building.

(Adam Jackaway)

Figure 2.2   View of the atrium looking east.

(Adam Jackaway)

Although daylighting strategies are common, the project is unique in the way it thoughtfully realizes design intentions on multiple levels, at different scales, and with attention to quality and detail. The designers weave together simple strategies to create high environmental performance and meaningful human experiences. The linear building is oriented on an east-west axis, with three stories of office spaces framed on either end by opaque masses containing service cores and vertical transportation. Sidelighting from the south and north is complemented by borrowed light from a centrally located atrium. The gently curving atrium brings light deep within the heart of the building, visually and physically connects lower and upper levels, and provides opportunities for informal human interaction. As Jackaway and Greene note, an unusual aspect of the atrium is the use of a curved white wall on the north side of the space to reflect light to offices on the south (similar in concept to Aalto's ceiling reflectors). In contrast to the openness of the south side (minimal handrails and columns separate the offices from the atrium), discreet openings provide borrowed light to offices on the north side of the wall. Baffles at the base of the skylight diffuse direct sunlight and control glare.

Figure 2.3 Detail of south facade and shading devices. (Adam Jackaway)

While the splayed windows on the north facade are modest in size (approximately 25 percent of the facade), the entire south facade is glazed from the desk surface to the ceiling. Large roof overhangs are combined with two layers of external louvered shading devices and internal blinds to control direct sunlight, glare, and thermal gains. High-performance fluorescent fixtures with photosensors and continuous dimming correlate the available daylight, electric lighting, and target illuminance levels. Fixtures are zoned so that dimming occurs from the perimeter of the office (where daylight is most abundant) to the center of the

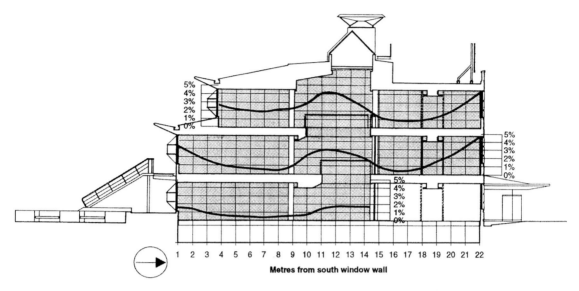

5%
4%
3%
2%
1%
0%

5%
4%
3%
2%
1%
0%

5%
4%
3%
2%
1%
0%

1 2 3 4 5 6 7 8 9 10 11 12 13 14 15 16 17 18 19 20 21 22

Metres from south window wall

Daylight factor measurements by Adam Jackaway, Research in Building Group, University of Westminster

Figure 2.4 Section with daylight factor measurements.
(Adam Jackaway)

offices (which is most remote from the daylight). All levels except the lowest on the north side of the building have sufficient, if not excellent, daylighting. According to Jackaway and Greene, the only problems occur during winter, when interior blinds are needed on the south facade to control direct sunlight and glare. Yet these concerns are predictable and fairly modest, and they can be internally controlled. Finally, operable windows and ventilation towers facilitate natural ventilation. Despite minor concerns, the project skillfully combines design strategies and off-the-shelf technologies to provide illumination, reduce electric lighting loads, and create a meaningful, luminous environment. (See Figures 2.1 to 2.4.)

PASSIVE HEATING AND COOLING

The passive solar movement of the 1960s and 1970s saw great advances in solar design and technologies. Despite these innovations, the design professions have been slow to adopt solar principles. This may be due to any number of factors, including inertia, lack of interest, not understanding the effectiveness of passive design, and perhaps even disdain for the solar aesthetic that is associated with these decades (an important issue which should not be underestimated). Many projects of the era represented the highest design standards, yet the more visually exuberant buildings are often the best remembered. While the sloping roofs, clerestory windows, bead and water walls, and other experimental devices played an important role in testing, exploring,

Figure 2.5 Aerial view of the Youth Hostel and Monastery.

(Peter Bonfig)

Figure 2.6
Facade details of
the Youth Hostel.

(Peter Bonfig)

and moving passive solar ideas forward, they can also leave a dated and exaggerated passive solar aesthetic in the minds of many people. Thomas Herzog addresses this notion of a passive solar stereotype when he explains his interest in thin buildings:

> There were various reasons why I continued to explore the narrow, elongated house type over a period of many years. One widely held opinion was that so-called "solar buildings" had to have a certain form and that the architectural range of expression was very restricted, due to the constraints of technical optimization. . . . In other words, there was fear of tight constraints and stereotypes. . . . After the triangular and cubic forms, we now tried something quite different—elongated forms with elegant proportions.[6]

The daylighting and thermal opportunities of solar design are particularly evident in the Youth Hostel at a monastery in Windberg, Bavaria (designed by Herzog + Partner). This thin linear building is tucked into the sloping topography that lies between the Bavarian forest and the Danube plain. In plan and section, the building consists of two major parts—sleeping areas to the south and service spaces (showers, rest rooms, stairs, etc.) to the north. A long corridor mediates the two zones. The south facade uses glazing and thermally insulated panels. The clear glazing provides daylighting, direct solar gains, and views to the stunning site, while insulated panels absorb solar gains for later use: "The wall thus becomes a thermal absorption element and a heating surface that begins to heat up as soon as the sun shines on it. The temperature reaches its maximum level in the early afternoon. Five to six hours later—during the night when the rooms are occupied—

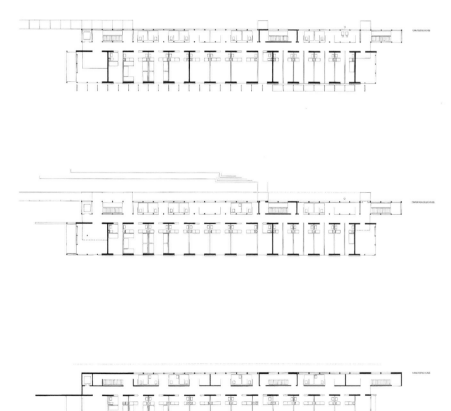

Figure 2.7 Plans of the Youth Hostel.

(Herzog + Partner)

Figure 2.8 Section of
the Youth Hostel.

(Herzog + Partner)

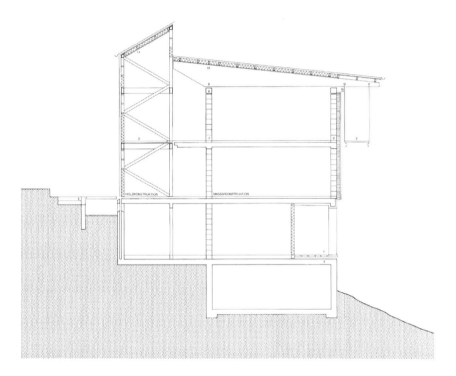

SCHNITT DER BAUKONSTRUKTION

1 OFFENER LAUBENGANG
2 ABGEHÄNGTER BALKON
3 NEBENRAUMZONE
4 SITZSTUFEN
5 STAHLBETON - UNTERBAU
6 KALKSANDSTEINMAUERWERK MIT TRANSLUZENTER WÄRMEDÄMMUNG
7 KALKSANDSTEINMAUERWERK GESCHLÄMMT
8 DURCHLAUFENDE PFETTE AUS LEIMHOLZ ALS RINGANKER
9 SPERRHOLZ- KASTENTRÄGER
10 WARMDACH MIT BLECHDECKUNG
11 WARMDACH MIT WELLBLECHDECKUNG

most of the heat is yielded in the form of radiation on the inside."[7] In contrast, the northern side of the building is made of timber frame and opaque infill panels combined with small windows for indirect illumination and ventilation. The formal clarity and elegance of the Youth Hostel is testimony to the architectural opportunities of passive solar design. Too few designers recognize that successful passive solar strategies and technologies can be independent of design aesthetics and architectural style. Principles of siting, orientation, percentage of glazing, thermal mass, materials, and shading provide criteria that can guide, rather than restrict, the design process. (See Figures 2.5 to 2.8.)

Daylighting is one avenue through which designers may begin to reconsider the ecological and aesthetic potentials of passive solar design. Jeffrey Cook, professor of architecture at Arizona State University, states that "Daylighting is a natural extension of passive solar heating. In larger buildings, daylighting is considered the prime cooling strategy."[8] Given many designers' apprehensions about the aesthetic implications of passive heating and cooling, it may be fruitful to also view passive solar design as a natural extension of daylighting. Daylighting, with its obvious experiential and form-giving implications, may be the prime means of reducing designers' negative associations and preconceptions about solar aesthetics.

As daylighting apertures gather visible light they can also gather solar radiation and wind. The integration of daylighting and passive design strategies is well documented and fairly easy to implement.[9] Apertures need to be properly sized, oriented, and shaded to respond to luminous and thermal criteria; appropriate thermal masses are needed for passive heating; and appropriately located and sized inlets and outlets are required for passive cooling. Although successful integration will depend on the building size, internal loads, and climate, many programs and building types can use some portion of passive heating and cooling to reduce the loads for mechanical systems. The benefits of the sun and wind are there for the taking; the decision to do so is dependent on the willingness of designers to reconsider the opportunities of passive solar design.

Hazel Henderson, director of the Worldwatch Institute, suggests that we need to move toward an "Age of Light":

> With new perspectives and new paradigms in the 1990s we can move beyond old conceptual prisons, whether the reductionist view of the Information Age or the, so far, literal interpretations of the Solar Age. When *The Politics of the Solar Age* was first published in 1981, it was catalogued among energy books. Many who heard my lectures asked me such questions as, "What percentage of my house's heating needs could be met by solar energy?" I would always reply that this was only one level of the meaning of the Solar Age, and then proceed to remind my questioner that if the sun was not already preheating their house and the earth, it would be about 400 degrees below zero! Thus I was referring to many other levels of the transition, from the Age of Fossil Fuels to renewable forms of energy, to the needed design revolution in our technologies and social structures, as well as to all the cultural and mythic levels of such a planetary transformation.[10]

If we focus on the pragmatic and technical details of Btu's, degree-days, footcandles, and daylight factors, we limit our ability to imagine the full opportunities of an "Age of Light." As Henderson suggests, solar design is not just about heat or light, but also about exploring the diverse opportunities of solar design within an ecological, technological, and sociological context. An increasing number of designers are carrying on and expanding the important solar advances and innovations that have been developed in the past several decades (and earlier). Some designers are also probing the social, cultural, and experiential implications of the "Age of Light" referred to by Hazel Henderson.

Louis Kahn once asked, "What is an architecture of the wind?"[11] One could also ask, "What is an architecture of the sun?"—a question that Kahn spent his life trying to understand. These simple questions imply that the sun and wind can shape and give form to architecture and that the expression of these forces can be visible in the built environment. The Center for Energy and Environmental Education at the University of Northern Iowa was designed by the architectural firm of Wells Woodburn O'Neil, with the Weidt Group, energy and environmental

Figure 2.9 View of the south facade of the Center for Energy and Environmental Education (CEEE) at sunset.

(King Au/Studio AU)

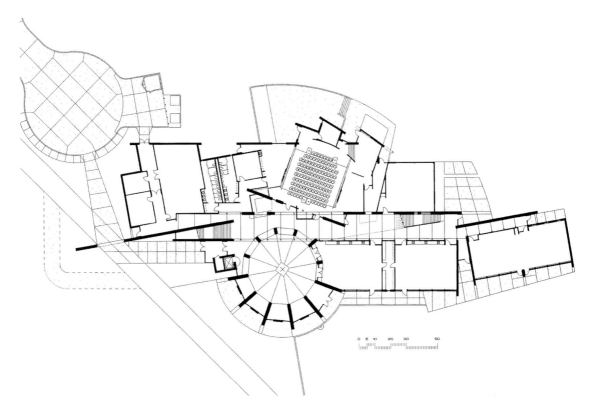

Figure 2.10   First-floor plan of the CEEE.
(Architects Wells Woodburn O'Neil)

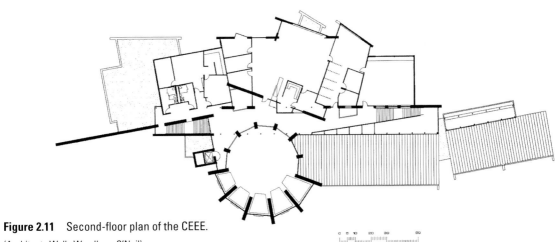

Figure 2.11   Second-floor plan of the CEEE.
(Architects Wells Woodburn O'Neil)

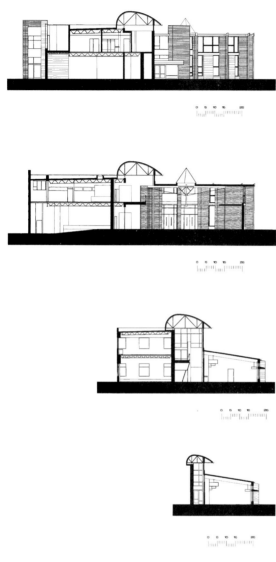

Figure 2.12 Sections through the CEEE.

(Architects Wells Woodburn O'Neil)

design consultants. The building was designed as part of a university project that integrates architecture, ecological design, and education. Despite many other ecological considerations, the primary goal of the UNI Center was to maximize daylighting and subsequently reduce electric energy consumption. Yet this project goes beyond these issues to also integrate passive heating, natural ventilation, and high-performance mechanical systems. The 29,300-square-foot building comprises three major elements: a circular toplit reception area, a central toplit circulation spine, and two wings oriented on east-west axes. Sidelighting, toplighting, borrowed light, thin room depths, shading, lightshelves, reflective surfaces, and electric lighting controls all contribute to excellent daylight levels, distribution, and quality throughout the building. Thermal mass, extensive south glazing, operable windows (with static pressure gauges to reduce mechanical ventilation when windows are open), and a variable-air-volume system are integrated to maximize energy performance. Based on energy simulations using DOE2, the Weidt Group predicts the following energy reductions: 37 percent in total energy load, 64 percent in peak electrical load, and 77 percent in electric lighting load.[12] While daylighting is the major contributor to increased building performance by reducing both electric lighting and cooling loads, the passive heating and cooling systems also help to reduce seasonal mechanical loads. The open, welcoming, and sensual qualities of the building expressed through siting, massing, and organization are reinforced by the judicious use of wood and limestone brought to life with light. (See Figures 2.9 to 2.14.)

The Allopro Administration Building in Dortmund, Germany, designed by Jürgen Hansen and Ralf Petersen, uses strategies similar to the UNI Center, but with a different architectural expression. This streamlined glass and steel building reflects daylighting and passive design strategies in virtually all aspects of its design. The linear building is also organized along an east-west axis, with office spaces located on the south and private meeting areas and support spaces on the north. A shallow roof slopes upward on the south facade; thermal mass is located on the floors of the upper and lower levels; glazing is concentrated on the south facade; exterior and interior shading are provided throughout; and operable windows are strategically located to enhance cross ventilation.

Figure 2.13 View of a classroom at the CEEE.

(King Au/Studio AU)

Figure 2.14   View of the
corridor at the CEEE.

(King Au/Studio AU)

Thoughtfully designed windows and shading systems are
essential in realizing daylighting and passive solar strategies.
Varying window sizes and placements on each floor create different luminous and thermal opportunities as well as distinct relationships to the site. Large panes of glass on the lower level
extend to the surface of the floor and subsequently admit abundant daylighting and solar gains while enhancing the connection
to the landscape. In contrast, the windows on the second floor
use smaller panes with sills located at the workplane for greater

Figure 2.15   South facade of the Allopro Administration Building.

(© Ralph Richter/ architekturphoto)

Figure 2.16   View of sidelighting strategies on the upper level.

(© Ralph Richter/ architekturphoto)

control of the luminous and thermal environments. Views from the upper level focus on the distant horizon and the sky. The extensive glass facade on the south is articulated by rhythms of light and shadow cast by balconies and colonnades alternating on the upper and lower levels. A single opaque wall and exterior stair provide a visual counterpoint to the expansive south glazing. The windows at the corners of the building wrap around the sides to admit light, heat, and expansive vistas of the site.

The extensive use of glazing for daylighting, passive heating, and natural ventilation would be disastrous without extensive shading on the exterior and interior. An elegant wooden roof, which appears suspended above the glass and steel facades, shades the upper floor. Simple adjustable fabric shades on the exterior of the building can be positioned horizontally to act as an overhang or lowered vertically to cover glazing as a blind. Located on upper and lower levels as well as on multiple orientations, the fabric shading provides tremendous flexibility in addressing varying sun angles and sky conditions throughout the year. White drapes are located on the interior to allow occupants to further modify the quality and quantity of light. Finally, operable win-

Figure 2.17 View of skylight strategy on the upper level of the Allopro Administration Building.

(© Ralph Richter/ architekturphoto)

dows and the thin north-south section facilitate natural ventilation. (See Figures 2.15 to 2.17.)

The C. K. Choi Institute of Asian Research at the University of British Columbia, designed by Matsuzaki Wright Architects, expresses the sun and wind with yet another architectural vocabulary. Soaring curved roofs and brick construction create unusual, but comfortable, references to both Asian and neoclassical archi-

Figure 2.18 Exterior view of the C. K. Choi Institute of Asian Research.

(Mike Sherman)

Figure 2.19   Interior view
of the C. K. Choi Institute
of Asian Research.
(Mike Sherman)

Figure 2.19   Interior view of the C. K. Choi Institute of Asian Research. (Mike Sherman)

tecture. One of the most distinguishing features of this 30,000-square-foot research facility is the expressive form of the five atria, which gather daylight for illumination and wind for passive cooling. The two-story atria are located along the north-south axis of the second and third floors. Natural ventilation is facilitated by the stack effect, which draws air from operable windows and fresh-air vents on the lower level of the second floor to be exhausted through the outlets at the top of the atria. Chimney stacks are used for ventilation on the first floor. North-facing glazing in the atria gathers indirect daylight, while sidelighting provides views of the site and additional illumination. Natural ventilation is used exclusively for cooling, while daylighting is combined with electric lighting to provide illumination. Given the temperate climate and predominantly overcast skies, passive heating was not a priority, yet the designers did include photovoltaic panels on the south-facing roofs of the atria. Other strategies to reduce energy and natural resources consumption include reused and recycled materials, composting toilets, and efficient fixtures and mechanical systems. (See Figures 2.18 to 2.20.)

In contrast to the stack ventilation and daylight monitors at C. K. Choi, sidelighting and cross ventilation are used at the Menara Mesiniaga office tower in Selangor Darul Ehnsan, Malaysia, designed by T. R. Hamzah & Yeang. The building includes public spaces, an auditorium, and a mezzanine on the lower levels; open-plan office spaces on the upper 10 floors; and a rooftop swimming pool and terrace. Similar to the Ionica Building, the offices are buffered on the east and west with services, terraces, and external louvers for solar shading. The north and south facades have curtain-wall glazing with operable windows that provide views and opportunities for natural ventilation. The surface of the cylindrical volume is carved out with terraces that spiral around the building from the south at the ground floor to the north at the roof deck. A berm wraps the base and lower levels of the building for thermal insulation, while the roof is crowned with a trellis that shades the swimming pool. Air-conditioning is provided in all spaces except the elevator lobbies and the rest rooms. Given the hot humid climate, the temptation to depend on the mechanical

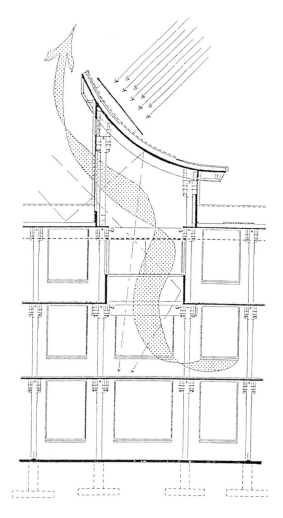

Figure 2.20 Section showing ventilation and daylighting concepts.

(Eva Matsuzaki and Matsuzaki Wright Architects)

Figure 2.21 Exterior view of the Menara Mesiniaga Tower.

(T. R. Hamzah & Yeang)

system needs to be tempered by occupant education and careful monitoring of outside temperatures and wind conditions so that natural ventilation can be used when appropriate. Maximum reductions in electric lighting and air-conditioning loads are dependent on the owner's and occupants' willingness to put the daylighting and natural ventilation to use. (See Figure 2.21.)

Despite common strategies, the architectural expression of the sun and wind are realized in different ways at the UNI Center for Energy and Environmental Education, Allopro Administration Building, C. K. Choi Institute, and Menara Mesiniaga Tower. These projects suggest that it is possible to integrate passive strategies with architectural integrity and virtually any formal vocabulary. As long as fundamental concepts are respected, designers have tremendous freedom and flexibility in interpreting the language and style of the architecture. In his essay, "A Post-industrial Culture of Regionalism," Jeffrey Cook emphasizes the design opportunities, rather than constraints, of the sun and wind: "Architecturally, the window and its many environmental opportunities should replace the thermostat and its supply grille. The architectural interest of exteriors articulated to modulate the qualities of walls in filtering the natural environment have suddenly expanded the aesthetic vocabulary and encourage buildings to participate with their climate's surroundings."[13]

WATER AND WASTE PROCESSING

Our survival and health depend on water and waste systems, yet little architectural attention is given to the labyrinth of pipes and plumbing components that deliver, process, or transport water and waste. Water, which nourishes and sustains life, has long been used as a means of removing waste in buildings. We continue to use high-grade water for low-grade tasks. Less than 10 percent of our water-related needs are dependent on potable water; meanwhile, water scarcity is increasing, and the quality of water continues to be a growing concern. Sandra Postel gets to the point in her essay, "Forging a Sustainable Water Strategy": "Without water, life and growth cease—a stark reality that may be taking on ever greater importance. . . ."[14] While water may be a global and regional issue, there is also a need to address water conservation and wastewater treatment at the scale of architectural design. At either scale we rarely know where our water comes from and where our wastes go. Equally elusive may be the connection between these issues and daylighting design. One point at which water, waste, daylighting, and passive heating intersect is in the design of spaces for solar aquatic waste systems (also known as Living Machines).

John Todd and Nancy Jack Todd, founders of Ocean Arks International, have devoted much of their lives to the development, testing, and monitoring of solar aquatic waste systems. John Todd explains the principles of Living Machines:

> A Living Machine is a device made up of living organisms of all types and usually housed within a casing or structure of "gossamer" materials. Like a conventional machine it is comprised of interrelated parts with separate functions used in the performance of some type of work. Living Machines can be designed to produce fuels or food, to treat wastes, to purify air, to regulate climates, or even all of these simultaneously. They are engineered with the same design principles used by nature to build and regulate its great ecologies in forests, lakes, prairies or estuaries. Their primary energy source is sunlight. Like the planet, Living Machines have hydrological and mineral cycles.[15]

Living Machines not only do more with less, but also enable occupants to observe the biological processes that transform waste into potable water, raise consciousness about where our water comes from and where our wastes go, and reveal natural cycles associated with ecological systems.

Many of the technical concerns for Living Machines are the same as those for daylighting. John Todd explains that technological, glazing, and daylighting innovations during the past decade have facilitated the realization of biological waste treatment:

Figure 2.22   Exterior view of the Boyne River Ecology Centre.

The containing vessels for the majority of the Living Machines I have developed need to be fabricated from lightweight, high-light-transmitting, flexible materials which can be bonded and waterproofed. They must be capable of handling a variety of stresses including high pressure and ultraviolet radiation. These materials started to become available in the 1970s. By the 1980s new transparent materials like heat mirrors were created to help reduce radiant heat losses. The next step will be materials capable of changing properties based upon internal and external conditions. Such materials will borrow their properties from strategies employed in nature, perhaps as dramatic as that of the skin of some lizards. Materials that are "intelligent" are on the verge of being produced commercially.[16]

Figure 2.23 View of the Living Machine in the solar aquatic room at the Boyne River Ecology Centre.

Unlike some other types of biological waste treatment systems, Living Machines can be located inside buildings. Their successful operation depends in part on a space that provides appropriate solar access, sunlight, and temperatures. As a result, daylighting and passive solar strategies are important considerations in the design of spaces for Living Machines.

The solar aquatic room at the Boyne River Ecology Centre (also known as the Grange) in Shelbourne, Ontario, contains a biological waste treatment system by Ocean Arks International. Doug Pollard Architects designed the building and its systems as teaching tools for environmental education. Therefore, the Living Machine is contained within the prominently and centrally located solar aquatic room, which is extensively glazed on the south facade and roof. Due to the experimental nature of the Living Machine, health inspectors required that adjacent classrooms and gathering spaces be separated from the solar aquatic room by glass. Students can either view the system from within the building or enter inside the solar aquatic room from outside. In addition to housing the Living Machine, the solar aquatic room acts as a heat sink for passive solar gains, a daylighting fixture through which light is borrowed to adjacent spaces, and an important educational space.

The Living Machine at the Boyne River Ecology Centre consists of opaque anaerobic tanks, a series of clear aerobic cylinders in a spiral configuration, and a sequence of interior marshes linked to

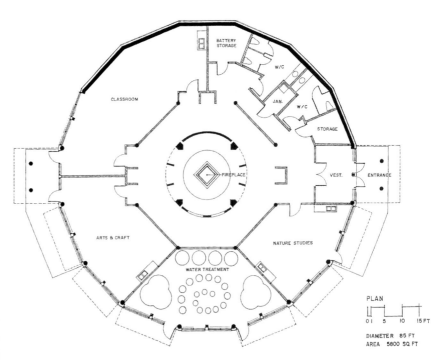

Figure 2.24 Plan of the Boyne River Ecology Centre.

(Doug Pollard Architect)

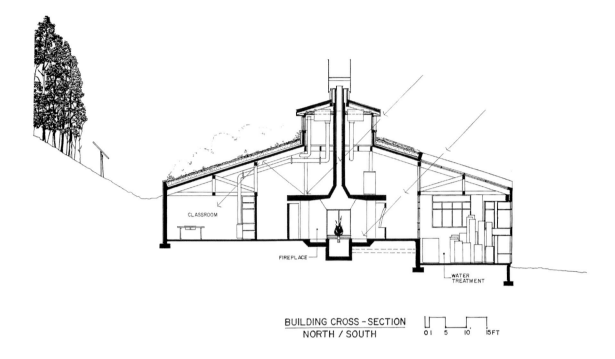

BUILDING CROSS - SECTION
NORTH / SOUTH

0 1 5 10' 15FT

an exterior marsh. Sunlight, fish, snails, plankton, and other microorganisms biologically process water and solid waste. The glazing area, thermal mass, orientation, and shading are designed to provide appropriate luminous and thermal conditions to support the Living Machine. As John Todd explains: "Another important attribute of living systems is that they are pulse-driven. Daily, seasonal, and sporadic variations stamp themselves deeply on the ecology. The background of pulse creates the ability and vigor of the systems to recover from external shocks, which is impossible for conventional machines. A living machine can be overwhelmed by overloading or by light deprivation, and in the process lose critical organisms and ultimately the ability to carry out the assigned task efficiently."[17] Although the Living Machine was intended to process water and waste for recycling and reuse within the building, at this time it plays only an educational role because building codes required a redundant septic system. It is hoped that as the system is monitored over time, building officials will allow the potable water, which results from the biological waste processing, to be recycled within the building. (See Figures 2.22 to 2.25.)

Figure 2.25 Section of the Boyne River Ecology Centre.

(Doug Pollard Architect)

Other recent projects that will help to educate designers, clients, and occupants about biological waste systems include demonstration projects at the Minnesota Children's Museum by Vince James and Julie Snow and the Oberlin College Environmental Studies Center by McDonough + Partners. Whether Living Machines will become more common in architectural design has yet to be determined. According to John Todd,

> The biggest blockade to the emergence of living technologies could be the very phenomenon Living Machines are intended to solve, namely, the estrangement of modern cultures from the natural world. Nature is "invisible" to many people in our culture. It is my hope that the aesthetic and emotional feeling that Living Machines can generate in us will yet carry the day. These machines can be made beautiful and evocative of a deep harmony that is nature. New economies wrapped in the wisdom of the natural world are capable of creating the future we all desire.[18]

ELECTRIC ENERGY GENERATION

Recent innovations in building-integrated photovoltaics (BIPV) combine daylighting, architectural design, and electric energy generation.[19] Designers are now able to integrate photovoltaic systems on or within roofs, cladding, glazing, skylights, and shading devices. New design and aesthetic opportunities have resulted from these innovations, as Theo Holtz notes in *Photovoltaics for Architecture:* "As with every new technology, photovoltaics are also changing architecture. Already today, houses without chimneys, gas mains or electricity are no longer fantasies. Architects are being invited to follow the sun and to avoid all ways which might lead to empty architectural formulas and thus to Icarus's crash. The challenge is to embrace these technical innovations and to find for them new forms of expression." Although some demonstration projects are found in the United States, explorations in the aesthetic and technological implications of BIPV are particularly prevalent in Switzerland and Germany. The popularity of BIPV in these countries is due in part to higher prices for fossil fuels that make the systems more economical, as well as to cultural and political forces that encourage and support new technologies. If the cost of fossil fuels increases during the coming decades and ecological momentum continues to grow, it is feasible that BIPV will become more common throughout the world.

Although the demand for photovoltaics slowed slightly during the past several years, the 10-year average for world shipments increased by 15 percent per year.[20] According to the Energy Efficient and Renewable Energy Division (EERE) of the U.S. Department of Energy, "It is predicted that photovoltaics and other direct conversions of sunlight will be the most rapidly growing form of commercial energy after 2030. . . ."[21] Based on trends in the photovoltaic industry, the design professions can anticipate further research and development in BIPV systems. According to Alan Paradis and Daniel Shugar from the company Advanced Photovoltaics: "The appeal of integrating PV into building materials is that the structure itself becomes an energy producer, providing some or all of the building's electrical energy requirements."[22]

There are also aesthetic and ecological advantages of using BIPV. Since the photovoltaics are integrated with the envelope, buildings on dense or small sites can generate electricity without losing land or roof surface to traditional photovoltaic panels, which leaves these areas free for other purposes. In addition, BIPV can appear more aesthetically integrated with the building—it is integral to the building, rather than something attached to the building. When placed in a visible location, BIPV can also make a statement about the ecological intentions of the building and its owner and can be used to educate occupants or visitors about related ecological, technological, and architectural principles. However, if desired, BIPV can be located less prominently to minimize the visual impacts of the system on the building aesthetic. When properly produced, used, and disposed of, photovoltaics promise tremendous environmental advantages. Timothy Wirth, undersecretary for global affairs, reminds us: "Enough sunlight reaches the earth's surface each year to produce approximately 1,000 times the same amount of energy produced by burning all fossil fuels mined and extracted during the same time period. Sunlight does not have to be explored, mined, extracted, transported, combusted, transmitted, or imported."[23]

A number of technical issues must be considered when integrating BIPV with architectural design, including selecting the type of system, providing adequate solar access, determining the location of the system on the building envelope, and evaluating construction implications, durability, and cost. The performance of BIPV will vary by system, orientation, climate, season, and sky condition. Maximum performance is achieved when the system is positioned to maximize solar exposure for the specific latitude and location. The additional cost of BIPV compared to other photovoltaic systems is another consideration. Othmar Humm and Peter Toggweiler suggest that cost should be considered within a larger context: "Facades with integrated photovoltaic cells are expensive; however, they cost no more than expensive conventional facades, such as natural stone or glass. In comparison to cost-effective standard designs solar facades certainly rate poorly, but their energy yield must be taken into consideration in the overall economic calculation. The use of standard components for fitting photovoltaic cells considerably reduces the cost of facades."[24] BIPV will also become more economically feasible as industry and government researchers continue to improve their performance.

Although optimal performance of BIPV systems is a primary concern, performance may not be the only factor in determining how a system should be integrated with architectural design. The decision of where to locate BIPV on the building envelope is a complex issue that also includes such concerns as aesthetics, solar exposure, construction, and access to daylight. Recent projects with BIPV illustrate that designers are juggling multiple variables and criteria in the design process and that there are many solutions to design integration. (Surprisingly, some designers compromise performance for other criteria, which may include aesthetics, daylighting, construction, etc.). Our focus will be on the opportunities and constraints of integrating BIPV with daylighting design at different building locations (on roofs and skylights, facades, and shading devices).

Roofs and Skylights

Perhaps the most obvious location for photovoltaics is on the building roof, which is typically a large uninterrupted area with good solar access. While attaching traditional solid photovoltaic panels to the roof may be appropriate in some cases, this solution does not present as great a design potential as BIPV, which can be integrated with the daylighting. When the roof is the location of choice, designers should consider whether there are windows, daylighting apertures, solid backs or sides of daylighting monitors, and shading devices or overhangs on the roof that could hold

Figure 2.26 Exterior view of a demonstration project for the Expo Wohnen 2000.

(HHS Planar + Architekten BDA)

photovoltaic glazing or panels. The size and design of skylights and apertures will need to account for the effect of the photovoltaics on the visible light transmittance, shading, and distribution and quality of light. (This impact is less significant if the solid surrounds or overhangs of the window contain the photovoltaics.) In addition, the performance of the photovoltaic systems and daylighting concerns must be weighed when determining the orientation and angle of the roof, skylights, or window surfaces that contain BIPV. The following projects will illustrate some of the distinct opportunities and constraints of roof- and skylight-integrated BIPV.

A demonstration project designed by HHS Planar + Architekten Heger for the Expo Wohnen 2000 in Stuttgart, Germany, integrates rooftop photovoltaics with daylighting and passive heating. The rectilinear building is covered on the south with a large roof surface that uses both clear and photovoltaic glazing. The clear glazing on the lower portion of the roof has adjustable photovoltaic louvers mounted above the glazing. Depending on the season and sky conditions, the louvers can be positioned to admit daylight or sunlight, block solar radiation, or automatically track the sun to produce electricity. The remaining portion of the roof is covered with fixed panels of insulated photovoltaic glazing. The extensive glazing and lightweight photovoltaic frame on the roof contrasts with the solid masonry walls of the building. (See Figures 2.26 to 2.28.)

A less visible approach to roof-integrated photovoltaics and daylighting is found at a school designed by Fritz Haller in Solothurn, Switzerland. A flat roof with gabled skylights brings daylight to the spaces inside while also producing electricity. The south side of the skylights contains photovoltaic glazing that is backlit by the sun. The translucent surface enables occupants inside the building to be aware of weather conditions and the movement of the sun, which powers the photovoltaics. The photovoltaic surface also acts as a shading device to control direct sunlight and glare from the south, while indirect daylight is admitted through clear glass on the north side of the skylight. The different north and south glazing visibly celebrates and informs students about photovoltaic technology and daylighting. In con-

Figure 2.27　Detail of photovoltaic louvers on the demonstration project for the Expo Wohnen 2000.

(HHS Planar + Architekten BDA)

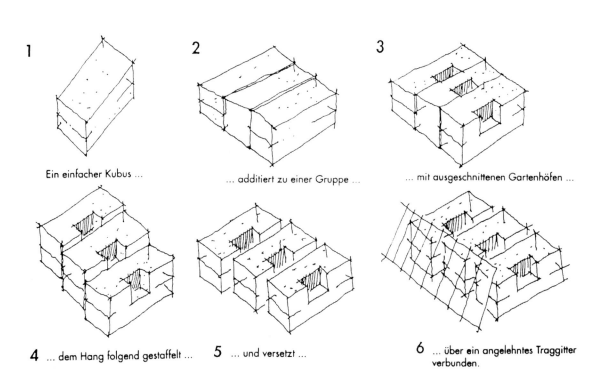

1 Ein einfacher Kubus ...

2 ... additiert zu einer Gruppe ...

3 ... mit ausgeschnittenen Gartenhöfen ...

4 ... dem Hang folgend gestaffelt ...

5 ... und versetzt ...

6 ... über ein angelehntes Traggitter verbunden.

Figure 2.28 Concept diagrams of the demonstration project for the Expo Wohnen 2000. (HHS Planar + Architekten BDA)

trast to using two types of glazing, photovoltaic panels could be mounted to the solid south side of a north-facing roof monitor. In this case the photovoltaic panels would not be revealed on the interior of the building.

These two projects represent opposite ends of the spectrum in integrating photovoltaics and daylighting on the building roof. The demonstration project at the Expo Wohnen 2000 is a visually dramatic statement that can be seen from the exterior and interior. Many types of glazing and adjustable components are combined to integrate electricity production with daylighting and passive heating. Photovoltaic glazing at the school in Solothurn is discreet, being visible only from the interior. The simple, fixed system uses two types of glazing to address daylighting, shading, and production of electricity. An infinite variety of programmatic and aesthetic solutions lie between these two alternatives.

Facade Systems

The integration of photovoltaics is technically less difficult on the facade than on the roof, which is due in part to simplified issues of weatherproofing, condensation, heat loss, and heat gain.[25] New photovoltaic glazing and cladding systems have been developed to facilitate installation on the facade and integration with daylighting. These systems can vary from opaque photovoltaic panels and translucent photovoltaic glass to systems that combine photovoltaic and clear glazing. Since the visible light transmittance of photovoltaic glazing is low, most designers integrate some combination of clear-vision glass with translucent photovoltaic glazing or solid photovoltaic cladding. Designers can choose from off-the-shelf products or specify custom assemblies for specific lighting, heating, cooling, acoustic, shading, or aesthetic concerns. Recent product innovations include opaque photovoltaic spandrel panels utilizing high-performance windows in curtain-wall systems for cladding, awnings, shading devices, and overhangs. Other developments include glazing systems that sandwich thin-film photovoltaic cells between two layers of glass to provide varying degrees of view and visible-light transmittance.

With roof systems, there is an opportunity to integrate photovoltaics with daylighting monitors, lightscoops, sunscoops, and skylights. On the building facade, the form and configuration of windows is typically more two-dimensional, and as a result the photovoltaics are not usually attached to the window itself. Instead, they are often assembled into a two-dimensional curtain wall that includes photovoltaic cladding, photovoltaic glazing, and/or clear-vision glass. In addition, facade glazing is typically oriented in a vertical position. This not only affects the performance of the photovoltaics, but also influences the rela-

Figure 2.29 Exterior detail of the photovoltaic curtain wall and shading device at the Advanced Photovoltaic System Factory.

(Kiss + Cathcart)

tionship between inside and outside. As a result, a variety of issues should be considered in the design of a photovoltaic curtain-wall system. What combination of clear glazing, photovoltaic glazing, or photovoltaic cladding will ensure daylight access and adequate electric energy production? What views and physical connections should be made to the site? Is privacy a factor? Are there sources of noise to consider in the window location? In most photovoltaic curtain-wall systems, the challenge is to design the appropriate pattern and amount of photovoltaics versus clear glazing to balance aesthetic, luminous, thermal, and electricity considerations.

The Advanced Photovoltaic System Factory by Kiss Cathcart Anders is a demonstration project that is evaluating the effect of orientation on the performance of BIPV. The designers placed BIPV on a south awning, on vertical curtain walls facing all cardinal orientations, and on the south side of a gabled skylight. Comparative studies found that the orientation of the photovoltaics has significant impact. According to Alan Paradis and Daniel Shugar from APS: ". . . the south-facing curtain wall generates 55 percent less energy than a proportionally sized section of the awning. While the vertical curtain wall orientation is not optimized for energy production, it offers one of the most attractive opportunities for offsetting conventional materials."[26] Not surprisingly, maximum performance is obtained in systems that are sloped in a south orientation. (See Figures 2.29 and 2.30.)

Figure 2.30 Interior view of the photovoltaic curtain wall at the Advanced Photovoltaic System Factory.

(Kiss + Cathcart)

The administration building for Stadwerke Aachen in Aachen, Germany, designed by Georg Feinhals, uses a clear and photovoltaic curtain wall in a bold geometric pattern. The clear glazing forms a cross-shaped window for views and sunlight penetration, with surrounding photovoltaic glazing consisting of translucent modules with a thin grid of clear glazing. Daylight enters around each photovoltaic module to cast a fine grid of sunlight on interior surfaces, which is contrasted by larger and more brightly illuminated patterns of sunlight from the clear windows. The resulting quality of light is dynamic and celebratory. Noncritical luminous activities are most appropriate in this location, considering the vibrant effect and southern orientation. Given the limits of any curtain-wall system, designers have great freedom in determining the patterns and proportions of photovoltaic versus clear glazing, qualities of daylight, transparency or translucency of the glass, and relationship between inside and outside.

Shading Systems

A final method of integrating photovoltaics and daylighting is to use the surfaces of shading devices for photovoltaic glazing or panels. This building location can provide great flexibility in positioning the photovoltaics for solar exposure and can reduce potential conflicts with daylight access (which can occur with systems located on the facade). Photovoltaic considerations such as orientation, performance, weather, and construction must be considered in conjunction with shading concerns such as diurnal and seasonal requirements, solar geometry, and the type of shading device (opaque, translucent, solid, louvered, etc.). The challenge is to design a shading device that meets both diurnal and seasonal shading needs and photovoltaic requirements. This can be a significant task, because in many climates shading is used only during the overheated period, while electricity is needed throughout the year.

An adjustable shading device (manual or automated) can help maximize photovoltaic and shading performance by allowing the device to be repositioned for different sun angles. Systems can be angled up, down, in, out, or can even be repositioned above the window if direct solar gains are beneficial in the winter. Although maintenance and cost are greater in adjustable systems, increased BIPV and shading performance make this option desirable. Fixed shading devices involve lower costs and maintenance; however, they inevitably compromise the performance of the photovoltaic system since their position relative to the sun is unchanging. As a result, the performance of the photovoltaic system varies over the course of the year. This seasonal performance discrepancy is a typical characteristic of photovoltaics, since fixed mountings are most common. Given these advantages and disadvantages, the designer and clients must determine which type of shading system is most appropriate for the project.

An innovative demonstration project designed by Reto P. Miloni for the Swissbau 93 Exhibition in Basel, Switzerland, maximizes solar control, daylighting, and photovoltaic performance. The system includes adjustable photovoltaic panels beneath operable high-performance windows and an adjustable shading device constructed of photovoltaic louvers. Photovoltaic panels beneath the windows are adjusted at various angles to maximize electricity production throughout the year. The photovoltaic louvers of the shading device are retracted (and subsequently do not pro-

Figure 2.31
Demonstration project for the Swissbau 93 Exhibition.

(Reto P. Miloni)

duce electricity) under overcast conditions or when direct sunlight is desired in the interior. When shading is needed under clear-sky conditions, the louvers simultaneously block sunlight and produce electricity. The performance of the shading device photovoltaics varies based on lighting needs. The two systems can be combined or used independently, depending on the time of year, luminous requirements, and electricity demands. Such dual systems challenge our assumptions about the integration of shad-

Figure 2.32 Photovoltaic shading devices on the CESTM.

(Gordon Schenck Jr. and Kawneer Company, Inc.)

ing, daylighting, and electricity production. They also suggest that we might better use surfaces that are often neglected yet optimally located for solar exposure. (See Figure 2.31.)

Another installation that integrates shading and photovoltaics is the Center for Environmental Science and Technology Management (CESTM) at the State University of New York at Albany by Cannon & Associates. The CESTM uses a BIPV curtain wall (developed collaboratively by Kawneer and Solarex) on the exterior of south-facing shading devices. As Kawneer explains: "The PV module consists of a piece of low-iron, tempered float glass. The solar cells are set between two layers of ethyl vinyl acetate (EVA) and laminated. The back of the ply on the interior side of the module is laminated with a protective layer of Tadlar film.

Figure 2.33 Distant view of the Wilkhahn Factory.
(© Dieter Leistner/Architekton)

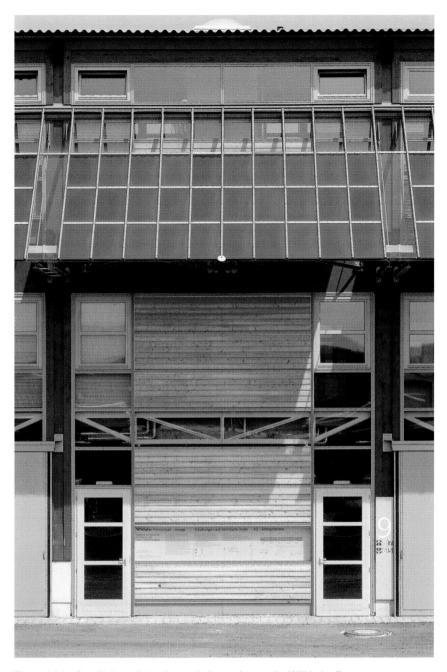

Figure 2.34   Detail view of the photovoltaic awning on the Wilkhahn Factory.

(© Dieter Leistner/Architekton)

Overall module thickness is ¼ inch."[27] Cannon & Associates integrate BIPV in a manner that is elegant as well as effective. The simple shading devices are used to generate electricity, reduce thermal gains and cooling loads, and control the quality of daylight. The Wilkhahn Factory by Thomas Herzog and the RWE AG Headquarters by Ingenhoven, Overdiek and Partner are two additional projects that integrate shading, daylighting, and BIPV with architectural integrity. (See Figures 2.32 to 2.35.)

A final example that illustrates how multiple concerns can be addressed through the design of a simple shading device is the Artvetro-designed awning-shaped shading device for an office building in Liestal, Switzerland. This shading device met the goals of controlling daylight, producing electricity, protecting the wood facade from rain, and even preventing the spread of fire between floors. It is constructed of a steel frame with translucent photovoltaic panels that diffuses direct sunlight while admitting abundant daylight. The depth, materials, and construction of the shading device are intended to prevent the vertical spread of flames between floors in case of fire. Whether photovoltaic systems are integrated on a roof, facade, or shading device, each

Figure 2.35 Detail of the photovoltaic awning on the RWE AG Headquarters.

(Holger Knauf)

location has the potential to weave together multiple layers of issues, from electric energy production to daylighting, solar control, passive heating, and weather and fire protection. Although there have been many innovations during the past decade, we have just begun to explore the ecological and aesthetic opportunities of BIPV.

PLANT GROWTH

Plants are rarely associated with architectural daylighting, yet they provide an excellent conceptual metaphor for ecological design and the principle of "doing more with less." As John Todd and Nancy Jack Todd explain in *Tomorrow Is Our Permanent Address:*

> From the point of view of design, a plant is noteworthy because of the way it fits into its larger ecology and has through its morphology and physiology devised methods of trapping and transforming energy, using nutrients, creating foods, and providing structure and shelter for itself so that it can withstand perturbation and change. It symbolizes a triumph in design. Plants do a great deal with very little, and yet they sustain many other forms of life. The biological metaphor or analogy may be the most important guide available.[28]

Plants also provide psychological and physiological nourishment. Most people take pleasure in nurturing plants, watching them grow, and watching their foliage and flowers change with the seasons. The psychological and physiological benefits of tending plants are reflected in the growing popularity of therapeutic gardens in arboreta, botanical gardens, healthcare facilities, and even correctional facilities. At a recent Healthcare Design Conference, Dr. Bernie Siegel emphasized the importance of plants in healing environments, "Put the plants and animals in the hospital—they don't charge for therapy. I have plants who teach me about life. . . . When you doubt life, go to nature. It has all the answers on how to deal with adversity."[29] Plants also nourish us by providing food, creating fragrances that enliven our senses, and filtering and purifying the air. A recent study by NASA found that plants can effectively reduce indoor air pollution, which is an increasingly serious problem associated with sick building syndrome (SBS) and building-related illnesses (BRI). According to

NASA, ". . . by including indoor house and office plants, one may reduce substantially the amount of exposure to now common VOCs [volatile organic compounds] one experiences daily."[30] Similar research by the Botanical Institute at the University of Köln found that hydroplants (which grow without soil) are particularly effective at reducing air pollution from formaldehyde, benzol, phenol, and nicotine. Only one or two hydroplants, such as *Ficus benjamina* and *Pothos aureus,* per 100 square feet are needed to absorb and transform pollutants into oxygen, sugars, and new plant growth. Other common plants that remove air pollutants include chrysanthemums, gerbera daisies, English ivy, peace lily, and bamboo palm.

It is typically in the design of sunspaces, greenhouses, glasshouses, and conservatories that we find an intersection of plants and daylighting design. While all of these are designated for plant growth, they vary in design, size, and intent. Sunspaces are usually small rooms adjacent or connected to a structure that is used to grow plants for food, pleasure, and health. While greenhouses can be residential (typically used for plant starts and winter gardening), they most often refer to larger commercial spaces for wholesale or retail growing. Glasshouses or conservatories include large public facilities with botanical exhibitions for pleasure, education, and research. Any space for plants, whether it is a building, room, or window niche, requires adequate light, humidity, temperature, soil, and water. As a result, the design of plant spaces requires careful attention to daylighting and environmental technologies. The following discussion will focus on the opportunities of different types of plant spaces: sunspaces and greenhouses for pleasure and food and conservatories for exhibition, research, and the preservation of biodiversity.

Sunspaces and Greenhouses

Personal sunspaces, greenhouses, and solaria for plants, vegetables, herbs, and fruits are popular in Europe, which may be due in part to tradition and climate and in part to energy-efficiency programs that encourage the use of passive solar design. Whether as a result of culture, land-use patterns and values, larger yards and gardens, or simply different priorities, these types of spaces are fairly uncommon in the United States. The sunspaces and greenhouses that do exist in the United States tend to focus on plants for pleasure rather than for food production. (Ironically, the low costs associated with transportation in the United States often make it more economical to obtain foods from other regions than to grow it in local greenhouses or gardens.) Despite the modest interest in these types of spaces in the United States, they still provide significant ecological lessons and benefits.

Contemporary greenhouses illustrate varied approaches to design, size, and intent. On one end of the spectrum we find huge research projects like the Biosphere II, designed by architect Phil Hawes of Sarbid Corporation and located south of Tucson, Arizona. Covering 3.15 acres, Biosphere II was intended to simulate the earth's biological processes within a contained and technologically moderated environment that was to house four men and women and over 3800 species of plants for two years. Michael Crosbie describes the peculiar mission of Biosphere in his article "Desert Shield": "While Biosphere's planners explain the project's value is understanding life on Earth, their long-term agenda seems more focused on creating a safe haven for eventual Armageddon. . . . Biosphere II isn't meant to live in harmony with nature, but to bottle it for export."[31] Crosbie describes Biosphere as "a building size petri dish recreating nature with a massive dose of technology." This huge glass and steel structure is a bizarre juxtaposition of ecology and technology that uses sophisticated environmental controls to sustain itself and regulate lighting, cooling, heating, air, waste, and water. The ecological integrity of Biosphere II was cast in doubt from its onset, given the climate, location, scale, and energy needed for its maintenance. (See Figure 2.36.)

The technological approach of Biosphere II contrasts sharply with the biological approach found in the pioneering "bioshelters" designed by John Todd and Nancy Jack Todd during the 1970s and 1980s at the former New Alchemy Institute (recent offshoots include Ocean Arks International and Living Technologies). Like the Todds' "bioshelters," Biosphere II explores the integration of food, waste, and energy production within an extensive system of greenhouses. The Todds' bioshelters were used for many purposes, including waste treatment, food and fuel production, climate regulation, and air purification. However, the biological processes associated with light, wind, plants, and water primarily drove the Todds' bioshelters, which were supported rather than driven by technological processes. The Living

Figure 2.36   Exterior view of the Biosphere II.

(Abigail Van Slyck)

Machines described earlier in this chapter represent a variation on the Todds' bioshelter research. An example is found in the Living Machine project in South Burlington by Living Technologies, which combines greenhouse design, plant growth, and biological waste treatment. (See Figure 2.37.)

At the other end of the spectrum, we find small greenhouses that are used to grow exotic and tropical plants or to produce food. At the Nyland Cohousing Community in Lafayette, Colorado, a solar-heated greenhouse supports and supplements organic produce from the gardens. Many of the 42 homes in the community also include small greenhouses or sunspaces, which enable residents to enjoy fresh locally grown vegetables and herbs throughout the year. Sunspaces, greenhouses, and solaria are also built for pleasure, health, and well-being, as we find in the small, passive solar greenhouse at the Rocky Mountain Institute (RMI) at Snowmass, Colorado. Dianna Lopez Barnett and William Browning describe the experience of the greenhouse at RMI: "It's December and snowing. Sitting in Rocky Mountain Institute's 4000-square-foot headquarters, you can watch the iguana laze in the flowering bougainvillea, listen to the waterfall splashing into the fishponds, and wait for the bananas to ripen."[32] The greenhouse acts as a solar collector, contributes daylight to adjacent spaces, and provides a refreshing retreat in which plants, ani-

Figure 2.37   Interior view of the South Burlington Living Machine.
(Natalie Stultz/Living Technologies)

mals, and water are combined to provide physiological and psychological renewal. (See Figures 2.38 to 2.40.)

Sunspaces can also be used to organize the space in a building and to admit daylight to areas with restricted solar access. The Mews House in Bloomsbury, London, designed by Greenberg & Hawkes, uses a plant conservatory to solve daylighting issues created by a dense urban site. Walls surround the building on three sides, with a street (or mews) immediately adjacent to the remaining facade. According to the architects, "If we were to achieve privacy in the mews at ground level and limit the size and number of windows, it would be necessary to light most of the ground floor from some kind of lightwell. But this would consume valuable space and would certainly be dark and uncongenial. This led us to the decision to have a roof-lit conservatory rather than an open lightwell."[33] The floor plan and section of the three-story building is organized around the toplit conservatory located in the northeast corner of the house. The ground floor contains a bedroom

Figure 2.38 Exterior view of the greenhouse at the Rocky Mountain Institute.

(Michelle Juneau)

Figure 2.39   Interior view of the greenhouse at the Rocky Mountain Institute.

(Michelle Juneau)

Figure 2.40 Axonometric drawing of the Rocky Mountain Institute.

(Rocky Mountain Institute)

and study adjacent to the conservatory, a bath, and a hall. The middle floor has an open plan with the kitchen, dining, and living areas, while the upper floor contains a large roof terrace and enclosed loggia with stairwell. Professor Simos Yannas, at the Architectural Association, suggests that there are thermal as well as luminous benefits of the conservatory: ". . . It receives heat gain from the surrounding heated spaces on three sides, with a smaller input coming from solar gain through the eastern-sloping-roof glazing. Such an arrangement should permit this space to maintain higher temperatures in winter than an ordinary attached

Figure 2.41   Exterior view of the Mews House.
(Tim James)

Figure 2.42   Interior view of the conservatory at the Mews House.
(Tim James)

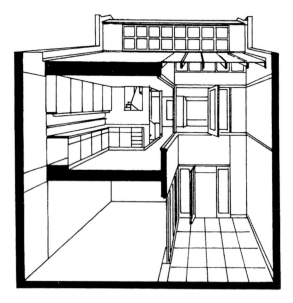

Figure 2.43   Axonometric drawing of the Mews House.
(Joe Ford)

conservatory and also enable it to act as a more effective thermal buffer to rooms facing onto it."[34] In addition, the plant conservatory spatially organizes the house, provides visual relief, and supplies indirect daylighting to adjacent rooms. Despite the extensive glazing requirements of a sunroom, greenhouse, or conservatory, these precedents suggest that it is possible to do more with less by integrating plants and daylighting while creating meaningful architectural experiences. (See Figures 2.41 to 2.43.)

Glasshouses and Conservatories

Finally, the design of glasshouses and conservatories integrates architecture, daylighting, plant conservation, and the preservation of biodiversity. In 1989, the World Wildlife Fund (WWF) developed the World Conservation Strategy, which included the first Botanical Garden Conservation Strategy. The WWF made a plea to botanical gardens throughout the world to adopt plant conservation as their primary mission.[35] Subsequently, the conservatories at many botanical gardens have come to play an important role in species preservation, education, research, plant propagation, and off-site conservation. According to a study by the Smithsonian Institution, "1.4 million plants and animals have been described, although estimates of the total number of species run as high as 5 million. If it is assumed that between twenty to fifty percent of all species will be extinct by the year 2000, we may be losing as many as six species per hour."[36] Although the role of the conservatory in species preservation is limited in comparison to the critical task of habitat preservation, work in plant reintroduction and off-site conservation may be the only alternative for critically endangered plants.

The practice of growing plants in a controlled environment can be traced back to the Romans, yet it was not until the sixteenth century that plants were placed inside buildings. Glasshouses were initially used for scientific inquiry, with a shift to the production of exotic fruits for the wealthy as international trade expanded. The design of early glasshouses responded to climate, site, and environmental forces through orientation, operable shading, natural ventilation, wind blocks, and solid masonry walls on the north.[37] Many of these simple climatic responses were abandoned during the nineteenth century with technological advances in heating, glazing, and iron construction. As a result, the conservatory became a distinct object in the landscape—a miracle of modern technology. At the same time, the philosophical mission of the glasshouse shifted from scientific endeavors to entertainment. Nineteenth-century glasshouses, particularly the large winter gardens, were places of refuge from the environmental exploitation and degradation of the industrial revolution, with its subsequent effects of urban growth, housing shortages, overcrowding, and poor sanitation.[38] The conservatory became a Garden of Eden.

The decline of the glasshouse during the early twentieth century was a result of a movement away from the machine aesthetic. In addition, many conservatories were destroyed or fell into disrepair during World War I. It was not until the 1960s and 1970s that there was a significant renewal of interest in the glasshouse. During this period "homegrown" greenhouses (many of which were influenced by Buckminster Fuller's geodesic domes) sprang up across the country in response to growing environmental concerns and owners' desires to get closer to the land and nature. For many reasons, the experimentation of the 1960s and 1970s was not sustained, and we find that the past two decades have seen yet another decline in small greenhouses. In contrast, a surprising number of large public conservatories were constructed during the past decade, and the design of many of these facilities explicitly addresses ecological concerns. New conservatories often combine lessons from the earliest climate-responsive glasshouses from the seventeenth century (orientation, siting, and building massing) with new technological innovations (glazing, mechanical systems, shading systems, and materials).

The Lucille Halsell Conservatory by Emilio Ambasz is just one example that combines lessons from history with new technologies. Reflecting the bermed masonry walls of early glasshouses, the Halsell Conservatory is recessed into the earth for thermal protection. Large glass roofs reach to the sky to gather daylight. Because the conservatory is located in San Antonio, Texas, heat gain rather than heat loss is the primary thermal consideration. Visitors enter the conservatory through an opening in a bermed wall that leads to a sunken courtyard. A shaded loggia surrounds the courtyard and links three glass conservatories which emerge from the landscape overhead. Ambasz explains the conceptual relationship between the landscape and the conservatories: ". . . the idea of a passage from earth to sky and from darkness to light drives the design . . . pushing it from mere utility toward myth."[39] The earth-sheltered form is a response to hot climatic conditions and southern vernacular traditions, yet the conservatory combines the shaded inner concrete loggia with steel and glass construction in a new way. In addition, the Halsell Conservatory is unique in its use of the loggia as a means of unifying separate conservatories. This arrangement enables the internal temperatures, humidity, and light levels to be varied for the specific plant species in each conservatory.

The regional approach to the Lucille Halsell Conservatory, which includes earth berms, glazed peaks oriented to maximize solar exposure, and a loggia that protects visitors from the hot Texas sun, is unprecedented in conservatory design, as David Dillon explains: "Traditional conservatories . . . are essentially gigantic glass sheds designed to admit as much sunlight as possible.

Figure 2.44 Exterior view of the Lucille Halsell Conservatory.

(Greg Hursley)

They are Northern phenomena. Ambasz recognized immediately that such a design would never work in San Antonio where summer temperatures often exceed 100 degrees and even the hardiest plants can get charbroiled. So he buried much of the plant rooms. . . . Light enters through the glass cones and triangles, which are equipped with operable windows and computerized sun screens that can be raised and lowered as light levels change."[40] The conservatory also uses a variety of lighting, heating, and cooling technologies. A custom shade cloth reduces light transmission by 37 percent; electric resistance heaters reduce the need for extensive piping, multiple boilers, and gas lines; and a fog machine keeps the plants moist and provides evaporative cooling. The conservatory is monitored by an environmental control system that operates shading, fans, vents, heaters, and fresh air.

Figure 2.45 View of the interior courtyard and loggia at the Lucille Halsell Conservatory.

(Greg Hursley)

The Lucille Halsell Conservatory is just one example of a building that combines traditional daylighting and thermal design with current environmental technology. Other projects that illustrate these and other ecological design concepts include the addition to the Steinhardt Conservatory at the Brooklyn Botanic Gardens as well as the Princess of Wales Conservatory at Kew Gardens in the United Kingdom. Recent innovations in conservatory design suggest that as natural species evolve, so must the process of design. By studying the typological evolution of the conservatory, we can see changes in designs that are making this building type more energy efficient and site and climate responsive. Greenhouses and conservatories are beginning to do more with less by combining daylighting with passive solar strategies to create lighting, heating, and ventilation conditions that foster and encourage plant growth while also providing human benefits. (See Figures 2.44 to 2.46.)

The preceding projects only hint at the potential opportunities of doing more with less by coupling daylighting with other solar strategies. If nothing else, we must begin by using daylight to provide illumination. From this point we can consider ways of adding passive heating, water and waste processing, production of electricity, plant growth, and other concerns. The integration of seemingly disparate issues requires innovation, experimentation, a willingness to take risks, and introspection. While reductions in the consumption of energy and natural resources inevitably result from doing more with less, this principle also challenges us to reconsider our patterns of consumption and personal values. An unanticipated byproduct of doing more with less is often a more conscious use of natural resources and redefinition of waste. As Duane Elgin suggests in his book *Voluntary Simplicity:* "The objective is not dogmatically to live with less, but is a more demanding intention of living with balance in order to find a life of greater purpose, fulfillment, and satisfaction."[41] Doing more with less has ecological, cultural, and even political implications. Yet underlying all these issues is the bottom line—we must begin to use the resources that we need rather than the resources that we can use. Wendell Berry cuts to the quick in his essay "The

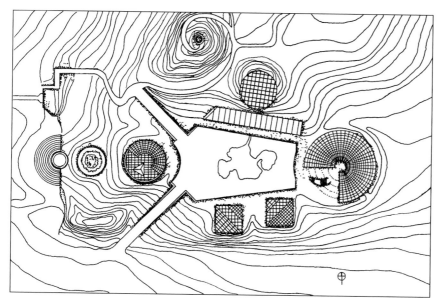

Figure 2.46 Plan of the Lucille Halsell Conservatory.

(Joe Ford)

Futility of Global Thinking": "We must achieve the character and acquire the skills to live much poorer than we do. We must waste less. We must do more for ourselves and each other. . . ."[42]

ENDNOTES

1. Michael Hough, *Out of Place* (New Haven: Yale University Press, 1990), 190.
2. Dianna Lopez Barnett with William D. Browning, *A Primer on Sustainable Building* (Colorado: The Rocky Mountain Institute, 1995), 17.
3. John Reynolds, "Glazing Forum," *Solar '95,* panel discussion at the American Solar Energy Society, *20th National Passive Solar Conference,* Minneapolis, Minn., July 1995.
4. For discussion of electric lighting controls, see Mark S. Rea, ed., *The Lighting Handbook* (New York: Illuminating Engineering Society of North America), 1995.
5. Adam Jackaway and David Greene, "Shedding Light on Ionica," *The Architects' Journal* (28 March 1996): 53.
6. Thomas Herzog, *Thomas Herzog: Bauten 1978–1992, Buildings,* Stuttgart: Hatje Verlag, 1993, 51.
7. Ibid., 65.
8. Jeffrey Cook, "A Post-industrial Culture of Regionalism," *Critical Regionalism: The Pomona Meeting Proceedings,* edited by Spyros Amourgis (Pomona Calif.: College of Environmental Design, California Polytechnic University, 1991), 173.
9. The American Solar Energy Society is an excellent source for information about recent innovations in passive solar design and technologies. American Solar Energy Society, 2400 Central Avenue, Suite G-1, Boulder, CO 80301, visit their website at http://www.sni.net/solar/.
10. Michael Tobias and Georgianne Cowan, eds., *The Soul of Nature* (New York: Penguin Books, 1996), 265.
11. Richard Saul Wurman, *What Will Be Has Always Been: The Words of Louis I. Kahn* (New York: Rizzoli International Publications, Inc., 1986), 87.
12. Burke Miller Thayer, "A Passive Solar University Center," *Solar Today* 10, no. 2 (March–April 1996): 37.
13. Spyros Amourgis, ed., 173.

14. Lester R. Brown, ed., *State of the World* (New York: W.W. Norton & Company, 1996), 41.
15. John Todd, "Living Machines for Pure Water: Sewage as Resource." Ocean Arks International Homepage, http://www.earthbase.org/guests/oai/oailivmachjt.html, 1995, Internet.
16. Ibid.
17. Ibid.
18. Ibid.
19. "PV is short for photovoltaics (photo = light, voltaics = electricity). PV is a semiconductor-based technology (similar to the microchip) used to convert light energy into direct current electricity, using no moving parts, consuming no fuel, and creating no pollution." Solar Energy Industries (SEIA) Fact Sheets, SEIA Homepage, http://www.ecn.nl/eii_138.html, 1995, Internet.
20. Lester R. Brown, Hal Kane, and Ed Ayres, eds., *Vital Signs 1993* (New York: W.W. Norton & Company, 1993), 52.
21. Energy Efficient and Renewable Energy Division (EERE), U.S. Department of Energy, "1998 Budget Briefing," SEIA Homepage, http://www.ecn.nl/eii/homepgnI/eii_138.html, February 6, 1997, Internet.
22. Alan Paradis and Daniel S. Shugar, "Photovoltaic Building Materials," *Solar Today* 8, no. 3 (May–June 1994): 34.
23. Timothy Wirth, *Second Conference of the Parties Framework Convention on Climate Change,* Geneva, Switzerland, July 17, 1996, Solar Energy Industries Association (SEIA) Homepage, http://www.ecn.nl/eii/homepgnl/eii_138.html, Internet.
24. Othmar Humm and Peter Toggweiler, *Photovoltaics in Architecture* (Basel: Birkhäuser Verlag, 1993), 114.
25. Ibid., 108.
26. Alan Paradis and Daniel S. Shugar, 37.
27. Kawneer Company, Inc., 1600 PowerWall Product Literature, Form No. 96-1268, Kawneer Company, Inc., 1996, 1.
28. John Todd and Nancy Jack Todd, *Tomorrow Is Our Permanent Address* (New York: Harper & Row, 1980), 55–56.
29. Bernie S. Siegel, "Healthcare Design in the Next Century," *Journal of Healthcare Design* 7, http://www.healthdesign.org/library/journal/journal7/j72.htm., Internet, 3.
30. NASA Clean Air Study—Sick Building Syndrome, "What Is Sick Building Syndrome?" http://www.zone10.com/Tech/

NASA/SICK_BLD.htm; and "Hydroculture: The Cure for Sick Building Syndrome," I.U.W.F., http://.interurban.com/hydroponics/articles/tap.html, Internet.

31. Michael Crosbie, "Desert Shield," *Architecture* 80, no. 5 (May 1991): 77–78.

32. Dianna Lopez Barnett and William D. Browning, *A Primer on Sustainable Building,* Colorado: The Rocky Mountain Institute, 66.

33. Simos Yannas, *Solar Energy and Housing Design,* vol. 2 (London: Architectural Association, 1994), 83–84.

34. Ibid., 85.

35. The growing interest in ecological approaches to conservatory design corresponded with a redefinition of the ecological mission of botanical gardens throughout the world. The *Botanic Garden Conservation Report,* developed by the World Conservation Union, had a significant impact on these ecological changes. For information see World Conservation Union, *Botanic Garden Conservation Report* (Switzerland: World Wide Fund for Nature, 1989).

36. Judith Gradwohl, *Saving the Tropical Rain Forest* (London: Earthscan Publications Ltd., 1988), 50.

37. John Hix, *The Glass House* (London, England: Phaidon Press Ltd., 1974), 13.

38. Georg Kohlmaier and Barna von Sartory, *Houses of Glass* (Cambridge, Mass.: MIT Press, 1981), 1.

39. David Dillon, "Drama of Nature and Form," *Architecture* 77, no. 5 (May 1988): 148.

40. Ibid.

41. Duane Elgin, *Voluntary Simplicity,* rev. ed. (New York: William Morrow & Co., 1993), 25.

42. Bill Willers, ed., *"Learning to Listen to the Land* (Washington D.C.: Island Press, 1991), 154.

Chapter 3

Design for Evolution

*A building is not something you finish. A building is
something you start.*[1]

—STUART BRAND

We live in a world that is constantly changing. The work we do,
where we live, the ways we communicate, even our cultural and
political institutions shift and alter from day to day. Change is
fundamental to life, yet so few of our buildings are designed to
accommodate this process. Adaptation and evolution are inherent
to an ecological design process, as John and Nancy Todd explain
in *Tomorrow Is Our Permanent Address:* "In the living world, evolutionary design, for some unexplained reason, is continuous and
highly adaptive. Inherent in its adaptability may be some of the
clues essential to attempting a synthesis of modern knowledge.
Such continuous adaptability is very important. It is at once
architecture and structure; it is also a dynamic process, developing unity where chaos would otherwise ensue. . . ."[2] The forces of
time, whether environmental or sociological, are influential factors in design. In *How Buildings Learn,* Stuart Brand suggests that
a building is something the designer starts rather than finishes; a
building has a life of its own, intimately linked to the users.

WASTE AND EVOLUTIONARY DESIGN

Underlying the concepts of building adaptation and evolution is a
desire to minimize waste and reduce resource consumption. From
discarded tin cans to discarded buildings, waste is part of the

American lifestyle. Stuart Ewen, professor of media services at Hunter College, provides a historical perspective of our consumptive tendencies in his essay "Waste a Lot, Want a Lot": ". . . the practice of obsolescence was part of a sometimes desperate attempt to build markets in a shrinking economy, the period following World War II saw obsolescence installed as a basic underpinning to the 'populuxe' ideal of suburban prosperity. . . . It is the prime mover of our national wealth."[3] Although we may not intentionally design buildings to become obsolete, it is all too rare that they are explicitly designed to grow and adapt with future users and needs.

A lack of foresight often leads to the architectural equivalent of planned obsolescence. Despite preservation efforts, many cities throughout the country are notorious for razing their old (and not-so-old) buildings. (The city of Minneapolis, which recently tore down an "obsolete" baseball stadium, is currently embroiled in efforts to build a new stadium—complete with retractable roof.) How can we reduce waste and obsolescence while meeting our desire for the new? How might old buildings be reclaimed, and how might we conceive of new buildings to address future needs? What role can daylighting design play in these efforts? If change is inherent to the American lifestyle, rather than discarding our buildings like so much waste, could the concepts and principles of adaptation and evolution shape our built environment and our design thinking?

Buildings that adapt and change over time are less likely to become obsolete, less likely to fall prey of the wrecking ball, and subsequently less likely to consume new natural resources and proliferate waste. The United States generates over 160 million tons of waste per year, with construction debris accounting for over 60 percent of the waste in our landfills.[4] In his essay "The Waste of Place," Kevin Lynch wrote: "Waste is what is worthless or unused for human purpose. It is a lessening of something without useful result; it is loss and abandonment, decline, separation and death. It is the spent and valueless material left after some act of production or consumption, but it can also refer to any used thing: garbage, trash, litter, junk, impurity and dirt. There are waste things, waste lands, waste time and wasted lives."[5] Our definitions and perceptions of waste must be challenged if we are to reconcile our desire for change with pressing environmental concerns. Ecologists remind us that there is no waste in natural systems. The natural cycles ensure that waste from one becomes food for another. From an architectural perspective, this ecological metaphor encourages us to explore waste as a resource. How might we reconsider wasted space, materials, energy, and even light?

Although the environmental benefits of designs that adapt and change to reduce waste and resource consumption are compelling, we can also consider the less tangible sociological and cultural benefits of evolutionary principles. Stuart Brand captures these more elusive issues in his quote from musician Brian Eno:

> We are convinced by things that show internal complexity, that show the traces of an interesting evolution. . . . An important aspect of design is the degree to which the object involves you in its own completion. Some work invites you into itself by not offering a finished, glossy, one-reading-only surface. This is what makes old buildings interesting to me. I think that humans have a taste for things that not only show that they have been through a process of evolution, but which also show they are still a part of one. They are not dead yet.[6]

Eno alludes to the human benefits of buildings and spaces that engage users and encourage them to participate in the processes of change, modification, and evolution. In addition to the human physiological and psychological benefits, there are also cultural and historical factors to consider. In *Out of Place,* Michael Hough discusses the importance of maintaining a sense of history: "The protection of natural and cultural history—the reuse and integration of the old into the new without fanfare while avoiding the temptation to turn everything into a museum because it is old—lies at the heart of maintaining a continuing link with the past and with a place's identity."[7] Providing a historical link through architecture implies extending the act of design through time. Is it possible to speculate on tomorrow? Can we imagine what will happen to and in a building over the months, years, and decades? In *Bridging the Gap,* Richard Roger examines this approach to design: ". . . We are looking for an architecture rather like some music and poetry which can actually be changed by the users, an architecture of improvisation."[8] Although no one can know what the future may hold, it is possible to balance our propensity for change with environmental concerns by employing design strategies that provide some degree of versatility to enable buildings and spaces to evolve with and for the users.

AN EVOLUTIONARY APPROACH TO DAYLIGHTING

The concept of evolutionary design reduces waste and resource consumption and also supports the changing needs of people, reinforces a sense of history and place, and invites occupants to participate in the life of the building. While design for adaptability and evolution generally focuses on materials, structures, and space planning, it is also possible to apply these concepts of change to daylighting design. Many building types and programs would benefit from greater flexibility and adaptability, including libraries, schools, museums, retail spaces, and housing.[9]

A surprising number of buildings and programs lend themselves to change. Museums have different luminous and spatial requirements for permanent and traveling collections. Libraries have new technological demands resulting from the digital revolution that challenge our preconceptions of how space is used and configured. Schools are exploring learning and teaching approaches that reconsider the organization and definition of a classroom. The concepts of home, family, and work are being transformed. As a result, approaches to space planning, the building envelope, structural systems, and even the role of windows need to be reconsidered. How can daylighting design help to facilitate future change, adaptation, and evolution?

We can begin with the popular expression "reduce, reuse, and recycle," concepts commonly associated with waste reduction. These concepts can also encourage innovative approaches to design that are based on flexibility, adaptability, and processes of change. To reduce is to use less in the first place. To use again, or to reuse, is to consider ways that spaces or buildings can be reconsidered or revitalized to accommodate new needs. This may involve minor or major alterations; however, it suggests that the integrity of the original building remains essentially intact. In contrast, recycling is a transformative process. To recycle is to use the materials (which could also be a structure, a space, or light) of the original object as the basis for something new and perhaps very different.

In existing buildings, reuse may imply optimizing the given daylighting strategies. This might involve rezoning a building; placing activities in areas with appropriate light levels, distribution, and quality; or it might mean making minor alterations to areas with problems such as glare, thermal gain, or excessive contrast. In new construction, reuse strategies might involve space planning that allows for varied configurations, window designs, and locations to accommodate multiple activities, as well as shading devices, blackout blinds, and filters to alter the quality and quantity of light for different uses. Flexible spatial organizations, movable partitions and furnishings, and dynamic window treatments could all be considered. Daylighting strategies that are developed so that spaces can be reused (particularly without major alterations) may create luminous environments less tailored for specific programs and qualities of lighting. Reuse therefore suggests a more general approach to daylighting, and perhaps a more uniform distribution of light, which could be easily altered for different activities, space planning, and uses.

If a space is to be recycled, or transformed from the old into something new (through more major alterations than those suggested by reuse), the daylighting design should consider the structural logic, window configuration, and building envelope to allow reconfiguration and adaptation of light over time. The structure might be designed for disassembly or adaptation to accommodate insertion of new windows, shading, reflectors, walls, or even interior partitions and plan configurations. An underlying structural logic could be used to accommodate these types of expansions or contractions over time. The massing and spatial organization could be designed to facilitate new additions without blocking solar access and daylight.

To reduce, reuse, or recycle requires additional effort and innovation that weighs the present within the context of the past and future. As Lester Milbrath explains in *Envisioning a Sustainable Society,* "Recycling an article is always more troubling than throwing it in the trash heap."[10] Yet the ecological, social, and cultural benefits of not throwing our buildings on the "trash heap" are worth the extra effort.

Adapting the Past for the Present

The structure and building envelope are the primary considerations if daylighting is to accommodate new users, programs, and spatial configurations. As Louis Kahn explained: "I cannot speak enough about light because light is so important, because, actually structure is the maker of light. When you decide on the structure, you're deciding on the light."[11] The lighting qualities,

Figure 3.1 View of the entry to the Stanislav Libensky and Jaroslava Brychtova Exhibition at the Corning Glass Museum.

(Paul Warchol Photography)

character, the opportunities for change derive directly from the physical characteristics of the structure and building envelope.

One approach to adaptability is to design interior walls, partitions, and furnishings so that they are independent of the structure, envelope, and windows. Daylighting could then be designed to provide general ambient illumination throughout the space, which would allow activities and tasks to occur freely within a uniform volume of light. Depending on the room depths and number of stories, sidelighting or toplighting could be used to provide either high or low levels of illumination. An example of this approach is found at the Corning Museum of Glass in Corning, New York. Originally designed by Harrison and Abramovitz, the 1950 museum was recently renovated by Smith-Miller+Hawkinson for a glass exhibit of works by Stanislav Libensky and Jaroslava Brychtova.[12] The original design was conceived as a glass box based on a 20- by 20-foot grid with an exposed steel structure and floor-to-ceiling windows around the perimeter. The open plan and regular structural module created a space with an industrial character, which could be transformed into a factory if needed during the Korean War.[13] In developing the new exhibit for glass artists Libensky and Brychtova, Smith-Miller+Hawkinson convinced their client to reclaim an L-shaped gallery from a portion of the building that over the years had been filled with support spaces. The clarity, simplicity, and elegance of the original design were rediscovered as the layers of former alterations were removed.

The new exhibition space wraps the south and west corners of the building, with galleries extending the depth of one bay on the west and two bays on the south. Circulation is remotely located from the building envelope at the interior edges of the exhibitions. Given the corner condition, sidelighting is admitted bilaterally through floor-to-ceiling windows. The daylighting gently defines the boundaries of the exhibit, while electric lighting is used to highlight the textures, colors, and depth of the glass artwork. The

Figure 3.2 Corner gallery in the Stanislav Libensky and Jaroslava Brychtova Exhibition.

(Paul Warchol Photography)

Figure 3.3 Sidelit gallery in the Stanislav Libensky and Jaroslava Brychtova Exhibition.
(Paul Warchol Photography)

space is divided into south and west exhibits with an enclosed video display and seating area located at the intersection of the two wings. Small artifacts are placed in elegantly detailed glass display cases on the west side of the gallery. The room is illuminated with ambient sidelighting, while the small works of art are accentuated with electric lighting. Larger pieces are exhibited on birch plywood plinths to the south.

An ephemeral, luminous environment is created as sunlight is diffused through metallic fiber-mesh shades forming a silvery backdrop for the glass artwork. As the sun moves through the day, delicate patterns of light and shadow are projected from the structure onto the back of the interior screens. The art is backlit with daylighting to reveal the depth and materiality of the cast glass. Supplemental incandescent track lighting further accentuates textures, details, and form. Rich patterns of projected color and shadow are projected from the glass onto the plywood plinths. Smith-Miller+Hawkinson also explore the different luminous qualities in the construction of glass partitions, display cases, and signage. The minimalist box designed by Harrison and Abramovitz is gracefully reclaimed in this simple and refined exhibition. The glass envelope, narrow depth of the space, and adjustable shading provide ample ambient daylighting. Future adaptability and versatility are ensured with volumes of soft diffuse light and the adjustable display cases, partition walls, and supplemental electric lighting. (See Figures 3.1 to 3.4.)

Another example of adaptability is found at the Showers Center in Bloomington, Indiana. Formerly a furniture factory, the building was recently converted to a multiuse facility for the City of Bloomington, Indiana University, and CFC, Inc. Architects Odle, McGuire & Shook skillfully include new users and activities

Figure 3.4 Axonometric drawing of the Stanislav Libensky and Jaroslava Brychtova Exhibition.

(Smith-Miller+Hawkinson Architects)

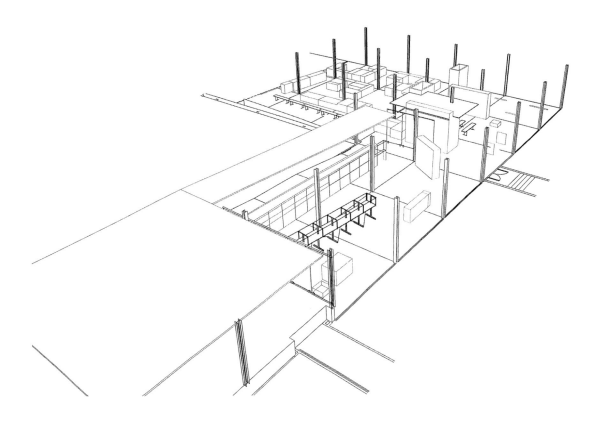

Figure 3.5 Aerial view of the Showers Center.

(Tim Hursley)

within an existing structure while remaining faithful to the daylighting logic of the factory. Over the years, the building has been used as a factory, a warehouse, and most currently as office and research spaces. The building is a trapezoidal form with a smaller rectilinear wing. The city hall and CFC, Inc., share the main body of the building, while the Indiana University Research Park is located in the northwest wing. The existing structure includes a grid of heavy-timber columns (which provide an underlying order for new floor plans), sidelighting (which was upgraded with a low-emissivity coating), and north-facing sawtooth skylights on the upper floor.

The daylighting challenges involved in adapting this building include the excessively large floor plate, subsequent depth, and the two-story construction. The lower level is particularly difficult; without insertion of a major daylighting feature such as a lightwell, atrium, or courtyard, the daylight is limited to the perimeter of the building. Several lower-level spaces such as the entry and council chamber in the city hall were opened the full height to provide soft indirect daylighting from the upper-level sawtooth skylights. Electric lighting is still needed in the inner-most portions of the building. In contrast, the upper level is toplit throughout. The skylights provide a continuous overhead datum under which wall partitions and furnishings can move depending on spatial and programmatic needs. Light-colored surfaces surround the skylights and further distribute daylight.

Although the addition of an inner atrium would have improved daylighting on the lower level, daylighting is still achieved along the perimeter of the lower level, within the entry and council chamber, and throughout the upper level. Considering the modest alterations that were made to the existing building, the daylighting results are significant. The designers used the underlying structural order to determine how rooms or partitions contract and expand, opened important lower-level spaces to daylight, and choreographed the space planning to maximize sidelighting and skylights for general illumination. (See Figures 3.5 and 3.6.)

Both of the preceding projects leave the building envelope unaltered and take a general or uniform approach to daylighting. A contrasting approach is found at the office of Meyer, Scherer &

Figure 3.6 Interior view of the council chamber at the Showers Center.

(Tim Hursley)

Rockcastle, where new daylighting strategies were used in an existing building to meet new luminous and spatial needs. The firm recently moved to a historic infill building in the Minneapolis Warehouse District. The daylighting challenge was to bring illumination into a narrow two-story building that had sidelighting only on the narrow north and south facades. A number of changes had occurred over the years, including the removal of a portion of the second floor to accommodate staging for large-scale photographic work. This opening was cut asymmetrically to create space on the north, south, and east sides of the second floor and a narrow balcony on the west. Because the photographer desired control of the luminous environment, no additional daylighting was admitted. Meyer, Scherer & Rockcastle's most significant change was to insert a large linear skylight over the second-floor opening. What had been a dark, electrically illuminated interior was transformed into a dramatically daylit space. Now the building is organized as a series of luminous layers around the new daylit atrium. The wall detailing and spatial organization create varied experiences of light and shadow. Much of the existing and new structure is exposed to reveal material detailing and mechanical integration, to create views through the building, and to suggest room boundaries without blocking borrowed light. The north entry and south meeting areas are located on either end of the linear axis, illuminated by existing sidelighting with new interior shading. Behind these spaces are the employee work areas which surround the inner atrium. The principals are located in the atrium, which is the most open and visibly accessible area of the building.

The atrium was a simple yet critical alteration that unifies the office by creating a luminous and spatial focal point. An asymmetrical layering of light and shadow creates visual interest, drama, and even mystery. One moves from the sidelit perimeter to an area of shadow, then to the brightly illuminated core. Inside this simple box lies a gem of unanticipated daylight. The work areas (primarily used for computers) surrounding the lower level of the atrium are in relative darkness even though low partition walls, open handrails, and reflective surfaces admit borrowed daylight. The resulting rhythm of light and shadow has intriguing spatial and qualitative affects. Small personal spaces are carved out of the shadows with electric task lighting to create a sense of intimacy, privacy, and calm within a larger community. In con-

Figure 3.7 View of upper- and lower-level spaces surrounding the atrium at the office of Meyer, Scherer, & Rockcastle.

(Meyer, Scherer & Rockcastle)

Figure 3.8　View of borrowed daylight on the lower level of the office of Meyer, Scherer & Rockcastle.

(Meyer, Scherer & Rockcastle)

trast, the principals' work area has a sense of disclosure and openness created by the dynamic multistory volume of daylight.

Depending upon the type of work, season, and sky conditions, the character and quality of light in the atrium can be adjusted with interior canvas shading devices. Fabricated by a boatbuilder, the shading devices are made up of a series of sails on pulleys that allow alteration of the luminous quality in part or all of the atrium. Translucent mesh shading is also provided on the north and south facades. These well-conceived design alterations transform a moderately daylit building from the past into a diversely daylit building in the present. (See Figures 3.7 and 3.8.)

Finally, the Mark Taper Center in Los Angeles successfully transforms a poorly illuminated auto-body garage into a light-

Figure 3.9   View of exterior courtyard at the Mark Taper Center.

(Erich Ansel Koyama)

Figure 3.10 View of
circulation, classrooms,
mezzanine, and interior
courtyard at the Mark
Taper Center.

(Erich Ansel Koyama)

filled art center for inner-city children. Michael Maltzan Architecture and Marmol & Radziner Architecture paid careful attention to the daylight zoning, strategies, and luminous qualities to reuse an old building and provide future flexibility. At the site scale the art compound can be viewed as a series of concentric rings with classrooms on the outer perimeter, a layer of circulation, and gathering spaces at the center. Half of the site contains the trans-

Figure 3.11   View of interior courtyard at the Mark Taper Center.

(Erich Ansel Koyama)

formed garage and the other half contains a new ceramic studio, shop, and centrally located outdoor room. Classrooms, circulation, and a large north-facing gathering space are located in the existing building. The outer area contains the classrooms, storage, and rest rooms, all of which are illuminated by new horizontal-diffusing skylights. Daylight is borrowed from the circulation corridor located between the classrooms and gathering space. A glazed office mezzanine for staff is located above the classrooms. Low interior-wall partitions, glazed doors, and light-colored finishes create a sense of connection between the different activities and rooms within the center. The central gathering space combines toplighting with sidelighting from large industrial garage doors to the north. In addition, clear glazing was inserted into the doors to provide views of the adjacent courtyard and to bring daylighting deep within the space. The glass garage doors delicately separate the interior from the exterior. When the doors are open, a larger gathering space is formed with varied luminous qualities and connection to climate. Students can move into the sunlight,

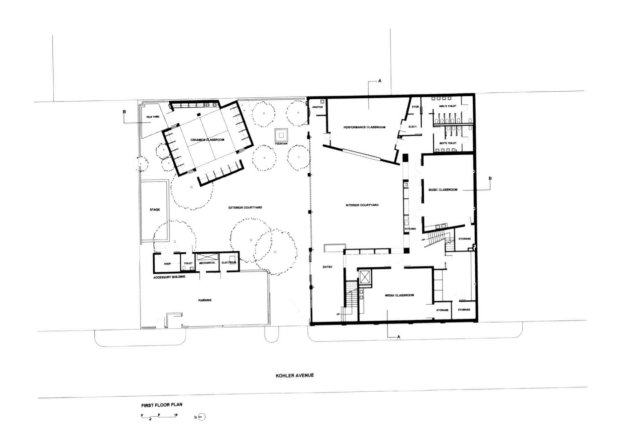

KOHLER AVENUE

FIRST FLOOR PLAN

N

Figure 3.12 Plan of the Mark Taper Center. (Michael Maltzan Architecture)

under a shade tree, near the water, or retreat to the protected interior. Depending on the activities and size of groups, this inside/outside space can expand and contract to meet varied spatial, programmatic, and luminous needs. Simple and effective daylighting strategies are used to transform the building, to foster visual and physical connections between the users, site, and climate, and to create a celebratory and dynamic learning environment. (See Figures 3.9 to 3.13.)

The adaptation of an existing building to a new program, user, or activity need not be elaborate or difficult. The Corning Museum illustrates the importance of understanding the original design intention of the building, the history of the project, and the opportunities of existing conditions and parameters. It also suggests the importance of studying the original daylighting design to determine whether strategies can reclaim or transform the building in a manner that respects the integrity of the initial design. Different opportunities will be present if the original design has toplighting, sidelighting, or both. At the Showers Center, the sawtooth skylights are left unaltered. The floor-to-ceiling height and abundant daylighting apertures provided the opportunity to move wall partitions anywhere beneath the skylights while still maintaining good daylighting distribution. In contrast, the sidelighting had greater limitations for light distribution and penetration. In this case, interior partitions and furnishings need to be carefully placed to admit daylight to areas distant from the window wall. Both projects illustrate that the existing conditions were carefully analyzed and coupled with thoughtful daylight zoning and interior planning to achieve successful daylighting results with minimal alterations.

In contrast, Meyer, Scherer & Rockcastle augment existing daylighting strategies to create new luminous experiences. The single skylight, shading devices, architectural detailing, and space planning create varied qualities and quantities of daylight to define distinct zones and layers. The project suggests that fairly minimal alterations can have a dramatic effect. If existing daylighting is limited, the challenge is to determine new alterations that will support existing conditions. While Meyer, Scherer & Rockcastle made minor alterations to significant effect, the Mark Taper Center transforms a previously electrically lit space with completely new daylighting strategies. Despite the significant modifications, the existing parameters of the site, structure, and

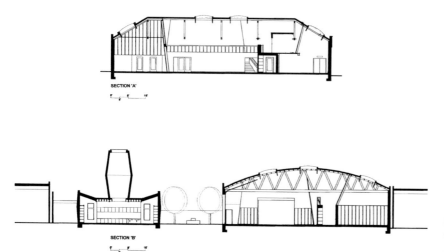

SECTION 'A'

SECTION 'B'

Figure 3.13 Sections of the Mark Taper Center.

(Michael Maltzan Architecture)

garage doors were still used as an underlying order for the new daylight zoning, envelope alterations, interior planning, and site development. Even the creation of entirely new luminous environments requires understanding of the logic and opportunities of the existing conditions to maintain the integrity of the initial design and possibly to retain a memory of the previous users.

Depending on the parameters of the existing building, daylighting alterations may vary from reclamation of earlier strategies to complete reconsideration of the design. Where a project falls on this spectrum can be determined only after careful consideration of existing conditions and the new program and users. Deciding whether a project is worthy of adaptation is a complex process that often defies logic, common sense, and intuition. As Jeffrey Cook explains in his essay "A Post-industrial Culture of Regionalism": "In Mies' time the economy could not afford to knock down usable buildings, but in our time, expense seems to be no object. Old hulks are 'born again' in renovation with a substance and style they never had originally. In contrast, great and memorable buildings of substantial significance are expensively removed to allow on-grade car parking. Thus, needs change, and choices are effected in spite of cost, and with neither logic nor affection."[14]

Daylighting opportunities are just one of many considerations that need to be weighed in determining whether adaptation is feasible. Many of the issues go beyond the program and users to include historic significance, contextual concerns, economics, safety, and even the care of ourselves and our environment. As Christopher Alexander suggests in *The Timeless Way of Building*: "What does it take to build something so that it's really easy to make comfortable little modifications in a way that once you've made them, they feel integral with the nature and structure of what is already there? . . . This kind of adaptation is a continuous process of gradually taking care."[15]

Planning in the Present for the Future

The adaptation of existing buildings provides opportunities and constraints particular to the existing design parameters and conditions. In contrast, the innovation of the designer is the only potential limitation to the exploration of concepts of adaptability, flexibility, and evolution in new construction. How could we design daylighting to meet the needs of the present users and programs while facilitating and perhaps anticipating the needs of the future? How can future daylighting flexibility, adaptability, and evolution be designed into a building today? The following projects explore strategies that meet present daylighting needs while planning for the future.

The gallery in the Sahara West Library and Museum by Meyer, Scherer & Rockcastle was designed to accommodate a variety of exhibitions.[16] Flexibility was a critical concern since installations could include large to small objects, two- or three-dimensional works, materials sensitive to daylight, different illuminance levels, and varied physical placements (on the walls or within the space). The gallery is a simple rectilinear box, which uses three main strategies to accommodate varied spatial and luminous requirements. These include an adjustable skylight, a retractable ceiling grid, and movable partitions. A thin linear skylight slices through the exhibition space on a north-south axis. A series of movable baffles are fixed beneath the skylight to alter the size of the opening. The positions of the baffles can range from fully open to fully closed, with any variation in between. As a result, the quality, quantity, and distribution of daylighting can be altered for different types of exhibitions. For example, study models illustrate that when the baffles are fully open (in the 100 percent open position) the daylight is concentrated in the center of the space, which is the preferable baffle configuration for three-dimensional work. Under this condition, daylight fills the space itself (rather than the perimeter) and helps to render three-dimensional and sculptural forms in light and shadow. In contrast, study models illustrate that when the baffles are closed at least 50 percent (in the 50 percent open position) the daylight is distributed to the walls at the perimeter of the room, which is optimal for the display of two-dimensional work. The baffles can also be completely closed for light-sensitive exhibits.

Figure 3.14 View of the entry into the Sahara West Museum.

(Tim Hursley)

Figure 3.15 Interior view of the Sahara West Museum.

(Tim Hursley)

An adjustable ceiling grid can be raised from 10 to 35 feet to alter the spatial parameters of the room for work of various sizes. Adjustable electric lighting fixtures are integrated into the ceiling grid to provide supplemental and accent lighting. Movable cabinets/walls can be configured in any position within the space, transforming it from a single gallery to a series of smaller galleries. (The partition walls are stored in hidden pockets within the gallery walls.) In their explanation of the gallery, Meyer, Scherer & Rockcastle parallel Richard Rogers's concept of improvisational architecture: "It might be said that the flexibility of exhibition space and infrastructure created for theatrical stages is the closest analogy to what is possible in this exhibition space."[17] Three well-conceived design strategies create a space that responds to a variety of spatial configurations and luminous requirements while anticipating the needs of the future. (See Figures 3.14 to 3.17.)

At the SEI Corporation Headquarters in Oaks, Pennsylvania, Meyer, Scherer & Rockcastle were also challenged to provide maximum spatial flexibility and high-quality daylighting. The financial corporation desired a nonhierarchical building in which everyone

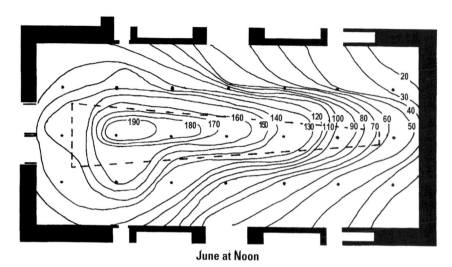

June at Noon

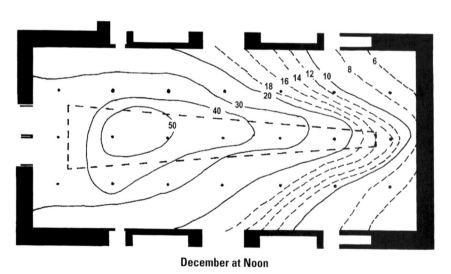

December at Noon

Figure 3.16 Daylighting contours at noon with the baffles open 100 percent, from a study model of Sahara West Museum.

(Joe Ford)

(from the CEO to entry-level employees) shares a common work space and a facility that accommodates frequent reorganizations of employee teams. These teams share large rectilinear open offices. A 6-foot circulation path runs along the perimeter and through the center of the space. Within this configuration, employee teams can organize workstations as they please. The large communal offices are completely free of wall partitions, creating a sense of lightness, openness, and community that is often lacking in typical office buildings. Sidelighting illuminates the perimeter of the spaces and

Figure 3.17 Daylighting contours at noon with the baffles open 50 percent, from a study model of Sahara West Museum.

(Joe Ford)

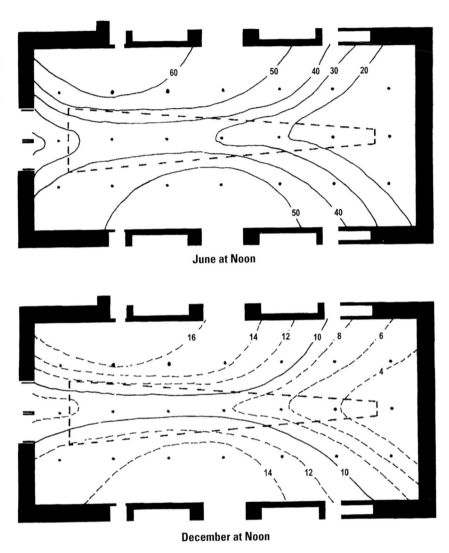

June at Noon

December at Noon

provides views to the rural site. Gable ends are glazed to reveal trusses and bring light gently down from above. Every employee is at least 32 feet from a window, which allows access to daylight from anywhere within the space. Desks, chairs, computers, and storage are on rollers to allow employees to easily relocate. An ingenious electrical system consisting of power and data coils on 8-foot centers is mounted to the trusses overhead. Employees simply unplug their workstations and move to a new area. Indirect electric lighting provides supplemental illumination. In addition,

all end walls are constructed of a structural system that can be dis-
assembled for future expansion. The linear offices can be extended
as future space is needed.

A fairly uniform and even distribution of daylight is found
throughout the SEI headquarters. The success of this approach
depends on activities that are best conducted under ambient daylight. Tasks requiring higher light levels or more particular qualities
of illumination require supplemental electric lighting. While the
design strives for and achieves an egalitarian approach to space
and lighting, the quality of daylight would be enhanced if the particular opportunities of each window orientation were further considered (size, shading, views, user interaction, etc.). Despite these
concerns, the daylighting design successfully creates a luminous
environment that supports the goals of the company, which desired
a flexible egalitarian space. (See Figures 3.18 and 3.19.)

Lindsay and Kerry Clare take a more diverse luminous approach to future flexibility with their house in Buderim, Australia.
Structure and daylighting are integrated to address the changing
needs of a young family. The house is a simple rectilinear box with

Figure 3.18 Exterior
view of SEI Corporation
Headquarters.

(Tim Hursley)

the shorter east and west walls slightly recessed to emphasize the parallel walls on the north and south sides of the linear two-story pavilion. Fin walls run perpendicular to the parallel walls to provide bracing and to transfer structural loads. As a result, interior partitions are non-load-bearing, spatial, and reconfigurable, as future needs require.

There are four types and shapes of daylighting apertures in the house: clerestory, crescent-shaped, floor-to-ceiling, and view windows. The upper-level clerestory windows rest on top of the parallel walls, creating a delicate transition between the sheltering structure below and the graceful roof above. Thin crescent-shaped windows above the shorter end walls articulate the soft curve of the roof and provide bilateral illumination. On the lower level, large floor-to-ceiling terrace windows and glass doors allow the landscape to move in and through the building. Small horizontal, square, and vertical windows frame unique views of the landscape.

The upper and lower levels have distinct daylighting concepts. The kitchen, living area, and master bedroom comprise the linear first floor. Daylighting apertures on this level are created by cuts in the parallel walls to provide illumination, to connect to the site, and to extend space into the landscape. The open plan allows rooms to be adapted to different uses in the future with respect to the structural logic and existing rhythm of windows. In contrast, the design of the upper level would easily accommodate insertion of new wall partitions and spatial configurations despite window location. Clerestory windows wrap the central portion of the upper floor, which is currently the children's play area. A gap is provided between the outside wall with the clerestory windows and an inner midheight wall (similar to a balcony). This illuminated void between the inner and outer structure allows new partitions to be added perpendicular to the clerestory windows. The play area could be reconfigured as a series of smaller spaces while still maintaining daylighting throughout. The children's bedrooms bracket the play area on the east and west, while the bathroom is contained by lower partition walls that allow daylight to penetrate to the play area.

Several distinct qualities and characteristics of daylight result from varied strategies used in the house. Small view windows cre-

Figure 3.20 East and north facades of the Clare Residence.

(Richard Stringer)

Figure 3.21   North facade
of the Clare Residence.

(Richard Stringer)

Figure 3.22   Interior view
of the lower-level
living areas in the
Clare Residence.

(Richard Stringer)

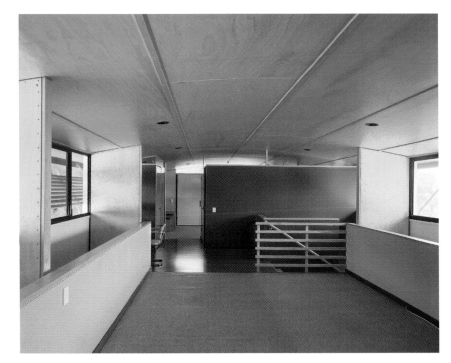

Figure 3.23 Interior view of the upper-level living areas in the Clare Residence.

(Richard Stringer)

ate intimate places throughout the structure. The kitchen is animated by a horizontal slice of morning sunlight; the wall of the bed alcove is grazed by the evening sun; and a thin band of light is glimpsed through the open risers of the stairs to create a luminous threshold between the upper and lower levels. Large terrace windows in the main living areas are sheltered from the high summer sun, while the low winter light is allowed to wash surfaces with a dynamic tracery of direct and reflected light from jalousie louvers. The exposed structure of the upper floor runs parallel to the windows, resulting in rhythms of light and shadow that emphasize the axial form of the pavilion and the logic of the structural system. Bilateral and unilateral lighting strategies alternate between the structural bays of the fin walls. The vertical transition of the stair passes through shadow to the soft, diffuse illumination of the clerestories above. Partition walls on the upper level are held below the roof plane to allow diffuse illumination from the crescent windows to enter the children's play area. Light is held within the gap between the clerestories and the low side walls, creating a band of soft illumination around the upper floor. The fin walls and large eaves soften the midday sun and provide thermal and visual

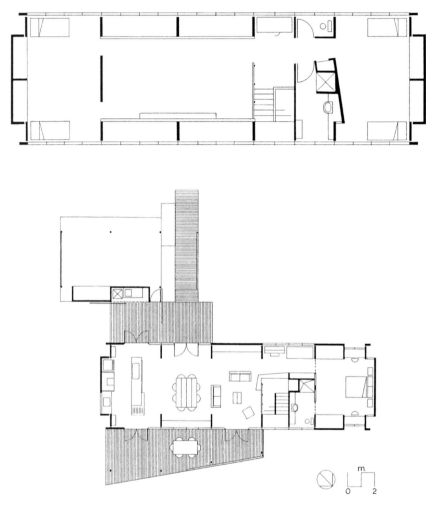

Figure 3.24   Upper- and lower-level plans of the Clare Residence.
(Clare Design)

comfort. The luminous experience is even extended to the outside of the house. Changing patterns of light and shadow are created on the end walls by rain gutters, structural reveals, and a horizontal banding of building components. The open plan, the void between the outer and inner walls, and the repetitive structural system allow future alterations and changes while also creating rich and varied luminous experiences. (See Figures 3.20 to 3.25.)

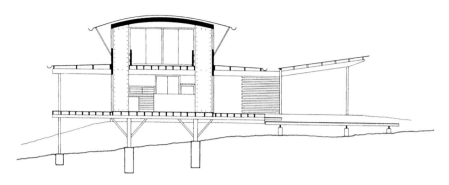

Figure 3.25 Section of
the Clare Residence.

(Clare Design)

In his essay "These Walls Around Us," David Owens captures
the significance of evolution in residential construction:

> Every house is a work in progress. . . . It begins in the imaginations of the
> people who build it and is gradually transformed, for better and for worse,
> by the people who occupy it down through the years, decades, centuries.
> To tinker with a house is to commune with the people who have lived in it
> before and to leave messages for those who will live in it later. Every house
> is a living museum of habitation, and a monument to all the lives and aspi-
> rations that have flickered within it.[18]

The daylighting concepts used in the preceding projects provide
lessons that can inform an evolutionary approach to daylighting
design. The adjustable skylight and the movable cabinets/walls
and ceiling grid at the Sahara West Museum illustrate that a variety of light levels, distributions, and qualities, as well as a variety
of spatial configurations, are possible. For programs that require
variable luminous conditions (museums, retail spaces, libraries,
etc.), we can consider the potential of shading, blackout screens,
filters, and layers to transform the window from a static to a
dynamic element. In contrast, at SEI the windows are fixed and
the quality of light is less particular to activities, program, or spatial characteristics. SEI illustrates a neutral luminous territory in
which space and activities shift and alter while respecting programmatic needs. Unless modifications are made, future activities
would be limited to those that are appropriate for this characteristic of light (offices, reading rooms, classrooms, etc.). The repetitive
structural system and building envelope are designed for disassembly—thus facilitating expansion and growth. In the Clare
House, the building envelope is separate from the interior partitions, allowing spatial reconfiguration independent of the window

location. (Building types that undergo frequent alterations would benefit from interior partitions that correspond with window heights and locations.) The projects illustrate that daylighting can accommodate change and evolution at a variety of scales and with strategies that include the design of the window, envelope, structure, space planning, and interior details.

DAYLIGHTING CONCEPTS FOR ADAPTATION AND EVOLUTION

People experience architecture most intimately at the scale of the room. Here we experience the rhythm of light and shadow, the comfort of a summer breeze through an open window, the intimacy of a well-proportioned window seat, the texture of stucco grazed by sunlight, and the color of passing time. According to Louis Kahn, "The room is the beginning of architecture. It is the place of the mind. You in the room with its dimensions, its structure, its light respond to its character, its spiritual aura, recognizing that whatever the human proposes and makes becomes a life."[19] We understand a room through time. We learn its seasonal and daily rhythms; we experience how it breathes; and we sense its thermal cycles. We interact with a room; we make modifications, adjustments, and alterations.

We also tune rooms to meet our needs. In *The Social Function of the Built Environment,* Robert Gutman explains that users transform the built environment in ways the architect may never have intended:

> . . . let me point out that there is one kind of built environment that does seem to have the power to dictate how its users should live. This is the built environment of the total institution, of the hospital, the psychiatric ward, and the prison. To realize this is to take comfort in the knowledge that building, for all its marvelous contributions to social functioning, is still only an enabling environment. . . . I think the message is clear: the freedom to practice architecture in modern society also implies the freedom of the user to ignore the intention of the designer.[20]

How can we prevent our rooms from becoming prisons for the inhabitants? In what ways can daylighting design help to facilitate the transformation of space through time? First, we must determine the relationship between daylighting, structure, and building envelope. Structural decisions are inseparable from day-lighting decisions. The sizes and forms of windows will vary depending on whether the structure is masonry, concrete, or frame. The degree of transparency or opacity of the building enve-lope will depend on the chosen structural system. The Corning Museum, SEI Headquarters, and Showers Center illustrate vari-ous approaches to simple, repetitive structural systems with fixed daylighting apertures to provide overall ambient illumination. Within this structural and luminous order the spatial organiza-tion, activities, and users can change. Alternatively, Lindsay and Kerry Clare provide a void between the load-bearing structure and non-load-bearing partitions to create an interior system that can be altered free of window location. The SEI Headquarters considers construction methods and materials that can be disas-sembled for future expansion, additions, or alterations. The Mark Taper Center and Meyer, Scherer & Rockcastle Office make day-lighting interventions in the existing structure to create varied luminous experiences directly linked to a new program and spa-tial configuration.

Second, what is the relationship between daylight and the building form, massing, and configuration? The building footprint, plan, section, room depth, ceiling height, configuration, window size, and window form all play critical roles in successful daylight-ing. The preceding projects provide insight into the opportunities and constraints of various building forms and configurations. Meyer, Scherer & Rockcastle's Office addresses the problems of limited access to daylight in a narrow multistory infill building. The existing sidelighting is enhanced by the insertion of an atrium to bring life to a formerly dark interior. The Showers Center reuses existing skylight monitors to provide illumination for new spaces on lower levels. In contrast, the Clare House uses a thin linear form with bilateral lighting to ensure access to daylighting.

Third, what is the role of the window design? Can the window be altered and changed to create new qualities and quantities of light? The Sahara West Museum illustrates the ability to vary illu-minance levels, distribution, and the quality of light with an adjustable baffle. The Mark Taper Center uses glazed garage doors to expand and contract space, to link the interior and exte-rior, and to provide programmatic and spatial flexibility. The Corning Museum of Glass integrates simple metallic screens to vary the illuminance levels and to control glare. Layers inside or out facilitate changing illuminance levels, light distribution, and programmatic needs.

Finally, what is the relationship between daylighting and the spatial organization, finishes, and furnishings? How can interior details, materials, and surface reflectances further enhance daylighting flexibility and adaptability? The SEI Headquarters combines movable furnishings, a versatile power/data system, and an open office plan with sidelighting. Portable walls/cabinets allow the Sahara West Museum to be transformed from a single gallery to multiple galleries beneath an adjustable skylight and electric lighting grid. The Mark Taper Center employs light-colored walls of various heights to maximize daylight distribution. (Virtually all of the projects employ light-colored surfaces for maximum reflectivity.)

These projects provide a glimpse of the possible strategies that can be used in reconsidering the opportunities and constraints of designing daylighting for the future. Designing for the present as well as the future requires new ways of thinking about space, materials, structures, and light. The motivations for this approach to design lie in the benefits of creating spaces that respond to human needs and desires, in maintaining links to our past, in anticipating a more responsive future and in the wisdom that the architectural marks we make on this earth have broader ecological implications. As Louis Kahn reminds us, the transformation of architecture through time has grown from a desire to create meaningful architectural and luminous experiences:

> Out of the wall grew the column.
> The wall did well for man.
> In its thickness and its strength
> it protected him against destruction.
> But soon, the will to look out
> made man make a hole in the wall,
> and the wall was very pained, and said,
> *"What are you doing to me?"*
> *I protected you; I made you feel secure—*
> *and now you put a hole through me?"*
> And man said, *"But I will look out!*
> *I see wonderful things,*
> *and I want to look out."*

And the wall still felt very sad.
Later, man didn't just hack a hole through the wall,
but made a discerning opening, one trimmed with fine stone
and he put a lintel over the opening.
And, soon, the wall felt pretty well.[21]

ENDNOTES

1. Stuart Brand, *How Buildings Learn* (New York: Penguin Books, 1994), 188.
2. John and Nancy Todd, *Tomorrow Is Our Permanent Address* (New York: Harper & Row, 1980), 46–47.
3. Stuart Ewen, "Waste a Lot, Want a Lot," in *Learning to Listen to the Land,* edited by Bill Willers (Washington, D.C.: Island Press, 1991), 188.
4. The American Institute of Architects' (AIA) *Environmental Resource Guide* is an excellent resource for information on the waste and energy implications of building materials and construction. See AIA, *Environmental Resource Guide* (New York: John Wiley & Sons, 1996).
5. Kevin Lynch, "The Waste of Place," *Places* 6, no. 2 (winter 1990): 12.
6. Stuart Brand, *How Buildings Learn,* 11.
7. Michael Hough, *Out of Place* (New Haven: Yale University Press, 1990), 186.
8. Stuart Brand, 71.
9. Sociologist Robert Gutman uses museums as an example to illustrate the process of evolution and change in architectural design: ". . . Buildings designed to serve a particular purpose in one historical epoch are now used for another; or buildings intended to serve a particular purpose in one way now achieve their goals by transformed means. The history of museum architecture illustrates both these statements. The Louvre, the Uffizi, and the Hermitage are three examples of buildings planned as palaces which now have been given over to the preservation and display of important collections of painting, sculpture, and prints and are no longer used as habitation." Robert Gutman, "The Social Function of the Built Environment," in *The Mutual Interaction of People and*

Their Built Environment, edited by Amos Rapoport (Paris: Mouton Publishers, 1976), 45.

10. Lester Milbrath, *Envisioning a Sustainable Society* (New York: State University of New York Press, 1989), 260.

11. Alexandra Tyng, *Beginnings: Louis I. Kahn's Philosophy of Architecture* (New York: John Wiley & Sons, 1984), 122, 173.

12. Architects from Smith-Miller+Hawkinson have recently designed a new addition to the Corning Glass Museum that demonstrates new glass technologies as well as additional daylighting concepts.

13. Charles Linn, "Jewel Box," *Architectural Record* 182, no. 9 (September 1994): 66.

14. Jeffrey Cook, "A Post-industrial Culture of Regionalism," *Critical regionalism: The Pomona meeting proceedings,* edited by Spyros Amourgis (Pomona, Calif.: College of Environmental Design, California State Polytechnic University, 1991), 171.

15. Christopher Alexander, *The Timeless Way of Building* (New York: Oxford University Press, 1979), 231.

16. See Chapter 7 for an additional discussion of the qualitative and experiential implications of the daylighting design at the Sahara West Library.

17. Meyer, Scherer & Rockcastle, firm literature on Sahara West Library and Art Museum, Minneapolis, Minn.

18. Stuart Brand, 163–164.

19. Alexandra Tyng, 122.

20. Amos Rapoport, ed., 49.

21. Louis I. Kahn, *Louis I. Kahn: Talks with Students* (Houston Texas, 1969), 4.

ARCHITECTONIC
CONSIDERATIONS

Shape Form to Guide Flow

Only where form arises at the same time as content or in faithful combination with it, as it were, can we speak of a step forward, but then form as a separate element no longer interests us.[1]

—ALVAR AALTO

In *Regenerative Design for Sustainable Development,* John Tillman Lyle describes the principle "shape form to guide flow" as a dynamic interaction between form and energy: "This principle could also be stated 'flow follows form follows flow.' Energy and material flows occur within the physical medium of the environment, and the medium largely determines the pace and direction of flow. By shaping the medium (the environment), we can guide the flow."[2] In the case of daylighting, the building massing, plan, section, and window design are the primary architectural determinants, or "forms," that shape and guide the distribution, or "flow of light," within and among spaces. The task is to determine appropriate forms based on ecological, lighting, and aesthetic criteria.

It is obvious that architectural form influences the quality of light, which in turn influences human experience and comfort. It may be less apparent that form relates to ecological issues such as resource consumption, energy, and our relationship to the environment. Yet the form of the building, rooms, and windows determines how much daylight will be admitted, how it will be distributed, whether electric lighting will be needed, the amount of heat gain or heat loss, and whether there will be appropriate ventilation. Form also determines the degree of connection with the site, with environmental forces, and with the climate. Each of these factors relates directly or indirectly to ecological concerns.

If architectural form is based on a relationship to natural light, then the window and even the building itself becomes what Louis Kahn described as a "daylighting fixture." Kahn explains this concept in a discussion of windows: "The window is a natural lighting fixture because it distributes the light and metes it out, all the things which are different from man. It's a device, a little locomotive. No motor is involved. It's simply a chosen shape—a design to allow in the natural light which would be good and not injurious."[3] Although Kahn is describing a window, his concept can be applied to the building itself. To shape form to guide flow suggests that we reconsider the inherent daylighting opportunities of architecture: the building massing, plan and section, ceiling form, room configuration, and window detailing. Yet to make decisions about form we must first understand the luminous program and design criteria.

FORM AND THE LUMINOUS PROGRAM

Aesthetic and formal opportunities are perhaps the most compelling reasons that designers are drawn to daylighting design. Yet shaping form to guide flow is more than an aesthetic exploration. Form is integrally linked to the program, whether in creating meaningful luminous effects, enhancing visual comfort, or illuminating a difficult task. Christopher Alexander elaborates on the relationship between form and program in *Notes on the Synthesis of Form:* "The ultimate object of design is form, physical clarity cannot be achieved in a form until there is first some programmatic clarity in the designer's mind and actions; and for this to be possible, in turn, the designer must first trace his design problem to its earliest functional origins and be able to find some sort of pattern in them."[4] It is only after we understand our design objectives (what daylight is intended to do) and criteria (how much daylight, where, when, and with what qualities) that we can begin to explore the relationships between daylight and form.

On the topic of architectural form, Louis Kahn suggests, "I think of Form as the realization of a nature, made up of inseparable elements. . . . Form precedes Design. It guides its direction for it holds the relation of its elements."[5] If form is "the realization of a nature," then we must first understand the "nature" of the luminous problem (the desired characteristics and qualities of light). During this process of clarification and exploration certain forms will be suggested and others will be eliminated. In *The Natural House,* Frank Lloyd Wright suggests there is an inherent relationship between the nature of something, its form, and simplicity: "Simplicity is a clean, direct expression of that essential quality of the thing which is in the nature of the thing itself. The innate or organic pattern of the form of anything is that form which is thus truly *simple.*"[6] Daylighting integrity and success depend on appropriate forms. In a time of often exuberant and excessive form making, simplicity (which can also lead to elegance) is a worthy ideal in the search for form. This is not to negate the challenge and difficulty of finding appropriate forms to achieve desired effects. Yet the more fully one understands the "nature" of the program, both qualitatively and quantitatively, the easier it will be to focus on appropriate forms.

The shaping of form should be based on explicit daylighting objectives and criteria. These might include how much light is needed, when, for what tasks, and with what qualitative, spatial, and aesthetic effects. One can begin by defining the daylighting objectives. What can daylighting do? How can it be used? What luminous effects are desired? Daylighting objectives can be defined from a variety of perspectives that might include ecological concerns (energy, natural resource consumption, and environmental impacts), tasks and activities (qualitative and quantitative lighting requirements), systems integration (lighting, heating, and cooling loads), human experience (visual comfort, health and well-being, wayfinding and orientation, environmental connections, etc.), aesthetic considerations (articulation of space, form, structure, and materials, hierarchy and order), and other factors. It may not be possible or even desirable to address each of these objectives. Yet exploring their potential will clarify design intentions, determine priorities, and reveal possible conflicts or necessary trade-offs. More important, daylighting objectives enable designers to understand what they are trying to achieve, why, and how they might achieve it.

Before exploring forms that will best realize design objectives, it is necessary to develop design criteria. How much light is needed? Where should it be located? What seasonal and climatic issues have to be addressed? Qualitative and quantitative day-lighting criteria might include illuminance levels (target foot-candle values or daylight factors based on program, tasks, and the desired quality of light), light distribution (patterns or distribution of daylight based on program, tasks, etc.), quality of light (direct and/or indirect light; luminous characteristics), seasonal factors (overheated and underheated periods; diurnal and seasonal luminous needs and concerns; shading requirements and profile angles; window orientation), and human comfort (view locations, glare control, contrast ratios, proximity to windows, etc.). These criteria can be used to inform the design process and to clarify the specific opportunities and constraints of given projects. The more explicit the daylighting objectives and criteria, the easier it will be to determine appropriate daylighting forms. After the luminous program is defined, the designer can begin to explore its relationships to form.

The following discussion will focus on the ecological implications of daylighting and form. Issues will include the building massing (linear, centric, and clustered forms), plan and section (the room depth and height, surface form, and journey through light and space), and window form (size, location, and detailing).

BUILDING MASSING

The prudent designer has always taken advantage of daylight to minimize the expense, maintenance, and resources needed for illumination. There are many precedents from nineteenth- and early-twentieth-century office buildings, schools, and hospitals that reveal successful daylighting strategies through thin building massing, atria, lightwells, and courtyards. These strategies were used to gather daylight, to reduce excessive contrast from unilateral (one-sided) light, to increase the distribution of daylighting, and to provide views. The desire for daylight resulted in a variety of typical building configurations, including L-shaped, U-shaped, doughnut, stepped, and thin linear forms. Each of these configurations was intended to reduce the apparent thickness of the building and ensure sufficient daylighting throughout the building.[7]

With the advent of electric lighting, the apparent need for daylight decreased, and subsequently the thickness of buildings increased.[8] As the building mass increased, contact with the environment, views, and opportunities for daylighting and natural ventilation decreased. While electric lighting can provide quality illumination, it can never substitute for daylight. Louis Kahn argues, "A space can never reach its place in architecture without natural light. Artificial light is the light of night expressed in positioned chandeliers not to be compared with the unpredictable play of natural light. . . . Natural light gives mood to space by the nuances of light in the time of the day and the seasons of the year as it enters and modifies the space."[9] If we are to capture the nuances of daylight described by Kahn, we need to pay attention to the inherent lighting opportunities of various building masses.

Quality daylighting is possible regardless of the size or shape of a building. The challenge is to determine how the massing of the building can respond to the plan and section to ensure daylighting throughout. Although a thin building naturally lends itself to bilateral or multilateral strategies, a thick massing is no excuse for not using daylighting. Even a huge mass can be transformed to a series of thin spaces by introducing lightwells, courtyards, and atria. Successful daylighting requires access to natural light, whether it is from the sides, top, or a combination of both. Interior access to daylight and its distribution in space can be achieved only by reducing the actual or apparent depth of the building mass.

In *Precedents in Architecture,* Roger Clark and Michael Pause discuss several common building forms that include linear, central, double-centered, clustered, nested, concentric, and binuclear configurations. Clark and Pause explain that "Configuration patterns describe the relative disposition of parts and are themes for designing space and organizing groups of spaces and forms."[10] Within these patterns we find variations on a theme. For example, nested, binuclear, concentric, and double-central forms could be considered modifications of clustered and/or central configurations. For a concise comparison, we will focus on the three most distinct patterns: linear, central, and clustered configurations. These three forms, which represent extremes in building configurations, illustrate a representative spectrum of daylighting opportunities and constraints.

Linear Forms

A building massing with a linear configuration has a length-to-width ratio that lends itself to sidelighting when the width is sufficiently narrow. Orientation is important because one aspect of the building is longer than the other aspect. If the length is oriented in an east-west direction, daylighting can be coupled with passive heating or cooling on a seasonal basis. In contrast, if the length is oriented on the north-south axis, symmetry is created between the building form and the east-to-west movement of the sun, which emphasizes diurnal solar patterns. In either orientation, the location of windows needs to be carefully considered within the context of luminous and thermal objectives. Since linear forms have a long and a short aspect, there are distinct opportunities on each side of the building. Depending on the orientation, climate, prevailing winds, and program, each facade might be treated differently to admit or control daylighting, solar gains, and ventilation.

Linear buildings can be organized with an infinite variety of configurations: as a single form, a compound of parallel or perpendicular forms, or at various angles (leading to the possibility of clustered configurations). Daylighting strategies for linear buildings relate to the depth of the massing and to whether the

Figure 4.1 South and east facades of the Carmel Mountain Ranch Library.

(© Hewitt/Garrison)

Figure 4.2 Interior view of the clerestory windows and bookstacks at the Carmel Mountain Ranch Library.

(© Hewitt/Garrison)

building is composed of one or more linear forms. A simple, single linear mass lends itself to bilateral or multilateral sidelighting. M. W. Steele uses sidelighting at the Carmel Mountain Ranch Library in San Diego. The single-story library is a trapezoidal glass pavilion tucked under a large rectilinear roof. Oriented on a northwest-to-southwest axis, the symmetrical building is completely glazed on the southern, northern, and eastern facades to bring daylight (and at times sunlight) deep into the interior.[11] Expansive overhangs, vertical sunshades, and exterior vegetation control glare and thermal gains on the south. As a pavilion in a garden, outdoor spaces, views, and site are integrated with the interior. Given the temperate climate, operable windows at the lower and upper levels provide natural ventilation during a significant portion of the year. An energy analysis by Chuck Angyal of San Diego Gas & Electric predicted a 50 percent reduction in energy consumption compared to typical libraries. Although building occupants have excellent access to daylight and views, supplemental shading may be needed on the south to control glare and to direct sunlight during the winter months. The suc-

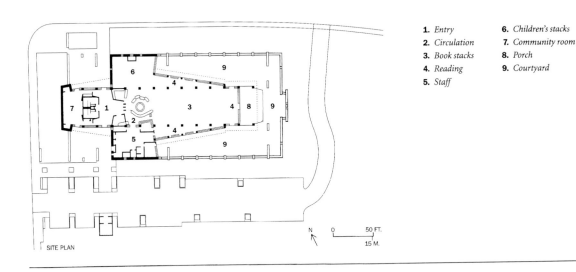

1. Entry
2. Circulation
3. Book stacks
4. Reading
5. Staff
6. Children's stacks
7. Community room
8. Porch
9. Courtyard

SITE PLAN

N   0   50 FT.
     15 M.

Figure 4.3   Plan of the Carmel Mountain Ranch Library.
(M. W. Steele)

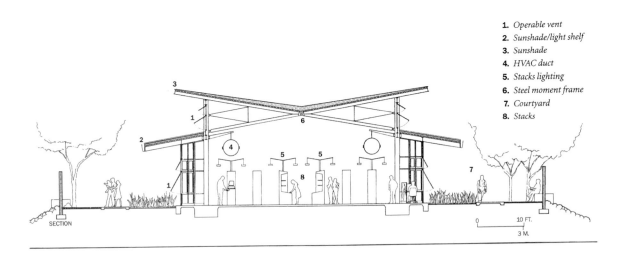

1. Operable vent
2. Sunshade/light shelf
3. Sunshade
4. HVAC duct
5. Stacks lighting
6. Steel moment frame
7. Courtyard
8. Stacks

SECTION

0   10 FT.
     3 M.

Figure 4.4   Section of the Carmel Mountain Ranch Library.
(M. W. Steele)

Figure 4.5 Exterior view of the Newton Library. (James Dow)

cesses of the strategies used at the library are dependent on a temperate climate and extensive shading. The transparency of the building would be inappropriate in all but the mildest of climates. (See Figures 4.1 to 4.4.)

A similar, yet more moderate glazing approach is taken by Patkau Architects at the Newton Library in Surrey, British Columbia. In this project the linear massing is oriented on an east-west axis. As in the Carmel Mountain Library, sidelighting and clerestory windows are located the south and north. Yet in contrast to the Carmel Mountain Library, the north and south facades are differentiated to respond to climate and distinct qualities of light from each orientation. The size of glazing is significantly reduced on the south, with overhangs and shading to control sunlight. Large expanses of glazing are found on the north to admit indirect daylight. Both projects use a linear form, relatively thin profile, and an appropriately tall section to provide

Figure 4.6   View of southern reading carrels at the Newton Library.

(James Dow)

sidelighting from both lower and upper clerestory windows. See Chapter 7 for additional discussion on the Newton Library. (See Figures 4.5 and 4.6.)

A variation on this theme is found in the Canadian Clay and Glass Gallery in Waterloo, Ontario, which was also designed by Patkau Architects. The massing is composed of a series of parallel linear forms oriented on a north-south axis. The interior has four distinct zones that essentially include the entry, lobby, information desk and stairs, and galleries. Three of the four zones are single-story spaces (the exception being the lobby, which contains staff spaces and library above). The parallel orientation of the four zones and close proximity of each to the other creates an overall building massing that is too deep for the exclusive use of sidelighting. As a result, the building is organized as a series of layers that alternately use sidelighting and toplighting. There are three distinct daylighting zones with sidelighting at the east (entry/lobby), toplighting at the center (information/ stairs), and the combined use of sidelighting and toplighting on the west (galleries). Large interior windows adjacent to the toplit zone provide daylight to the adjacent lobby and gallery. Interior windows and glazed doors also provide visual connections between the building masses and different activities.

The gallery is a rectilinear space that contains several smaller spaces. The overall gallery is illuminated primarily by sidelighting from the west. Three smaller spaces, inserted within the larger gallery, are contrasted by their distinctive use of toplighting, side-lighting, and electrical lighting. The Canadian Clay and Glass Gallery illustrates rich and contrasting luminous qualities that result from the combined use of toplighting and sidelighting. Although the depth of the plan mandates the use of toplighting, it also creates opportunities for a different character and quality

Figure 4.7 Exterior view
of the Canadian Clay
and Glass Gallery.

(Terri Meyer Boake)

of light. Toplighting gathers daylight from the zenith of the sky, while sidelighting gathers it from the horizon. As a result, spaces are brought to life by varying luminous qualities and patterns that dramatically change on a diurnal and seasonal basis. (See Figures 4.7 to 4.14.)

Another approach uses repetitive linear forms to create a large and deep overall massing. The Kimbell Art Museum by Louis Kahn is an example of such an approach, using a parallel configuration of repetitive forms. Given the overall depth of this type of massing, toplighting will play a predominant role in providing illumination. Like the Canadian Clay and Glass Museum, the massing of the Kimbell Art Museum is composed of a series of linear spaces on a north-south axis. The footprint of the building is organized into eighteen linear masses, three deep on a north-south axis, and six deep on an east-west axis (with the space for two masses left as voids to form the entry court). Galleries are located on the north and south sides of the building, with the

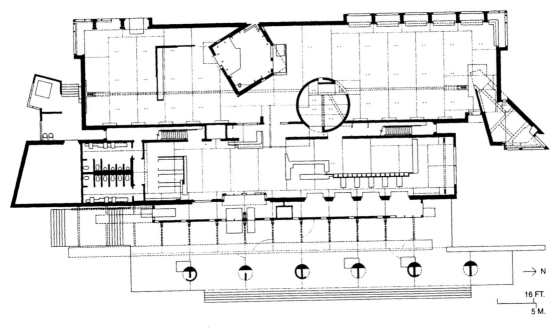

Figure 4.8   Main-floor plan of the Canadian Clay and Glass Gallery.

(Patkau Architects)

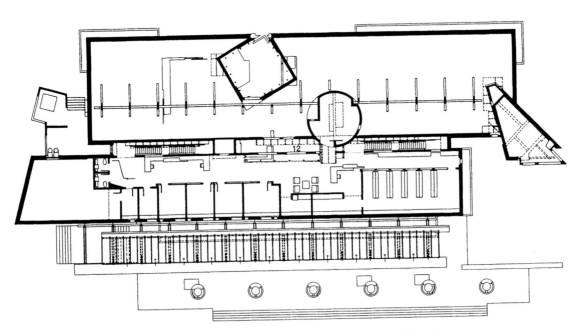

Figure 4.9   Upper-floor plan of the Canadian Clay and Glass Gallery.

(Patkau Architects)

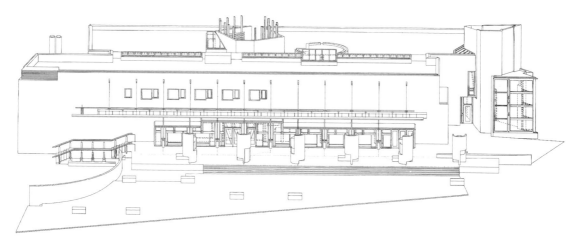

Figure 4.10   Axonometric drawing of the Canadian Clay and Glass Gallery.
(Patkau Architects)

entry, bookshop, and library at the center. The volume of each mass is articulated though materials, forms, and light so that the visitor is aware of moving through a series of adjacent parallel spaces. Kahn's famous skylight (a thin horizontal aperture at the center of a cycloid with a convex perforated reflector below) admits daylight that is reflected to the ceiling and subsequently to the gallery. The overall massing is punctured by the light courts, which are open to the sky above. Glazed walls provide daylight to adjacent spaces, provide a counterpoint to the toplit galleries, and create visual relief. Kahn ingeniously uses a series of thin masses illuminated by skylights and light courts to provide daylight

Figure 4.11   Entry to the Canadian Clay and Glass Gallery.
(Terri Meyer Boake)

Figure 4.12   Skylight in the stair corridor at the Canadian Clay and Glass Gallery.
(Terri Meyer Boake)

Figure 4.13 Exhibition area in the Canadian Clay and Glass Gallery.
(James Dow)

Figure 4.14   View of the sky from the outside gallery at the Canadian Clay and Glass Gallery.
(James Dow)

Figure 4.15 Interior of a gallery at the Kimbell Art Museum.
(Craig Johnson/CALA Visual Resources Collection)

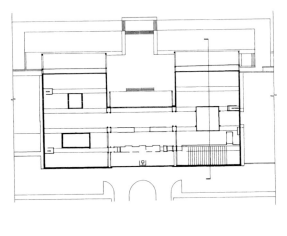

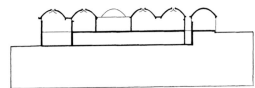

Figure 4.16   Plan and section of the Kimbell Art Museum.
(Donovan Nelson)

in a challenging building form. (See Figures 4.15 and 4.16.)

If we compare the sidelit Carmel Mountain Library, the Canadian Clay and Glass Gallery with layers of sidelighting and toplighting, and the Kimbell Art Museum, which uses toplighting as the primary strategy, we find that the type of daylighting strategy employed will depend to a great extent on the overall depth of the building massing. With linear forms, designers have the opportunity to admit daylighting from multiple facades as well as from the roof plane. If the building is not excessively deep, sidelighting may be sufficient. Deeper spaces can use toplighting to infill and supplement areas that are located far from the building perimeter. Toplighting becomes an increasingly important strategy as the overall depth of the form increases. Linear forms configured perpendicular to each other or at various angles present unique opportunities that are common to clustered configurations. These will be considered in a later discussion.

Centric Forms

Centric forms have an internal core that is typically a focal point around which other spaces are organized. They tend to be internally focused, though there may be views to the outside as well as the inside. A dense building massing may result from centric forms since they generally have a fairly equal length-to-width ratio. It is common to reduce the apparent depth of centric forms by inserting atria, lightwells, or courtyards, all of which tend to become focal points of the building. Centric massings may use only one of these strategies, although it is not uncommon to find atria, courtyards, and lightwells in the same building. Where it is not feasible to use atria or courtyards, a thin building profile and careful zoning of luminous activities (i.e., placement of services, storage, and circulation on the interior versus luminous tasks near the perimeter) can best help to use available daylighting.

When a thick massing with multiple stories is unavoidable due to site, programmatic, aesthetic, and economic concerns, the mass must be sculpted to maximize daylighting.

Louis Kahn's Phillips Exeter Library is a good example of a centric massing that uses a single atrium as a means of spatial and luminous organization. Kahn uses a variation on this theme at the Center for British Art, in which he includes two atria to create double foci within the building. Both approaches transform a thick massing into a series of thinner spaces. The atrium generally plays an important role in a centric form, with sidelighting often used along the perimeter of the building along with additional types of toplighting. These strategies are particularly successful in large multistory buildings, which can be a challenge to illuminate with daylighting. Depending on the height and depth of the building, even combined toplighting and sidelighting may be insufficient to provide daylighting throughout. Unless very wide and deep atria or courtyards are used, toplighting is usually most effective on the upper floors. Both the light levels and the distribution of daylight diminish at lower levels, which often leaves the bottom portion of the building in need of additional sidelighting. (See Figures 4.17 to 4.20.)

Figure 4.17 View of the atrium in the Phillips Exeter Library.

(J. Stephen Weeks)

We find classic daylighting strategies for a multistory building with a dense massing in Exeter Library. The square mass of the building has an atrium with clerestory windows on all sides. A light monitor admits both direct and indirect light, which is reflected off the walls to create indirect illumination for the atrium and the adjacent library stacks. Shading louvers modify the light based on seasonal and diurnal variations. Sidelighting along the perimeter of the building illuminates the study carrels and circulation. Sliding wooden louvers that recess into the wall

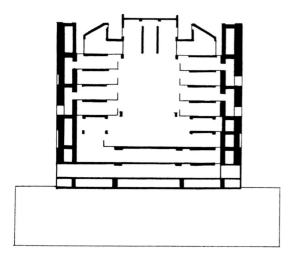

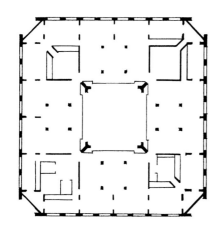

Figure 4.18   Plan and section of the Phillips Exeter Library.
(Donovan Nelson)

cavity can modify the quality and quantity of daylight in the carrels. Kahn protects the books from direct sunlight by placing them between the perimeter of the building and the inner atrium. While borrowed light provides ambient illumination beyond the atrium, the size of the clerestory windows is insufficient to fully illuminate the library stacks. Despite this limitation, Kahn creates meaningful and high-quality luminous experiences; for daylight also reveals form and space, aids in wayfinding, and creates distinct places of light.

William Bruder's Phoenix Central Library, in Phoenix, Arizona, represents a variation on the Exeter Library theme. Although the massing of the Phoenix Library could be characterized as a hybrid configuration, in part centric and in part linear, the overall density of the building, depth of the floor plate, and building height lead to daylighting strategies typical in centric forms. In contrast to Exeter, each facade is treated differently to address the particular lighting conditions of north, south, east, and west. The library is a rectilinear form oriented on a north-south axis that is embraced on the east and west by two thin linear masses containing service spaces. Sidelighting, toplighting, an atrium, and extensive shading are used to admit and control daylight in different portions of the building. Floor-to-ceiling glazing admits sidelighting from the south and north, with the solid mass of the support spaces blocking sunlight and thermal gains from the east and west.

Bruder uses simple but elegant shading strategies to overcome the problems inherent to such large areas of glazing in hot climates. The expansive south glazing has adjustable external horizontal louvers that modify the sunlight and thermal gains. In

Figure 4.19 View of an atrium in the Center for British Art and Studies.

(Dale Mulfinger/CALA Visual Resources Collection)

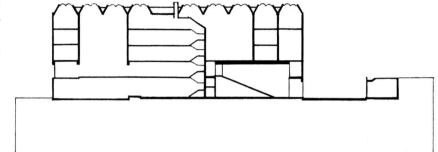

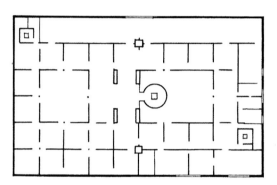

contrast, the north facade has vertical sailcloths that block sunlight while maintaining views of the city and surrounding landscape. An asymmetrically located atrium (described as a "crystal
canyon" by Bruder) brings daylight to areas located away from the
perimeter. The top of the atrium contains nine automated sunscoops that track and project light into the "canyon" and onto
reflecting pool below. As with the Exeter Library, the quantity of
daylighting provided by the atrium is insufficient to meet all the
luminous needs for the building. Yet the atrium plays other
important metaphorical and experiential roles. As an architectural
interpretation of the stunning geography of the Southwest,
Bruder used the atrium (or crystal canyon) to create a cool, shadowy oasis that is appropriate for the climate and evocative of
place. It also provides a focal point, marks the vertical circulation, adds visual interest, and creates internal views throughout
the heart of the building.

In addition to sidelighting on the lower floors, toplighting

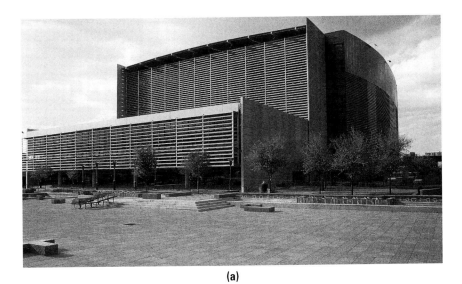

(a)

(b)

Figure 4.21 Distant views of the Phoenix Central Library: (a) south facade and (b) north facade.

(Abigail Van Slyck)

strategies are used in the 40-foot high public reading room on the upper floor. Thin horizontal skylights, at the junctures of the ceiling and the east and west walls, make the ceiling appear to hover over the space. Depending on the time of day, slivers of sunlight enter the thin skylights to wash along the concrete walls on the

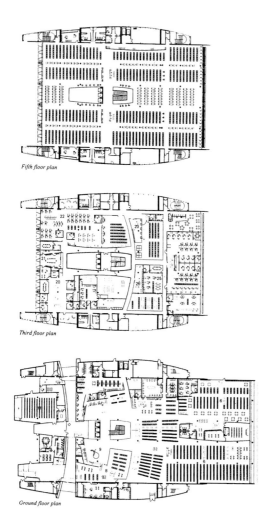

Fifth floor plan

Third floor plan

Ground floor plan

Figure 4.22 Plans of the Phoenix Central Library.
(William Bruder Architect)

east and west. The delicacy of the ceiling and its appearance of weightlessness are further enhanced by the design of the stainless steel structure. Vaguely reminiscent of Frank Lloyd Wright's daylit columns at the Johnson Wax Building, Bruder marks each column, which stops just short of the ceiling, with an oculus. An elegant structural connection transfers loads from the roof to the thin column without blocking daylight from the oculus. The field of columns, marked by dynamic pools of light, creates a stunning space in which light celebrates the structure as well as the public gathering. While the primary role of the oculus is aesthetic and experiential, some ambient daylight is also provided to the reading room and stacks. Additional sidelighting is provided on the north and south. Despite the many striking aesthetic and experiential uses of daylighting in the building, it is difficult to overlook its limited use for illumination. Although not always needed, electric lighting is used throughout the day. Modest design modifications could have resulted in better daylight for illumination while still maintaining the experiential concepts and aesthetic effects. (See Figures 4.21 to 4.26.)

A distinctly different daylighting approach is used to illuminate the compact massing of the Cy Twombly Gallery in Houston, Texas, by Renzo Piano. The design is based on a nine-square grid, with one double bay for large paintings. The solid and protective qualities of the building are maintained by limiting sidelighting to the two centrally located entries; otherwise, the galleries are completely toplit. An ingenious toplighting system, constructed of a series of external and internal layers, provides daylight and protects the art from sunlight and ultraviolet radiation. A structural frame,

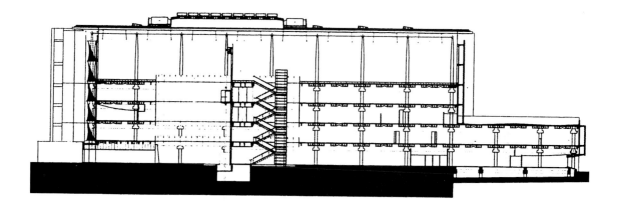

HVAC system, and solar control grilles are suspended over the roof of the building on the exterior. Under this structure is the glazing of the skylight, beneath which a cotton fabric ceiling is suspended. This three-dimensional roof filters and controls sunlight outside, at the glazing surface, and inside the building. The lack of outside views (except at the entries), neutral interior, and soft ambient daylight allow the artwork to dominate the spaces. Contrary to the preceding examples, toplighting is the primary daylighting strategy used to illuminate the building. Given the small scale and single story, the introduction of atria and lightwells is unnecessary. An intriguing aspect of the design is the use of a single daylighting aperture to illuminate multiple spaces. Similar strategies can be found in buildings of much larger proportion, such as the Roman Pantheon, which is illuminated by a dynamic pattern of light projected through a single oculus. Robert Mark, in *Light, Wind, and Structure,* describes the effects and characteristics of this small aperture, which is less than 4 percent of the floor area: ". . . This relatively small opening . . . is oriented to admit a maximum of light from the brightest area of the sky. No glass is present to reduce transmission, and the orientation of the opening with respect to the temple floor allows close to 100 percent of the radiated source light to reach the floor some

Figure 4.23 Section of the Phoenix Central Library.

(William Bruder Architect)

Figure 4.24   View of the
atrium from ground
level in the Phoenix
Central Library.

(Tim Hursley)

43 meters (143 feet) below."[12] The Pantheon is a striking example of the effectiveness of a small aperture illuminating a large
building mass. At the other extreme is the Cy Twombly Gallery,
where the glass area is equal to the area of the floor. The large
glazing area, which is intended to provide even, diffuse illumina-

Figure 4.25 View of reading room and skylights in the Phoenix Central Library.

(Tim Hursley)

Figure 4.26 Exterior view of the north facade and reading room at night.

(Tim Hursley)

Figure 4.27   Interior view of the Pantheon.

(Terri Meyer Boake)

Figure 4.28   Exterior view of the Cy Twombly Gallery.

(Jim Wasley)

tion throughout the galleries, is successful only because of the extensive layers of shading inside and outside—a lesson we also see expressed in different ways at the Exeter and Phoenix Central Libraries. These examples illustrate a range of approaches to daylighting buildings with dense footprints and large massings. While a variety of daylighting strategies may be used, toplighting is unavoidable. In each of the projects, we find toplighting, whether in an atrium, a lightwell, or a skylight, used as a strategy that organizes and unifies aesthetic, experiential, and luminous concerns. (See Figures 4.27 to 4.32.)

Figure 4.29   Entry to the Cy Twombly Gallery.

(Jim Wasley)

Figure 4.30   Interior view of a gallery.

(Jim Wasley)

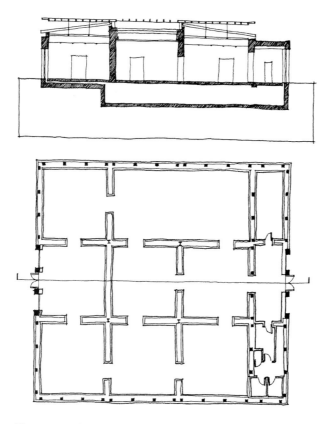

Figure 4.31 Plan and section of the Cy Twombly Gallery.

(Donovan Nelson)

Clustered Forms

Clustered building forms are inherently less difficult to daylight than dense building forms. Because clustered forms are composed of a series of smaller masses in variety of configurations, extensive surface areas abound for either toplighting or sidelighting. Negative spaces between masses (whether inside or outside) and the wings of the buildings can also be used to gather and borrow light to adjacent spaces. The Type/Variant House by Vince James is an example of clustered massing that takes advantage of linear

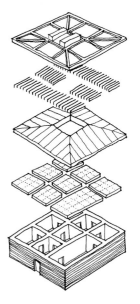

Figure 4.32 Axonometric drawing of the Cy Twombly Gallery.

(Donovan Nelson)

Figure 4.33 Exterior view of the Type/ Variant House.

(Don Wong)

forms that are configured perpendicular to each other. As a result, it benefits from the thinness and multilateral access to daylight that is typical of thin forms, while also taking advantage of space between the clustered masses to gather daylight and to connect to the landscape. Located on a lake in Hayward, Wisconsin, the site provides a stunning context for the house, which was designed as a vacation retreat for a couple with five adult children. The building is a compound of rectilinear masses unified by a series of exterior spaces. The title of the house, "Type/Variant," refers to the repetitive use of rectilinear forms or "types" while "variant" describes the ways in which each form is altered to respond to program, site conditions, views, and daylighting. The primary mass of the house, oriented on a north-south axis, contains lower-level living areas, the kitchen and dining areas, and the upper-level bedrooms. A master bedroom wing with a roof deck is located perpendicular to the north end of the living area (on an east-west orientation). Moving in an opposing western direction at the south end of the living area is another perpendicular mass containing a porch, courtyard, garage, and bedroom. A separate vertical mass with a studio loft is located farther to the south.

Sidelighting is used exclusively throughout the house, with the sizes and placements of the windows varying to capture particular qualities of light and to frame specific views of the lake, forest, earth, and sky. Large areas of glazing are typically located on

Figure 4.34   Interior view of the living area.

(Don Wong)

Figure 4.35   Interior view of the dining area.

(Don Wong)

the short ends of the linear masses on both the upper and lower levels. The living area is an exception, with floor-to-ceiling windows placed on the long aspect of the wall to overlook the lake to the east. The lake is not the only focus in this compound; there are also places throughout the house where the walls disappear to engage different views of the site along the cardinal directions. These large apertures minimize the boundaries between inside and outside, while a series of smaller windows discreetly frame the landscape. The smaller windows tend to define particular qualities of light for activities: a clerestory window tucked within a sleeping loft, a low horizontal band of windows over a work surface or sink, and a corner window to mark an entry. Light and shadow create varying experiences and rhythms, empha-

Figure 4.36   Distant view of Rainbow Shores.

(Richard Stringer)

size expansions and contractions in the building, and reinforce external versus internal foci. For example, the shadows of the corridor along the upper bedrooms contrast with pockets of light in the sleeping nook, and a narrow passage behind the fireplace is juxtaposed with the openness and brightness of the adjacent living room. As a result, spaces are marked by distinct experiences of light. (See Figures 4.33 to 4.37.)

Clare Design uses a different approach to clustered forms at the Rainbow Shores housing project near the Sunshine Coast in Australia. This beachfront community consists of a series of multifamily units designed to provide views, daylighting, and ventilation. A ziggurat configuration ensures that each mass has maximum exterior surfaces and exposure to sun and wind. The

Figure 4.37   Interior view of the master bedroom of the Type/Variant House.

(Don Wong)

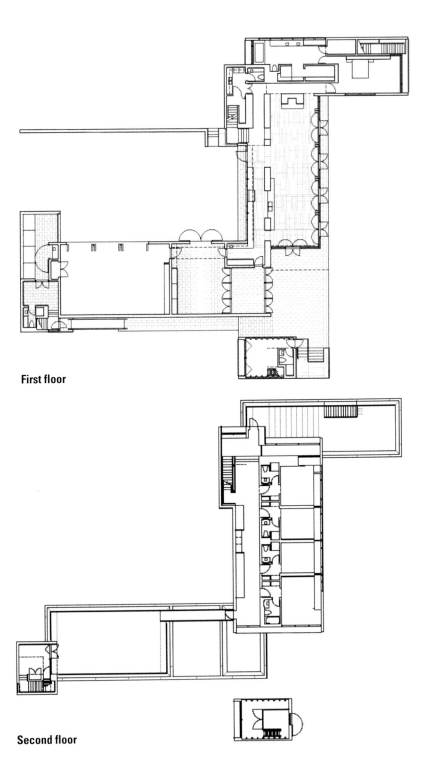

Figure 4.38a
Plans of the Type/
Variant House.

(Vince James Associates)

First floor

Second floor

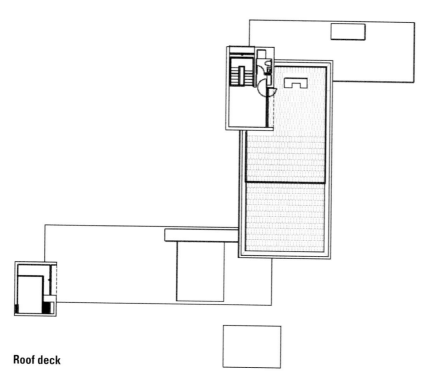

Figure 4.38b
Plan of the Type/
Variant House.

(Vince James Associates)

Roof deck

lower levels of each three-story house include a carport, stair, and two exterior terraces; the midlevels contain bedrooms; and the living areas are located on the top floors to maximize light, wind, and views. Distinct sidelighting strategies are used on each level. On the ground floor, vertical trellises visually screen terrace openings to maintain privacy while selectively connecting to the site and community. The upper floors, clad in vertical wood, appear to perch on top of the concrete lower level. Small horizontal and vertical windows with awnings provide bilateral sidelighting and cross ventilation in the bedrooms. Depending on the location within the cluster of housing units, rooms occasionally have only one outside wall, which results in unilateral daylighting. By offsetting the building masses, the architects minimize the frequency of this condition. Large windows wrap the upper levels to provide maximum ventilation and daylight in the living areas. Given the hot climate, a large roof plane extends beyond the mass to provide shading. Smaller awnings provide additional shading on the upper-level verandas. Windows are carefully located to maximize breezes while providing daylight in all rooms.

Figure 4.39 Facade
detail of Rainbow
Shores.
(Richard Stinger)

A significantly dense housing compound has been developed at Rainbow Shores to minimize the ecological impact to the site while also maintaining privacy and human comfort. Although the forms and configuration of the masses are different, both Vince James and Clare Design take advantage of the daylighting opportunities of a clustered massing. They each keep the profiles of the buildings thin; they configure the masses to integrate daylight, ventilation, site connections, and views; and they embrace the landscapes and light in the surrounding negative spaces. (See Figures 4.38 to 4.40.)

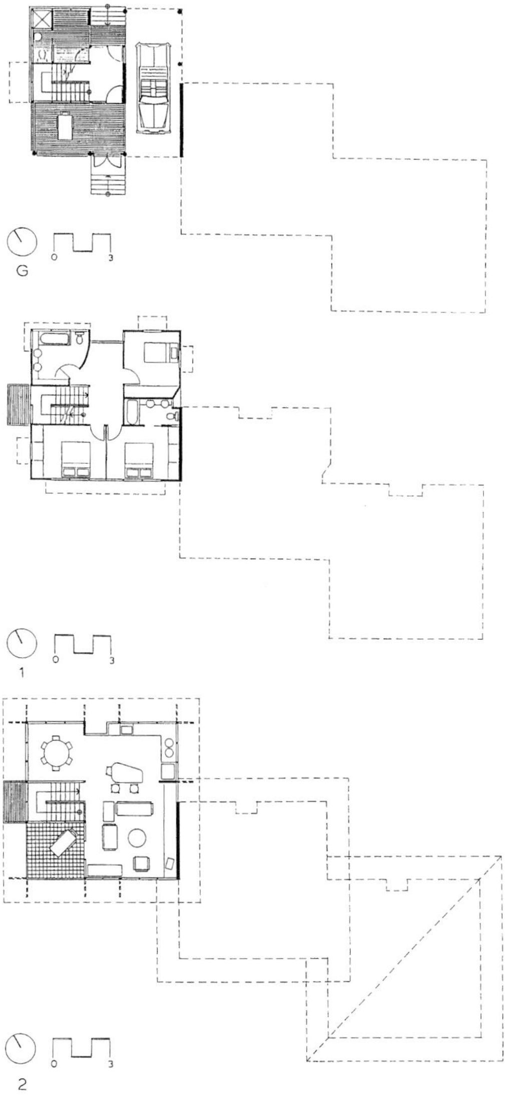

BUILDING PLAN AND SECTION

The plan and section are two-dimensional representations that define three-dimensional relationships between the parts of a building and the whole. Through plan drawings we are able to understand how deeply light will penetrate, to determine patterns of light in rooms, to explore the relationships between spaces, to size shading devices and overhangs, and even to study the moods and qualities of light. Plans and sections describe the sequence of luminous events and the interaction between spaces inside and outside. The following discussion will use plans and sections as means of exploring and understanding three issues of particular importance to daylighting: room depth and height, surface characteristics, and journey through space.

Room Depth and Height

In daylighting design, plans and sections can be used to understand whether appropriate qualities and quantities of light reach the appropriate locations for which the room depth and height are issues of particular significance. Plans and sections are also helpful in understanding the limitations of daylighting—what it can and cannot do depending on the strategies and desired programmatic and aesthetic effects. Simple guidelines such as

Figure 4.40 Plans of Rainbow Shores.
(Clare Design)

Figure 4.41 Exterior view of Sahara West Library and Museum.

(Tim Hursley)

the 15/30 and the 2.5H rules of thumb illustrate the daylighting boundaries that need to be respected when designing room depth and height.[13] There are limits to how deeply daylight will penetrate and how widely it can be distributed for particular strategies. Unilateral sidelighting is particularly problematic because daylight quantities drop quickly away from the window wall. Approaches that use bilateral and/or multilateral strategies can greatly improve the quantity and distribution of sidelighting. Because these strategies bring light from the walls or perimeters of the space, the depth of the room is particularly critical. In contrast, toplighting can easily admit daylight over virtually any area of the plan. Subsequently, the height of the room (as well as the size and location of the windows) becomes increasingly important in determining how much light will reach the lower portions of a toplit space. The depth and height of the room will also influence which portions of a space "see" a window, skylight, or monitor. If areas of contrast (light and shadow) are desired, then the section and plan can be designed to prevent a particular location from seeing the window. The plan and section can also be used to determine whether rooms or subspaces are unintentionally blocked from the windows by partitions, furnishings, or structures.

The plans and sections of Sahara West Library and Museum in Las Vegas, by Meyer, Scherer & Rockcastle are useful in understanding fundamental concepts and principles concerning the room depth and height. The reading rooms and library stacks illustrate how the form of the plan and section can be developed in response to activities, human experiences, and design aesthetics. The two-story library wing is a fairly dense linear form oriented on a north-south axis. The lower level contains an infor-

Figure 4.42a Plan of the Upper Level at Sahara West Library and Museum.

(Meyer, Scherer & Rockcastle)

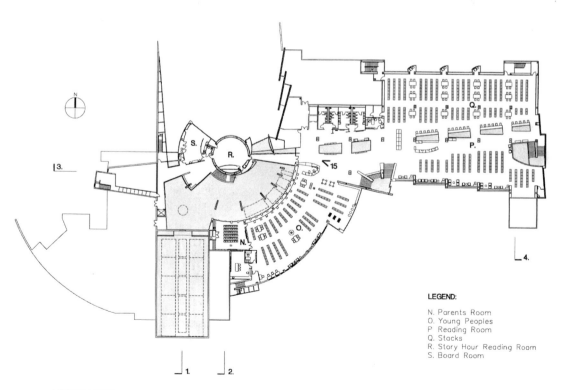

LEGEND:

N. Parents Room
O. Young Peoples
P. Reading Room
Q. Stacks
R. Story Hour Reading Room
S. Board Room

UPPER LEVEL

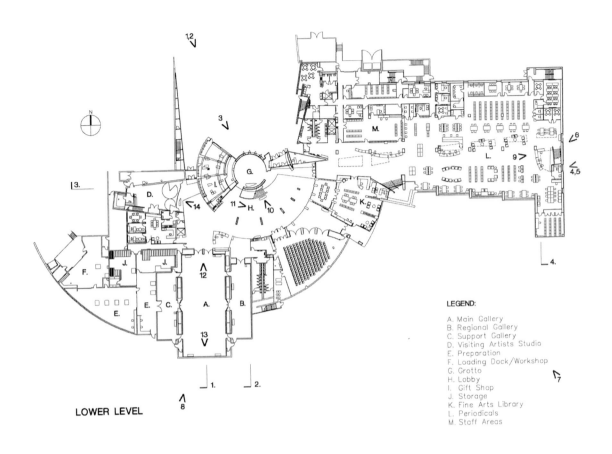

LEGEND:

A. Main Gallery
B. Regional Gallery
C. Support Gallery
D. Visiting Artists Studio
E. Preparation
F. Loading Dock/Workshop
G. Grotto
H. Lobby
I. Gift Shop
J. Storage
K. Fine Arts Library
L. Periodicals
M. Staff Areas

LOWER LEVEL

Figure 4.42b   Plan of the
Lower Level at Sahara
West Library
and Museum.

(Meyer, Scherer &
Rockcastle)

mation area, references, reading areas, stacks, periodicals, and support spaces, while the upper level contains additional stacks and the main reading room. The plan reveals that the spaces on both floors are divided into southern and northern zones, which are separated by a line of lightwells that extend vertically through the upper level to gather daylight. The southern zone has windows that provide sidelighting on both floors. Small three-dimensional windows project out from the north facade on the second floor to create intimate reading rooms. The northern zone on the lower level has no access to sidelighting due to service spaces and meeting rooms at the building perimeter. The east wall of the lower and upper floors is framed by a "celestial wall," which animates the stairwell with changing patterns of light. The western portion of each floor continues on to adjacent library and museum spaces.

The building section reveals that the southern and central zones are particularly well daylit. Large south-facing windows with lightshelves control direct sunlight, reduce excessive contrast at the window wall, and redistribute indirect daylight deep into the space. A vaulted ceiling distinguishes and celebrates the southern zone of the building, and a clerestory window adjacent to the vaulted ceiling reflects indirect northern light to the main reading room below. The northern zone of the building has a lightwell immediately adjacent to the vaulted reading room. This centrally located lightwell slices through the second floor to bring daylight to the lower level. While its contribution for illumination is limited, the lightwell opens the center of the building to views of the upper level, creates a vertical connection, and enhances a sense of spaciousness. The sidelighting, lightshelves, clerestory windows, and lightwell in conjunction with the room form, depth, and height are thoughtfully conceived to address illuminance requirements and visual and thermal comfort—particularly on the upper level and within the main reading room. Traditional window forms that provide light for specific tasks are contrasted by a range of irregularly shaped and idiosyncratic windows that

Figure 4.43 Section renderings of Sahara West Library and Museum.

(Meyer, Scherer & Rockcastle)

Figure 4.44 Interior view of lightwell adjacent to the library stacks at the Sahara West Library and Museum.

(Tim Hursley)

create dramatic luminous events at special locations within the library and museum. For example, the intriguing forms and dynamic luminous effects of the windows on the "celestial wall," "grotto," and "young people's" room create a striking counterpoint to the even, soft illumination in the larger public spaces. (See Figures 4.41 to 4.44.)

The particular strategies at the Sahara West Library are less important than the general concepts and principles that are embodied in the design of the plan and section (and therefore in the three-dimensional spaces). Most important, form has been conceived to get light where it is needed. The section clearly reveals which areas of the space see the windows and/or reflected light and which areas are problematic. The sections and plans also illustrate how deeply light will penetrate. Careful zoning in the north and south sections minimizes the apparent depth of the building, as does the central lightwell, the reflective ceiling, and the lightshelves. Similarly, the heights of the spaces are designed to maximize light distribution. This is particularly evident in the daylighting relationship between the ceiling vault, clerestory monitor, and lightshelves in main reading room. Varied spatial depths and heights also create a variety of luminous events, with differing illuminance levels and the play of darkness and shadow combining to create distinct and rich luminous experiences.

Surface Form and Characteristics

The surfaces of a room can be shaped to gather, reflect, filter, and redistribute daylight. The relationship between a daylighting aperture and the room surfaces is an important consideration for both sidelighting and toplighting. By placing windows adjacent to surfaces, designers can use the room itself as a means of modify-

Figure 4.45 Interior detail of the clerestory at the Bagsvaerd Church.

(J. Stephen Weeks)

Figure 4.46 Interior view of the ceiling reflectors at the Menil Gallery.

(Jim Wasley)

ing, manipulating, and controlling daylight. For example, a room with a single double-hung window isolated within a wall creates a pool of light that has distinct seasonal and diurnal patterns. In contrast, a window placed adjacent to a wall, floor, or ceiling surface will reflect the daylight, increase light penetration, and potentially control glare. There are many ways in which the windows can interact with architectural surfaces. We will focus on three areas of particular daylighting potential: ceiling and walls, window reflectors, and exterior surfaces.

Because the floor of a room may be covered with furniture, carpet, or other nonreflective finishes, the walls and ceilings often

have the greatest potential to interact with the windows. Ceilings merit special consideration given their size, distribution over the space, and potential geometric relationship to the window. A ceiling can even be shaped to modify daylight, as in Alvar Aalto's Seinäjoki Library, where a curved ceiling surface adjacent to a clerestory monitor captures light and redirects it to the library stacks below. Glenn Murcutt uses a double-curved ceiling oriented in opposite directions to similar effect in the Magney House at Bingie Point. A large curved surface faces north (toward the sun in the Southern Hemisphere), reflecting daylight to the living spaces, while a smaller curved surface facing south redirects and concentrates daylight to service areas. A variation on this theme is found at Jørn Utzon's Bagsvaerd Church in Copenhagen, Denmark, where a high clerestory window is located adjacent to a ceiling sculpted of multiple curved surfaces. Daylight is interreflected between the ceiling surfaces before softly reaching the sanctuary below. At the Menil Gallery in Houston, Texas, Renzo Piano uses multiple curved reflectors for a similar effect. Long

S-shaped reflectors placed parallel to each other are oriented on an east-west axis to create ceiling surfaces that diffuse and distribute sunlight throughout the galleries. Sunlight strikes the upper surface of one reflector and is redirected to the lower surface of an adjacent reflector before finally reaching the gallery below. At the Los Angeles Museum of Contemporary Art, by Arata Isozaki, a deep pyramidal ceiling is used to achieve multiple reflections, control direct sunlight, and redistribute daylight. Variations on the theme of solar control are found in different galleries. One gallery uses a simple, deep skylight well to diffuse daylight; another adds a translucent laylight (or ceiling) beneath a deep skylight; while yet another diffuses daylight with huge triangular baffles. (See Figures 4.45 to 4.48.)

Windows can also be placed adjacent to specially designed surfaces in the room itself. As we saw earlier, Louis Kahn locates a reflective surface directly below the skylight at the Kimbell Art Museum. Sunlight entering the skylight is reflected off the surface to the concrete ceiling and space below. Direct light is also diffused through small perforated openings in the reflector, which provide a glimpse of the sky from within the galleries. Meyer, Scherer & Rockcastle take a similar approach at the Sahara West Museum in Las Vegas, Nevada. Two large adjustable parabolic

Figure 4.48 South gallery with daylight baffles at the Museum of Contemporary Art.

(Bruce Haglund)

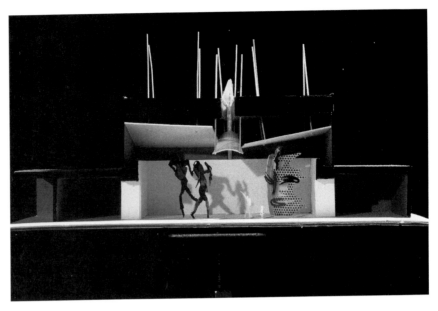

Figure 4.49 Section study model of the Sahara West Museum.
(Meyer, Scherer & Rockcastle)

Figure 4.50 Exhibition niches in the entry to the Anthropology Museum.

Figure 4.51 Study models of reflected light for the Chapel of St. Ignatius.
(Stephen Holl Architects)

Figure 4.52 Reflected light in the choir area at the Chapel of St. Ignatius.
(Nicolas McDaniel)

Figure 4.53 Interior rendering of the Capuchinas Sacramentarias del Purismo Corazon de Maria Chapel.

baffles are located directly below a deep skylight. The baffles can be positioned to modify illuminance levels and reflect daylight to either the ceiling or wall surfaces. (See Figure 4.49.)

In contrast to approaches that use a special daylighting reflector, windows or skylights can simply be positioned adjacent to an interior surface. In the Anthropology Museum at the University of British Columbia, Arthur Erickson places deep skylights adjacent to walls to create diffused daylight niches for archaeological artifacts. The softly illuminated niches frame a shadowy path that descends to a brightly illuminated exhibition hall. As we saw in Chapter 1, Steven Holl uses wall surfaces to create distinct and dramatic effects at the Chapel of St. Ignatius at Seattle University. Sidelighting in the chapel is screened by solid wall partitions that are suspended in front of the windows. Daylight enters the window, is reflected off the interior surface, redistributed to an adjacent wall, and finally reflected to the room itself. A mysterious luminous effect results because the source of the daylight is not visible. In addition, the back of the reflective surface is painted and colored lenses are placed on the windows. In the sanctuary, Holl uses either blue or yellow for the reflective surface and window glazing. We find a variation on this strategy in the choir area, where Holl uses a green reflector with a red window. Luis Barragan creates a similar effect using direct, rather than reflected, daylight at the Capuchinas Sacramentarias del Purismo Corazon de Maria Chapel in Tlalpán, Mexico. A small niche containing a single vertical window and large cross is hidden from direct view in the sanctuary. Daylight enters the stained glass window to be reflected off the wall and floor surfaces. Golden daylight fills the niche and projects a shadow of the cross into the sanctuary. (See Figures 4.50 to 4.53.)

Exterior surfaces can also be used to modify daylight. The

Carmel Mountain Library by M. W. Steele uses the roof adjacent to a south clerestory to reflect daylight onto the ceiling, which redistributes the light to the library stacks below. In contrast, Carlos Scarpa uses the ground surface to reflect light to the interior of the Brion Family Chapel near Treviso, Italy. Low windows adjacent to a shallow pool of water reflect shimmering and ethereal light onto the altar. These ingenious windows frame the corner of the altar and provide soft, reflected backlighting. An inverse approach is found in Scarpa's elegant addition to the Passagno Plaster Cast Gallery in Passagno, Italy. Here Scarpa uses toplighting to "capture a slice of the sky." Three-dimensional windows frame a mysterious view of the sky while also illuminating sensuous plaster figures. Abundant daylight is also reflected from a reflecting pool outside the south window (adjacent to the figures of the Three Muses) and from a slot that Scarpa has inserted between the existing building and the new addition. This thin slice of space allows light to be reflected from the vertical surface of the existing building into the new gallery. Yet

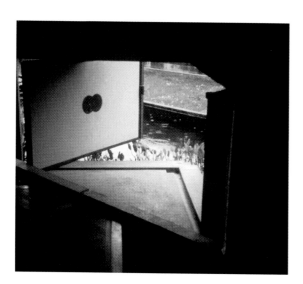

Figure 4.54 Interior view of the Brion Family Chapel.

(Eric West)

Figure 4.55 Interior view of the Passagno Plaster Cast Gallery.

(Leon Satkowski)

perhaps most memorable are Scarpa's three-dimensional sky-lights, which, as he explained "capture a slice of the sky." These projects illustrate that plans and sections must be carefully conceived if architectural surfaces are to be used to modify daylight. The daylighting opportunities are limitless if the form and characteristics of the ceiling, walls, floors, and exterior surfaces have a conversation with the daylighting apertures. (See Figures 4.54 and 4.55.)

WINDOWS

The design and form of the window is our final consideration. Its size, position, sectional characteristics, and relationship to other surfaces ultimately define the luminous experiences within a space. Windows play many roles and take on many tasks. They can be spaces in and of themselves, stages for activity, filters to the outside, frames for views, and much more. Many programmatic, aesthetic, and experiential factors must be weighed in determining appropriate window forms. Of particular concern are the window size, location, and detailing.

Window Size

Attention is often paid to the size of windows (or glazing area) because of the impact of glazing on energy consumption.[14] The size of the window and its influence on daylighting must also be considered from a broader conceptual perspective which might include the connection to the site, desired quality or mood of the light, human comfort, wayfinding, articulation of form, and visual relief. In order to determine the size of a window one needs to return to the programmatic objectives and criteria discussed earlier in this chapter. First, how much light is needed? Are low levels or high levels of illumination appropriate? Next, how does the light need to be distributed? Should there be pools of light to correspond with distinct tasks? Should the light be distributed uniformly? Are there areas that have greater or lesser needs for daylight? Finally, what is the desired quality of light? Is there a particular mood or character that is appropriate for the program? What is the role of light and shadow? Based on these types of questions, the designer can begin to assess the relationship between the size of the aperture and the luminous program.

Small windows typically create distinct pools of daylight that punctuate a space with rhythms of light and shadow. A small window defines a boundary between the inside and outside which is accentuated by the contrast between the mass of the wall and the small area of glazing. As the size of the window increases there is a corresponding decrease in both the contrast of light and shadow and the boundary between inside and outside. A small window can be used to frame a particular view or relationship to the outside, focusing attention on a special or unique environmental feature. In contrast, a large window creates a less discriminating boundary between inside and outside—it can welcome the site and landscape to the interior. Small windows also define a space of light within shadow. When located in close proximity, small windows can create dappled rhythms of light and shadow. If clustered together they can form larger openings that wash the room or surfaces with light. As the window size increases, contrast of light and shadow decreases.

There is a delicate balance between an appropriate amount of light and the desired luminous effect. A small, carefully placed window can be as effective at providing illumination as a large (and potentially resource-consuming) window. This is particularly true when a small window is located adjacent to a wall, floor, or ceiling surface to redistribute light. Good daylighting does not require large windows. In order to use daylight most effectively it is critical to put light where it is needed. This approach minimizes problems with visual and thermal comfort and helps to avoid the creation of monotonous luminous environments that can result from overillumination. Jun'ichirō Tanizaki reminds us of the importance of shadows in this discussion of Japanese aesthetics from his book *In Praise of Shadows:* ". . . we find beauty not in the thing itself but in the patterns of shadows, the light and the darkness, that one thing against another creates. A phosphorescent jewel gives off its glow and color in the dark and loses its beauty in the light of day. Were it not for shadows, there would be no beauty."[15] The celebration of shadows can lead not only to energy- and resource-efficient daylighting, but also to rich and varied luminous experiences. This concept suggests that windows can be used sparingly, yet within the context of the program and climate. Window size is of particular importance in hot and cold climates. Unless passive heating is an objective, it is judicious to minimize the size of the window while maximizing its luminous effect.

At the Sahara West Library and Art Museum in Las Vegas, Nevada, architects Meyer, Scherer & Rockcastle use window size and form as a means of creating particular qualities of light. This is especially evident in the "celestial wall" on the east facade,

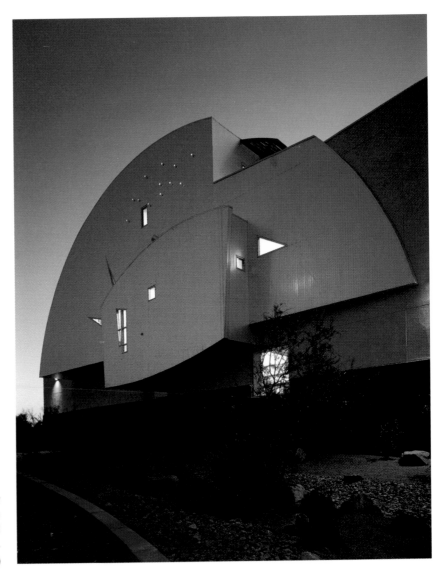

Figure 4.56 Exterior view of the celestial wall at the Sahara West Library and Museum at night.

(Tim Hursley)

Figure 4.57 Interior view of the celestial wall at the Sahara West Library and Museum.

(Tim Hursley)

where a composition of intriguing, irregularly shaped windows marks the vertical circulation from the lower to upper levels. One of several window types includes tiny circular apertures with glass rods that project from the outside to the inside. Daylight is transmitted through the cylindrical rods to create the effect of stars hovering along the interior of the wall. These tiny apertures concentrate and collect a brilliant light, which contrasts with shadows on the surface of the wall. Three slightly larger windows are located within and below this celestial field. One of these windows is a three-dimensional cylindrical aperture that focuses light from the southeast. The second window is a triangular wedge that cuts through the depth of the wall to provide a glimpse to the northeast. Finally, a rectilinear window is beveled to capture northern light, creating a wash of light that illuminates the interior surface of the bevel, while the mysterious source of the light remains obscured. While the form of the windows is critical, the size is equally important. Sufficient darkness must be maintained on a wall to realize the unique luminous effects of each window type. The resulting qualities of light are reminiscent of the elegant daylighting that is created by the south windows at the Chapel at Notre Dame du Haut in Ronchamp, France, by Le Corbusier. (See Figures 4.56 and 4.57.)

At the Frye Art Museum in Seattle, by Olson Sundberg Architects, we find that the size of the window can also be used to modify or control daylight, determine the visual hierarchy of a space, and create particular luminous experiences. In the information area, a tiny asymmetrical oculus provides abundant ambient light while animating the domed ceiling of the rotunda. Shifting patterns of light draw the visitors' attention to the sky and the architectural feature overhead. The luminous events of the entry create a transition between the outside and the soft indirect daylight of the galleries, where modestly sized clerestory monitors are positioned to reflect light to the walls. Earlier, we saw an even smaller aperture used by Louis Kahn at the Kimbell Art Museum, where a thin horizontal skylight and reflectors provide ambient illumination throughout the gallery. (See Figures 4.58 and 4.59.)

Neither the Frye nor the Kimbell are fully daylit museums. Both use low levels of ambient daylight to illuminate the space and supplemental electric lighting to accentuate the artwork. While it is possible to use daylight for illumination during a great portion of the day, it is not uncommon to find this task-ambient approach to lighting in museums. Although it is less energy- and resource-efficient, the use of daylighting for ambient, rather than task, illumination helps to avoid the difficult

Figure 4.58 Section rendering of the rotunda at the Frye Art Museum.

(Olson Sundberg Architects)

Figure 4.59 View of galleries in the Frye Art Museum.

(Robert Pisano)

challenge of getting light to the artwork in appropriate levels and without its potentially damaging effects. This approach often uses darkness and contrast as a means of focusing attention on the artwork. While there are strategies to control the damaging effects of daylight (ultraviolet filters, shading devices, rotating the artwork, etc.), the exclusive use of daylight may be inappropriate for some programs, curators, and clients. In these cases, a task-ambient approach that combines electric light with daylight may be the most feasible strategy. If the program and artwork can withstand greater exposure to daylight, then the size of apertures can increase accordingly. As we have seen at the Cy Twombly Gallery, Renzo Piano uses a glazing aperture that is the same size as the floor area. The entire roof of the museum is one large aperture, which filters daylight through a series of shading louvers, glazing, and fabric to provide diffuse ambient and task illumination throughout. Although electric lighting is provided, it is rarely needed. The program, the curator's objectives, the light sensitivity of the artwork, and issues of control will help determine the appropriate size of the window, which in turn affects the illuminance levels, distributions of light, and daylighting qualities. At

Figure 4.60 Lightscape renderings of the Chapel on Mount Rokko during the summer and winter solstices.

(Lars Peterssen and Tim Guyette)

the Frye and Kimbell Art Museums, contrasting illuminance levels are used to create a hierarchy in which the artwork predominates. At the Cy Twombly Gallery, a relatively even distribution of illuminance is found throughout. As a result, there is less contrast and differentiation between the artwork and the space of the gallery. These contrasting approaches establish different relationships between the artwork, viewers, and gallery as a direct result of window sizes.

Ando's Chapel at Mount Rokko illustrates how the size of windows can be used to express a relationship to the environment and to reveal the architecture. As we saw earlier, the chapel is a simple rectilinear box that contains a series of different-sized apertures. Small, thin apertures articulate the junctures between walls and ceiling at opposing corners of the east and west walls. Two additional apertures are oriented horizontally as ceiling slots above the east and west walls. These small windows play multiple roles. They mark the movement of the sun as it tracks from east to west, define time and seasons as sunlight or daylight animate different surfaces, and reveal the cardinal directions. These washes of light also emphasize the perimeter of the room and the nuances of its concrete construction. In contrast, a large south-facing window (located at the center of the southern wall) illuminates the volume of the space and provides a visual connection to a walled garden adjacent to the chapel. Windows are used differently to emphasize space, site, materials, orientation, and the passage of time. These examples suggest that the sizing of windows relates not only to energy and resource consumption, but also to a great variety of human and aesthetic factors. The size of the window determines the character of light in space, the relationship between inside and outside, whether the room volume or perimeter will be illuminated, how a surface or an object will be revealed, how time and seasons will be emphasized, whether electric lighting will be needed, and many other qualitative and quantitative aspects of the luminous program. (See Figure 4.60.)

Window Position

The position of a window on a wall or ceiling affects how light will be distributed and what relationship it will have with the tasks, activities, and experiences in a space. Low windows, for example, provide an opportunity to take advantage of ground-reflected light, which can be redirected from exterior surfaces and floors to bring light deep within the space (assuming that light-colored surfaces are used and that the floor is not covered with objects). The lower the window, the greater the opportunity to provide direct visual connection to the site and landscape. Mid-height windows are popular for combining views, reflected light, and an optimal location for ventilation in proximity to the occupant. As the window height increases, so does privacy. High windows shift the visual relationship from the earth to the sky, while also allowing light to penetrate deep into the space. Care must be taken with high windows because the surface below the window may be cast in shadow, which can create excessive contrast between the window and the wall. Bilateral illumination or reflective surfaces can be used to overcome this effect (as in Aalto's Seinäjoki Library).

As we saw earlier at the Newton Library, by Patkau Architects, windows are positioned to respond to the site, program, and different zones within the building. Low windows, adjacent to the study carrels, provide views, ventilation, and illumination for reading. In contrast, high clerestory windows bring light deep into the space to illuminate the library stacks and large reading tables. At the Frye Art Museum, windows are positioned to bring light to different surfaces of the room by positioning a clerestory monitor adjacent to walls. Daylight is reflecting off the wall to provide ambient illumination within the space. At the Sahara West Library and Museum, a series of low windows are positioned at a seated eye level, while other windows correspond to the eye level of a child rather than an adult. Other windows evoke metaphorical allusions, such as the starlike windows located high on the celestial wall and the low vertical windows in the grotto that suggest

Figure 4.61 Exterior view of the Chapel at La Tourette.
(Radford Oliver)

geological fissures. Still other windows are positioned to illumi-nate a volume of space instead of a particular surface.

At the Chapel at La Tourette in Eveux-sur-l'Arbresle, France, Le Corbusier places the windows to articulate different activities and subspaces. At the front of the chapel, a tall vertical window with a south-facing sunscoop gathers daylight and washes the south wall adjacent to the altar. The asymmetrical light at the altar is the primary focus of the chapel. Borrowed light from adja-cent spaces on the north and south softly complements the bright illumination from the sunscoop. Pews at the opposite end of the chapel are accentuated with a series of small horizontal windows positioned slightly above and behind the pews. The deep reveal and splay of these windows emphasizes the depth of the wall, in contrast to light that washes the surface adjacent to the altar. A skylight and high, thin horizontal window articulate the ceiling above the pews. The skylight marks the center of the area and admits a sliver of sunlight in the late afternoon. A thin horizontal window located at the juncture of the wall and ceiling makes the ceiling appear to float overhead. Both of these mysterious apertures have ethereal luminous effects, which allude to the heavens above. (See Figures 4.61 and 4.62.)

Window Detailing

The detailing of windows concerns window depth, sectional characteristics, and materials. Window depth has a significant impact on the relationship between inside and outside—the deeper the window the greater the distinction. As windows increase in depth, there is also a greater opportunity to use the section of the window itself to modify, reflect, or redistribute daylight. In contrast, as the mass of the wall diminishes, light is more easily reflected from adjacent room surfaces than from window surrounds. Supplemental shading becomes increasingly important for many programs and climates with diminishing wall mass. With a deep window, the sill and jamb can provide daylight control; with a thin profile, additional layers (inside, at the window, or outside) will be needed for solar control. The sectional characteristics of

Figure 4.62 Interior rendering of the Chapel at La Tourette.

the window also play important roles in determining the quality of light, where it will be distributed, and whether light will be concentrated, distributed, reflected, filtered, or otherwise modified. The window can even be detailed to bring light to a particular place at a particular time.

One of the most famous examples of using window depth and sectional characteristics for luminous effects is found at Notre Dame du Haut. Le Corbusier elegantly uses the sectional properties of the window itself (rather than external or internal layers) to create a sacred luminous experience while also addressing thermal and visual comfort. Small, deeply recessed windows emphasize the distinction between the inside and outside, between the

(a)

(b)

Figure 4.63 Views of the south wall of Notre Dame du Haut: (a) exterior and (b) interior.
(Radford Oliver)

Figure 4.64 Detail views of the Phoenix Central Library: (a) south facade and (b) north facade.

(Abigail Van Slyck)

sacred and the profane. The windows, which appear to be carved out of the massive south facade, have splayed forms to correspond with the sun's altitude and azimuth at different times of year and day. In addition, some windows splay to the exterior, creating pockets of shadow on the facade, while other windows splay to the interior to capture pockets of light that contrast with the dark window wall. The small openings create three-dimensional volumes that contain sunlight or darkness within the depth of the wall. A rich and varied tapestry of light and shadow results from the massiveness of the wall, the depth of the window, and the form of the section. (See Figure 4.63.)

In Chapter 1 we saw that Kaija and Heikki Sirens use a contrasting approach to window detailing in their Chapel at Otaniemi, Finland. A wood-framed northern window wall with a very thin sectional profile brings the landscape inside and extends the chapel outside. The window is detailed flush to the ground plane to suggest that the earth extends into the chapel. A high, south clerestory monitor admits direct sunlight behind the parishioners to wash the ceiling and walls with dynamic patterns of light. In contrast to Notre Dame du Haut, the Chapel at Otaniemi breaks down the boundaries between inside and outside. Sectional characteristics of the window are minimized, and the relationships to adjacent rooms and outdoor surfaces are of great importance.

The detailing of window layers can also be used to create particular qualities of light in relation to program, site, and climate. At the Phoenix Central Library, the exteriors of the large north and south windows are detailed to provide solar control. Motorized horizontal louvers on the south respond to the varying altitude of the sun during the year, while vertical sails on the north respond to the apparent movement of the sun during the summer. In contrast, the skylight at the Cy Twombly Gallery has layers on the exterior, at the glazing, and on the interior. The outermost layer has a solar control grille; beneath this plane is the glazing with movable louvers; and finally, an inner layer of ceiling fabric further diffuses and controls sunlight. At the Exeter Library, Louis Kahn provides only an interior window layer of simple wooden louvers that recess into wall pockets. (See Figure 4.64.)

There are advantages and disadvantages as well as climatic implications that influence where window layering might occur. Layering on the inside can be detailed to control sunlight and glare, but it is less effective at reducing solar gains than is layering on the exterior of the building. Exterior layering is of particular importance with large apertures, programs that require high quantities of daylight, and where there are climatic or programmatic needs for control. Yet layering is more visible on the exterior of the building and is more likely to make a statement that must be integrated with the architectural vocabulary. On the other hand, exterior layers create an aesthetic opportunity that can be celebrated. In their essay "Shady Aesthetics," Fritz Griffin and Marietta Millet explain: ". . . shading is more than comfort control—it has been and can be an aesthetic vehicle. . . . To achieve fullness in architecture, these concerns must be integrated with the fundamental meaning of the building and be a conveyor of its beauty. . . . Forces, such as shading, are modifiers of the generators of the architectural form. Shading is an expressive medium of form."[16] Designers such as Nicolas Grimshaw, Renzo Piano, Herzog and de Meuron, and Glenn Murcutt have illustrated the integration of aesthetics and function through elegantly designed and detailed window layering.

We have only begun to explore the many innovative ways to reconsider and detail the window. Louis Kahn said, "Every assumption about what a window is, is open to question and redefinition." Form defines the flow of light in space, whether it is at the scale of the building massing, the plan and section, or through the detailing of a window. While we are all aware of the aesthetic and human implications of form, we should not underestimate its important ecological implications. Form defines the amount of natural resources that will be needed for lighting, heating, and cooling; the subsequent environmental impacts that result from our consumption of these resources; and our physiological and psychological relationships to the environment. Form that is considered independent of the aesthetic, human, and ecological aspects of the luminous program may result in intriguing architectural effects, but rarely will it result in meaningful daylighting design.

ENDNOTES

1. *Alvar Aalto: 1898–1976* (Helsinki: The Museum of Finnish Architecture, 1978), 155.
2. John Tillman Lyle, *Regenerative Design for Sustainable Development* (New York: John Wiley & Sons, 1994), 43.
3. Richard Saul Wurman, *What Will Be Has Always Been: The Words of Louis I. Kahn* (New York: Rizzoli International Publications, Inc., 1986), 235.
4. Christopher Alexander, *Notes on the Synthesis of Form* (Cambridge, Mass: Harvard University Press, 1967), quoted in Dean Hawkes, *Environmental Tradition: Studies in the Architecture of Environment* (London: E & FN Spon, 1996), 66.

5. Alexandra Tyng, *Beginnings: Louis I. Kahn's Philosophy of Architecture* (New York: John Wiley & Sons, 1984), 74.

6. Frank Lloyd Wright, *The Natural House* (New York: Horizon Press, 1954), 187.

7. The relationship between the section, window height, and the plan will determine how deeply light penetrates into space. The "2.5H rule" is a rough guideline used to study the relationship between the room depth and the window height and size. It assumes that light will be admitted into a room approximately 2.5 times the height (H) of the window as measured from the workplane (typically 30 inches above the floor). For example, if a window is 5 ft 0 in high (measured from the workplane to the top of the window) then light will penetrate approximately 12 ft 6 in into the room (5 ft × 2.5 = 12 ft 6 in). Although this rule of thumb is useful in estimating the room depth, it provides no information about the quantity or quality of the light. Use of the 2.5H rule of thumb should be limited to the early conceptual stages of design. Physical and/or computer models are needed as schematic design and design development progress.

8. For a history of architectural daylighting and window technologies see H. E. Beckett and J. A. Godfrey, *Windows* (London: Crosby Lockwood Staple, 1974) and David Button and Brian Pye, eds., *Glass in Building* (Oxford: Butterworth Architecture, 1993).

9. Alexandra Tyng, 162.

10. Roger H. Clark and Michael Pause, *Precedents in Architecture* (New York: Van Nostrand Reinhold, 1985), 196.

11. The daylighting design would have greater clarity if the symmetrical building were reoriented to correspond with the east-west symmetry of the sun (which is difficult due to site constraints), or by developing a more asymmetrical configuration and window composition to respond to the distinct luminous qualities in each facade orientation (qualitative and quantitative differences on the east, south, west, and north).

12. Robert Mark, *Light, Wind, and Structure* (Boston, Mass: Massachusetts Institute of Technology, 1990), 44.

13. For additional discussion on the quantitative and qualitative performance of various daylighting strategies, see Fuller Moore, *Concepts and Practice of Architectural Daylighting* (New York: Van Nostrand Reinhold, 1985); William M. C.

Lam, *Sunlighting: As Formgivers for Architecture* (New York: Van Nostrand Reinhold, 1986); Gregg D. Ander, *Daylighting: Performance and Design* (New York: Van Nostrand Reinhold, 1995); and Marietta Millet, *Light Revealing Architecture* (New York: Van Nostrand Reinhold, 1996).

14. To determine the appropriate area of glazing, designers have to specify the desired quantity of light that is needed—the *target illuminance level*—based on the task. In addition to the amount of light that is being sought, designers have to decide in which month they will try to achieve this target. The target illuminance levels allow designers to estimate the glazing area for a predetermined target month. This means that during some months the illuminance levels will fall both below and above the target illuminance level. The target month is typically the average or midyear condition (such as during the equinoxes) rather than the extreme conditions during the solstices (June and December). Physical and computer models can be used to estimate the required glazing area needed to achieve target illuminance levels. Given the dynamic quality of daylight, designers have to accept and celebrate the variability of daylight while still respecting programmatic concerns. This often means providing some degree of daylighting control and adjustability to accommodate seasonal and diurnal variations.

15. Jun'ichirō Tanizaki, *In Praise of Shadows* (New Haven: Leete's Island Books, 1977), 30.

16. Fritz Griffin and Marietta Millet, "Shady Aesthetics," *Journal of Architectural Education* 37, no. 3 (spring–summer 1984): 59.

Chapter 5

Use Appropriate Technology

If we look more closely at the progress of human life,
we find that technology is only an aid and not a final
and independent phenomenon in itself.[1]

—ALVAR AALTO

During the past several decades there has been much debate over the beneficial and detrimental roles of technology in the twentieth century. Sandra Postel states, in her essay "Carrying Capacity: The Earth's Bottom Line," that: "As a society, we have failed to discriminate between technologies that meet our needs in a sustainable way and those that harm the earth."[2] Given the abundance of new daylighting technologies, it is appropriate and timely to reconsider which technologies move us toward—or away from—a more sustainable future. A variety of technological approaches to daylighting have captured our imaginations. Light pipes, heliostats, high-tech glazing, photovoltaic cladding, and environmental control systems reflect our belief in the promise of new technologies. The daylighting benefits and performance of these and other technological approaches have varied greatly. As we move forward with continued innovations and research, we must clarify the purpose of technology.

In *Ecological Literacy,* David Orr cautions us against seeing technology as a solution to ecological concerns: "Advocates of technological sustainability tend to believe that every problem has either a technological answer or a market solution. There are no dilemmas to be avoided, no domains where angels fear to tread. Resource scarcity will be solved by materials substitution. . . . Energy shortages will be solved by more efficiency improvements."[3] We must look at what can and cannot be achieved by technology. What role can technology play in daylighting design? What are the strengths and limits of daylighting technologies? What can be achieved through architectural daylighting strategies or through the design of the building, room, and window form?

Understanding the differences between technological and architectural approaches to daylighting is an essential issue in fully realizing the benefits of each. If, for example, the objective is to get daylight into the inner reaches of an office building, does the solution lie in new technologies, in reconsidering architectural form, or in both? What are we trying to do, and how can it best be achieved? Lester Milbrath suggests that technology redefines the types of questions we ask: "Technologies, by their very presence, force us into searching for solutions to problems that become defined as technological, even though they may not have been technological or a problem to begin with."[4] In the case of the office building, the problem of poorly distributed daylighting could be addressed through technological means such as light pipes, beamed daylighting, and heliostats. Yet it could also be solved through architectural strategies that consider the building form and massing, the room height and depth, and the window form and configuration. While both approaches may solve the problem, the question remains: What is gained or lost by each approach? How do we decide whether an architectural or a technological solution is most appropriate?

Developing daylighting performance criteria is one means of assessing the possible role of technology, yet care must be taken to include both quantitative and qualitative considerations. With questions of technology, we might benefit from Alvar Aalto's reminder to stay focused on the nature and purpose of architecture: "In recent decades, architecture has often been compared with science. . . . But architecture is not a science. It is still the same great synthetic process, a conglomeration of thousands of significant human functions, and it will stay that way. Its essence can never become purely analytical. Architectural study always involves a moment of art and instinct. Its purpose is still to bring the world of matter into harmony with human life."[5] Glazing technologies are a case in point. While the benefits of new glazing assemblies and glass technologies may provide increased energy efficiency and thermal comfort, the success of a window goes far beyond the standard performance criteria of the solar heat gain coefficient, or U-value, and visible light transmittance. How a window frames a view, admits the smell of fresh rain, creates a particular quality of light, or connects occupants to the sounds of life all have sociological and cultural significance that elude quantification. This is not to suggest that our only means of assessing the performance of a window has been or will ever be limited to quantitative measures. Rather, it suggests that the issues and questions we include—or do not include—in our criteria will determine the role and prevalence of technology in design. New glazing technologies answer only a particular set of concerns related to daylighting design. Many other issues still need to be answered at the drawing board (or at the computer). In considering the role of technology, we might ask essential questions raised by David Orr in *Ecological Literacy:* "Whether (technology) can be controlled and harnessed to the long-term benefit of humanity is *the* question of our civilization. If so, the goal of a sustainable society based on the model of natural systems is not necessarily antithetical to technology. The question then becomes what kind of technology, at what scale, and for what purposes."[6]

DAYLIGHTING TECHNOLOGIES

Technology can be defined as the tools that humans use to shape the built environment and subsequently to modify the natural environment. Peter McCleary, professor of architecture at the University of Pennsylvania, describes recent shifts in our perceptions of technology: ". . . a new concept of technology has arisen, one that does not limit itself to building materials and processes, but defines technology more broadly as the understanding (skills and knowledge) of the dialectical relationship between humans and their environments (natural and built) in the production of a new superimposed built environment."[7] McCleary brings an important element to the discussion of technology—that of the relationship between humans and their environment. Our values and how we choose to use technology will determine whether ecological characteristics are present in what McCleary characterizes as the "new superimposed built environment." We can only hope that we have the wisdom to use technology for both human and ecological benefit.

Daylighting technologies are generally employed as a means of modifying, filtering, or even controlling natural forces. We frequently use the term *control* in discussions of daylighting design, as though light is a force that needs to be restrained, tamed, and regulated. Environmental control systems, daylighting controls, electric lighting controls—all suggest dominance over natural forces. If technology is perceived as a means of control, then an adversarial relationship is established that overlooks the opportunity to create a conversation between the natural and the built environments. From an ecological perspective the term *control* might more accurately refer to ways of modifying, altering, or shaping daylight. It is in this way that the term (which is so deeply entrenched in daylighting vocabulary) will be used in this discussion.

As technology has played an increasingly important role in architectural design, environmental and climatic responses have generally diminished. In *House, Form, and Culture,* Amos Rapoport discusses this relationship: "While I have suggested that climatic determinism fails to account for the range and diversity of house forms, climate is, nevertheless, an important aspect of the form-generating forces, and has major effects on the forms man may wish to create for himself. This is to be expected under conditions of weak technology and limited environmental control systems, where man cannot dominate nature but must adapt to it."[8] At one extreme you could argue that an increased use of technology distances us from the environment, ecological awareness, and perhaps even from a sustainable future. On the other hand, if appropriately used, is it possible that technology could move us forward in an ecologically responsive way?

Despite extensive research on the environmental and human benefits of daylighting, it is still most common to find electric lighting as the predominant means of illumination in buildings. The technology needs to be there, but it should be coordinated with the daylighting design so it can be shut off during the day. How many office buildings in the United States really use daylighting for illumination? How many have operable windows? How many use natural ventilation? Even some designers who are interested in ecological issues perceive certain building types as inappropriate for daylighting and passive solar strategies. In contrast, Louis Kahn believed that every room merited daylight, whether it was a rest room, mechanical room, or storage space. It is intriguing that Asian and European countries are leading the way in developing new prototypes for office design that include extensive use of daylighting and passive strategies. Natural resources and energy may be motivating factors, but human considerations are equally important. Technology can be used as a means of responding to the environment and defining a dialogue between the occupants and natural forces. In Hand's End: Technology and the Limits of Nature, philosopher David Rothenberg describes this opportunity: "Technology claims to liberate us from the constrictions of a hostile and fierce environment, while in fact it ties us more tightly to the ecology as we extend ourselves through tools and techniques. To be human means to be extended through technology into the world, defining nature along this course. As we try to bend the world toward human need, we find ourselves closer to those parts of it that seem unwavering 'facts' of nature."[9] Daylighting technologies can be used to extend into the environment, to respond to natural forces, and to increase awareness of ecological phenomena and the laws of nature. While the motivations for using daylighting technologies are generally to reduce energy, resource consumption, and environmental impacts, technology can also tell a story about our relationship to the world in which we live. The story we create is dependent on our perceptions of the ecological role of technology in design.

ARCHITECTURAL AND TECHNOLOGICAL APPROACHES TO DAYLIGHTING

It is often difficult to distinguish between an architectural and a technological approach to daylighting. One could argue that successful daylighting design does not differentiate between the two approaches. As Alvar Aalto explained: "A building is not a technical problem at all—it is an archi-technical problem."[10] Yet the term *architectural daylighting strategies* generally refers to approaches that focus on the building form and massing, while *technological daylighting strategies* emphasizes supplemental systems and components such as shading and glazing assemblies. Given this distinction, there are at least three views of daylighting and its relationship to technology.

On one extreme is an approach that is independent of technology. This perspective sees daylighting primarily as a question of design, integrally related to the building massing, section, plan, and window form. Technology plays little or no role in resolving daylighting objectives. The work of Le Corbusier (Ronchamp or La Tourette), Utzon (Bagsvaerd), and Ando (Mount Rokko) all embrace a decidedly architectural approach to daylighting. In these examples, the plan organization, section of the wall and windows, structure, and materials interact to create distinct luminous experiences. The quality, character, and quantity of daylight are directly dependent on decisions concerning the articulation of architectural form.

A second approach uses technology to support architectural decisions. Technologies such as shading, glazing, and electric lighting controls supplement and enhance design decisions. Daylighting objectives are first addressed though architectural form and then further refined through the integration of technology. Glenn Murcutt's house at Bingie Point uses the building plan and section to either gather or redistribute daylight. A gently curving roof shades the north side of the house and reflects indirect daylight to the service corridor on the south (the building is located in the Southern Hemisphere). The roof appears to hover gracefully over the interior partition walls, an effect created by clerestory windows that borrow daylighting between spaces. Shading and glazing technologies provide a second level of environmental response. The north facade, which is entirely glazed, uses simple horizontal louvers to provide shading during the summer. Double-glazed, operable jalousie windows regulate natural ventilation.

Finally, there is an essentially technological approach to daylighting. This approach uses technological systems such as light pipes, solar concentrators, advanced glazing systems (holographic gratings, prisms, switchable glazing, etc.), or heliostats to gather, distribute, and control daylight. An example of a technological approach to daylighting is found in a corridor at the Energy Resource Center in Los Angeles. A solar heliostat is mounted on the exterior of the building to track the apparent movement of the sun and to reflect daylight through a diffusing skylight to a space below. The heliostat is a demonstration of new technology; however, one could argue that given the low illumination required for the corridor, the resulting daylighting effect could easily be achieved through a simple skylight. TIR Systems Ltd. uses an even more elaborate technological approach in the Victoria Park Place Office Building in Toronto, Canada. A solarium on the top floor houses eight heliostats that reflect sunlight to parabolic mirrors mounted on the ceiling. The parabolic mirrors reflect the sunlight to an aperture that directs the light to a prism light pipe for redistribution in the offices. Daylighting is supplemented with metal halide lamps during overcast weather and in the evening. The light pipe, although conducting daylight, creates a distribution and quality that is similar to electric lighting. The system provides no views, visual relief, connection to weather, or natural ventilation. (See Figure 5.1.)

What is gained and lost with an approach such as that used in the Victoria Park Place Office Building? How far should we take technology? When is its use appropriate or inappropriate? What architectural gymnastics must we undertake to bring daylight into a building? These are difficult questions, for one could argue that even though occupants at Victoria Park Place do not perceive the source of the daylight or receive the typical benefits of view and site connection, the daylighting system is still preferable to electric lighting. The appropriate use of technology often depends on whether one is considering daylighting for a new or an existing building. New construction is a clear example in which architectural rather than technological solutions should dominate. De-

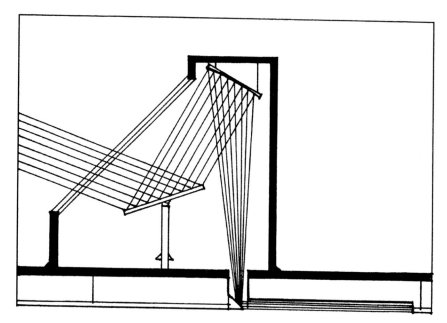

Figure 5.1 Section of a solar heliostat at the Victoria Park Place Office Building.

(Joe Ford)

signers of new buildings have much greater latitude to address issues of building massing, room configuration, and window design. Technological solutions may be more reasonable for building retrofits, because architectural modifications may be too costly or difficult.

While each of the three approaches discussed has strengths and weaknesses, the most critical issue is to determine when technology furthers design objectives and when solutions could more easily be met by architectural strategies such as thinner building profiles, atria, and light courts. The second approach, which combines both architectural and technological strategies, may offer the greatest daylighting opportunities. If designers depend solely on architectural or technological approaches, the spectrum of daylighting and ecological solutions is limited. Daylighting design should maximize the potential of architectural form while taking advantage of technologies to further refine and enhance solutions.

DAYLIGHTING TECHNOLOGIES AND THE BUILDING ENVELOPE

The attitude and approach to the building envelope is a determining factor in daylighting design. It is at this stage that designers realize the role and intention of windows. What purpose will they achieve? What story will they tell? The window is one of the single most important elements in establishing the character (perhaps even the personality) of the building. The same repetitive window, marching endlessly down a facade, evokes a sense of order and formality. Irregularly shaped windows in asymmetric composition have a sense of playfulness and spontaneity that express varied activities within. Windows evoke different moods and activities through their form and placement: the small, barred window of a prison that keeps someone in, the large storefront window that welcomes shoppers, the whimsical window of a child's attic hideaway, or the window seat that beckons a reader. Louis Kahn regarded the window as the most "marvelous element of the room."[11] As Kahn's work illustrates, a window is more than a hole in the wall; it defines a particular relationship between inside and outside and reveals the characteristics of the climate, site, program, and occupants.

Although glazing technologies have increased the transparency of buildings, occupants have become further removed and disconnected from the environment because of nonoperable windows and technological means of providing lighting, heating, and cooling. Professor Roger Stonehouse of the University of Manchester discusses this concern in his essay "Dwelling with the Environment," pointing out that an ". . . increase in active, energy intensive means of environmental control is associated with the paradox seen in much modern architecture where the layer between inside and outside has become increasingly thinner and transparent, yet increasingly impermeable, leading to a disassociation of inside and outside world, physically, environmentally, and socially."[12] This is a widespread and profound problem that not only has immediate physical impact on human well-being, but also on our perceptions of the environment. How can we expect to increase our ecological literacy if we have limited contact with the environment or place we live? Do these types of separations lead to ecological and environmental insensitivity? The following discussion will focus on recent design and technological innovations that have begun to strengthen ecological connections by reconsidering the role of the building envelope.

Several projects will be used to illustrate recent trends in the design of the building envelope and the increasingly important role of daylighting technologies. Three levels of concern will be addressed: glazing assemblies and glass technologies, daylighting systems within the glazing cavity, and integrated glazing and shading systems. The three approaches frame different attitudes about the role of technology in daylighting design and reveal distinct opportunities and constraints. Each of the approaches creates new opportunities for using the building envelope and daylighting technologies as a means of expressing the relationships between the occupants, the building, and the environment.

GLAZING ASSEMBLIES AND GLASS TECHNOLOGIES

New glazing technologies have been developed to harness solar energy and natural forces and to diminish the thermal and energy consequences of windows. While windows were once considered "thermal wounds," an adept analogy by Professor Lance Lavine of the University of Minnesota, today new glazing innovations allow us to do what was never possible (or responsible) with standard windows. New glazing technologies, with their increased thermal performance, can be perceived both as a means of controlling the forces of nature and as a liberating force that provides designers freedom from essential environmental considerations such as climate, weather, sun, and wind. John Carmody, Steve Selkowitz, and Lisa Heschong allude to this perspective in their book *Residential Windows*:

> There has been a long-established set of window design guidelines and assumptions intended to reduce heating and cooling energy use. These are based, in part, on the historical assumption that windows were the weak link in the building envelope. These assumptions frequently created limitations on design freedom or generated conflicts with other performance requirements, such as view. Traditional considerations include orientation, amount of glazing, and shading requirements for windows. The new technologies, however, raise questions about the validity of many of these restrictive assumptions. It can be argued that many assumptions developed over the last twenty years about energy-efficient home design require rethinking in light of the new window technologies.[13]

These authors remind us that energy is just one part of the design challenge. Equally important are ecological and experiential considerations such as views, ventilation, illumination, passive heating, and aesthetics. Despite advances in the thermal performance of windows, the designer must still address other luminous and design concerns (how the window connects to the site, increases awareness of weather, responds to human comfort, glare, veiling reflections, light levels, etc.).

A variety of glazing assemblies and glass technologies have been developed over the past decade that use the characteristics of the glass as a means of responding to environmental forces. Although the new glazing technologies may be excellent in controlling thermal gains, or in other cases addressing direct sunlight or glare, these technologies have limited potential to enhance an ecological relationship between inside and outside (in some cases, the technologies diminish this relationship). Yet benefits that have resulted from glazing advances in thermal performance and visual comfort should not be underestimated. It is important to understand what new glazing systems and glass technologies can and cannot do for daylighting design. There is always the risk that some designers will mistakenly believe that a plane of glass can solve all their daylighting concerns. When appropriately used and coupled with other strategies, a comprehensive approach can be achieved that addresses the environment and its relationship to human experience. New glazing technologies are a baseline or point of departure that illustrates, on one hand, the current state of the art for glass technology, and on the other hand, the distance that we still need to go. The further we can develop glazing innovations that address not only energy and natural resources (which tend to be the focus of the glass technologies discussed subsequently), but also the human relationship to the environment, the closer we come to the development of technologies that benefit all of life.

Recent Glazing Innovations

The specification of windows with low-emissivity coatings, selective films, multiple air gaps, and inert gas fills is now considered standard practice. Low-e glazings have gained popularity due to increased performance for both the heating and cooling seasons. Designers are now able to specify assemblies that respond to varying climatic and thermal criteria. The early low-e coatings improved passive solar performance by transmitting shortwave solar radiation and reflecting long-wave thermal energy; new low-e coatings are available that reject solar gains while still providing good visible light transmittance. Although design has benefited from low-e glazings that control thermal gains and provide good visible light transmittance, this technology does not ensure high-quality daylighting. In most cases, additional types of solar control will be needed to respond to changing daylight conditions and potential sources of glare.

The same is also true of superwindows, which combine selective films, multiple air gaps, and high-performance frames. These innovations have resulted in higher R-values and reduced thermal consequences of windows.[14] Some designers are even using multiple glazing assemblies to respond to different thermal and luminous conditions within the same building. For example, the Solar Energy Research Facility in Golden, Colorado (Anderson DeBartelo Pan, Architects) uses six different types of glazing based on window orientation and daylighting and thermal criteria. The ability to selectively filter infrared and ultraviolet radiation has also opened new options for designers concerned with degradation of materials and fading of fabrics. Improved window performance has led to a rapid increase in their specification. Only a few years ago, the low-emissivity glazing used at the National Audubon Headquarters and the National Resource Defense Council's Headquarters, both by Croxton Collaborative, was considered unusual and innovative. Some of the first high-profile ecological projects, such as the work by Croxton Collaborative, have helped to redefine the standard for windows. Yet glazing technologies are just one of many daylighting strategies used in these projects. Attention has also been paid to building form, space planning, finishes, furnishings, and electric lighting integration. (See Figure 5.2.)

Fritted and laminated glazing systems are also gaining popularity as a means of shading sunlight, reducing thermal gains, responding to glare, and providing privacy. Ground-glass particles (called *frit*) are oven-dried and fired onto the glass, creating integral shading through a translucent overlay. An increasing number of buildings are using fritted glass because of the simplicity of this system, which provides shading and diffuses sunlight without external or internal shading devices. Standard or custom frit patterns can be applied to a variety of glazing assemblies that include additional selective films, insulation, air gaps, and inert gas infills. The Federal Judiciary Building in Washington, D.C., by Edward Larrabee Barnes, uses frit glass for the interior glazing of offices facing a five-story atrium. The frit is patterned as a series of horizontal stripes that are reminiscent of louvers. It is intended to provide diffusion and control glare while allowing some visibility through the clear portion of the glass. Although thoughtful daylighting strategies are used in the building, solar control was a challenge. Despite the frit glass, internal blinds were added after the project was completed to provide additional shading and privacy. Frit glass offers no options to adjust or modify the daylighting for different uses or qualities of light. Yet despite this limitation, it continues to be a popular solution to solar control. The question is, when is frit glass appropriate? The advantages of this technology are the simplicity of an integrated shading device with low maintenance. The drawbacks are that it is static and cannot be altered to meet changing daylight conditions or needs, to provide views, or to connect to the site. Potential glare at the window should also be considered, because the diffuse light captured on the surface of the frit can become a

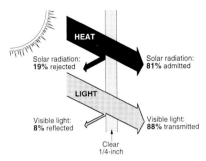

NOTE: U-Value = 1.09; SHGC = 0.81; SC = 0.94; VT = 0.88

SINGLE GLAZING—CLEAR GLASS

NOTE: U-Value = 0.45; SHGC = 0.70; SC = 0.81; VT = 0.78

DOUBLE GLAZING—CLEAR GLASS

Figure 5.2 Solar characteristics of common glazing systems.

(John Carmody)

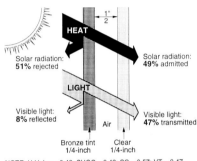

NOTE: U-Value = 0.48; SHGC = 0.49; SC = 0.57; VT = 0.47

DOUBLE GLAZING—GRAY/BRONZE TINT

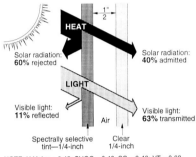

NOTE: U-Value = 0.48; SHGC = 0.40; SC = 0.46; VT = 0.63

DOUBLE GLAZING—SPECTRALLY SELECTIVE (GREEN/BLUE) TINT

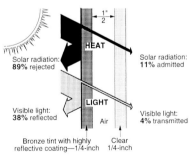

NOTE: U-Value = 0.48; SHGC = 0.11; SC = 0.13; VT = 0.04

DOUBLE GLAZING—BRONZE TINT WITH HIGHLY REFLECTIVE COATING

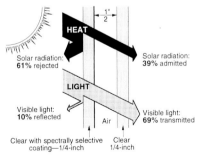

NOTE: U-Value = 0.29; SHGC = 0.39; SC = 0.46; VT = 0.69

DOUBLE GLAZING—CLEAR GLASS WITH SPECTRALLY SELECTIVE COATING

Note that all figures on this page give these characteristics for the center of the glass only—the characteristics of the frame must be included to provide performance information on the whole window assembly. The performance numbers shown in these figures is calculated using a computer program, WINDOW, developed at Lawrence Berkeley National Laboratory. In these examples, all glass is nominally 1/4-inch thick, and double-glazed windows have 1/2-inch gaps between glazings.

potential source of glare or a troubling light source within the room. Adding additional shading to a frit-glass system is redundant. If flexibility is needed, it is easier simply to use operable shading. Even in situations where continual daylighting control is needed, it may be wise to consider other alternatives, such as the orientation of the window, external shading, or the use of reflected daylight, which provide control while still allowing views of the sky, site, and weather. (See Figure 5.3.)

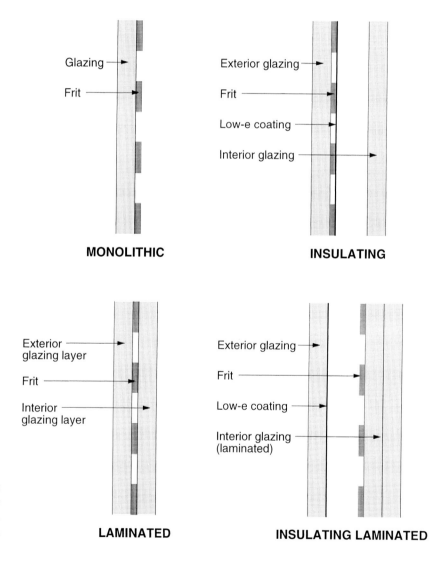

Glazing

Frit

MONOLITHIC

Exterior glazing

Frit

Low-e coating

Interior glazing

INSULATING

Exterior glazing layer

Frit

Interior glazing layer

LAMINATED

Exterior glazing

Frit

Low-e coating

Interior glazing (laminated)

INSULATING LAMINATED

Figure 5.3 Construction characteristics of various types of frit glazing.
(John Carmody)

Laminated glass is also being reconsidered in response to day-lighting and thermal concerns. Selective films, air gaps, tinting, infills, and insulation allow designers to reduce solar gains and provide shading within structural glass members. The New Plenary Chamber Complex of the German Bundestag in Bonn, by Behnisch & Partner, uses laminated glass in both interior and exterior applications to address such diverse concerns as cladding, daylighting, shading, acoustic privacy, and security. The desire to have a visually accessible plenary hall connected to the outside presented potential security conflicts in the Bundestag. Walls of laminated glass were chosen to meet security requirements for bullet-resistant glazing and to provide acoustic privacy without compromising the daylighting and views into the hall and out to the surrounding landscape. As Günter Behnisch explains:

The Plenary Chamber itself is integrated into the landscape dominated by the Rhine. . . . A limit was placed on the quantities of materials permitted for the Plenary Chamber. The purpose of this was to help ensure that the true "event" lay not in the architecture, but in the gathering of parliamentarians. And this gathering should take place on the banks of the Rhine, protected from the "rigours" of the world outside but linked to it as far as possible, e.g., via the large skylight.[15]

The huge skylight above the Plenary Chamber is designed to provide high-quality daylighting and to create a focal point within the building. The skylight consists of exterior and interior layers. On the roof of the building, a series of louvers diffuse and redirect daylight to the chamber below. Beneath the skylight, a deep grid of metal baffles diffuses daylight while accommodating electric lighting, ventilation outlets, sprinkler heads, and other services. Soft, diffuse sidelighting surrounds Plenary Chamber. A variation

Figure 5.5   Detail view of the ceiling in the Plenary Chamber for the German Bundestag.

(Behnisch & Partner/ Christian Kandzia)

Figure 5.6 View of the daylighting louvers on the roof of the Plenary Chamber for the German Bundestag.

(Behnisch & Partner/ Christian Kandzia)

of the rooftop louvers is found on the exterior walls, where glass louvers are used to control solar gain through the laminated glass cladding. (See Figures 5.4 to 5.6.)

New Glazing Research

As we found in the discussion of building-integrated photovoltaics (BIPV) in Chapter 2, new innovations in the generation of electricity are also influencing glazing research. Photovoltaic screens, spandrel panels, cladding systems, and shading devices are enabling designers to simultaneously enclose buildings, provide daylighting, and generate electricity. While BIPV is more common in Europe, it has begun to emerge in projects in the United States. For example, a photovoltaic curtain wall developed by Kawneer and Solarex was recently installed on the entrance

Figure 5.7   Detail view of photovoltaic curtain-wall system from inside the entrance canopy of the Aquatic Center, Callaway Student Athletic Center, Georgia Institute of Technology.

(Larry Thomas and Kawneer Company, Inc.)

canopy for Rosser Fabrap's Aquatic Center at the Georgia Institute of Technology. There is still much to learn about the most effective applications for BIPV and its opportunities and constraints. For example, the Advanced Photovoltaic System factory in Fairfield, California, designed by Kiss Cathcart Anders Architects, has been studying the effectiveness of BIPV for several years. The factory tests photovoltaic glazing systems in various locations on the building envelope, such as vertical curtain walls, a skylight, and an awning. The project has been used for comparative studies on the effects of orientation on the performance of BIPV. Not surprisingly, maximum performance is obtained in south-sloped orientations. As the costs of BIPV decrease, it may be more economically feasible to install the systems in a vertical position despite decreased performance. Examples in Chapter 2 illustrate that BIPV is being used in multiple orientations and in innovative ways to explicitly address daylighting. Given the increased attention to photovoltaics in general, and the specific developments in BIPV, it is likely that we will continue to see technological innovations that push the integration of photovoltaics, daylighting, and architectural design. (See Figure 5.7.)

Switchable glazing is a technological advance that holds the promise of providing variable glazing characteristics within a single glazing system. Systems are under development that will alter the visible light transmittance, reflectance, thermal capacity, transparency or translucency, and even the color of glazing. Although switchable glazing has been used in some demonstration projects, it is still under development. Whether it will gain wide application has yet to be determined; however, the concept of this dynamic system is to allow designers greater flexibility in responding to changing programmatic requirements, daylighting, and thermal conditions. Electrochromic, photochromic, and thermochromic systems switch the characteristics of the glazing by modifying electrical current, light levels, or temperature. There are many questions about the advantages and disadvantages to these systems. First, should glazing (rather than the occupants) respond to varied programmatic, lighting, or thermal needs? Why, when, and where would we use glazing of this type? What are the benefits of this type of glazing flexibility and versatility? Would we no longer need layers of shading inside or outside? Would we lose a degree of connection with the places where we work and live? If the glazing automatically adjusts the visible light transmittance to keep illuminance at a constant level (for example, 75 footcandles), do we become less aware of the time of day, the changing weather, the movement of the earth? If the glazing automatically blocks the sun from a west window at 1:30 P.M. on June 21, are we less aware of the seasons? What are the aesthetic implications of this glazing system? These and other questions will persist until we better understand the opportunities and constraints of switchable glazing. Continued research in this area must consider not only the implications of the technology in terms of energy, natural resources, and visual comfort, but also its physiological and psychological impacts on humans.

Other areas of continued research include glazing systems that have integral louvers, prisms, and holographic gratings. The concept of these systems is to integrate shading or light-directing mechanisms directly into the glazing assembly. Current investigations range from louvers that are laser-cut into the window assembly to prismatic coatings and microlouver films.[16] The control or modification of sunlight occurs within the glazing assembly, which makes external or internal shading devices unnecessary. The challenge of these types of glazing technologies is to determine when integral solar or luminous controls are needed. Any system that is fixed or nonadjustable runs into difficulties in responding to changing lighting conditions. With the exception of light-sensitive programs, hot climates, and predominantly clear skies, it is rare that daylight control is continually needed. It is far more common to have a few hours in the morning, midday, or afternoon (depending on the window orientation and program) that sunlight needs to be modified, filtered, or controlled. Even with the promise of these new innovations, caution should be taken in their application to ensure that daylighting flexibility and versatility are maintained.

While there are clear advantages to new glazing technologies, their limitations must also be considered. Glazing technologies have increased thermal performance, high-visible-light transmittance, and opportunities to control glare and the diffusion of sunlight. At the same time, these technologies have decreased flexibility, adjustability, and opportunities for views. The visual and physical connections to the environment are particularly limited by glass technologies or glazing assemblies that are fixed, nonoperable, and that use diffusing or light-modifying techniques that block views. Glazing technologies are not a quick fix to what is often a complex set of daylighting issues. Solutions with technological and architectural integrity can be found only if the benefits and limitations of glass technologies are carefully weighed with other architectural daylighting strategies. Glass technologies are not a daylighting solution, but rather an important component of a larger package of strategies and systems.

DAYLIGHTING SYSTEMS WITHIN THE GLAZING CAVITY

While the preceding examples focused on the characteristics of the glass itself, the following examples explore the opportunities of the glazing cavity (or the void within the glazing assembly) to accommodate additional levels of daylighting response. Manufacturers currently use the space between panes of glass to increase thermal performance by inserting inert gasses or creating air gaps. The following examples go beyond such techniques to use the cavity, which in some cases may be several feet in depth, to integrate daylighting filters, solar shading, passive heating, natural ventilation, and mechanical systems.

Opportunities of the Glazing Cavity

The glazing cavity can range from a narrow slot between the panes of glass to a large three-dimensional volume. New daylighting opportunities are presented as the panes of glass are pushed away from each other. The glazing assembly becomes a three-dimensional system that has a potentially useful space between external and internal glazing. The ways in which this space can be used may range from the modest insertion of diffusers, shading, and insulation to a more elaborate integration of daylighting and passive solar systems. Several projects by Thomas Herzog illustrate simple and effective approaches that maximize the thermal and daylighting opportunities of the glazing cavity. At the Wilkhahn Factory in Bad Münder, Germany, Herzog combines technology and architectural form to achieve excellent luminous and thermal performance. The large rectilinear building is divided into three production spaces that are separated and framed by four vertical towers (or monitors). Daylighting is provided by toplighting from the monitors and diffuse sidelighting from the building perimeter. A translucent white fiberglass quilt between the exterior and interior layers of glass increases thermal resistance and diffuses daylight. Operable vision glass below the translucent panels ensures that visual comfort as well as pragmatic daylighting and thermal objectives are met within the over-

Figure 5.8   Exterior view of the Wilkhahn Factory.

(© Dieter Leistner/Architekton)

all system. The glazing technology enhances the performance of an already thoughtful design that integrates natural ventilation and abundant daylighting. In some areas, additional solar and glare control is provided with awnings and interior blinds. In contrast to the vertical monitors, the flat roofs above the production areas are planted with vegetation to control heat loss and heat gain, provide sound insulation, and control rainwater runoff. (See Figure 5.8.)

While insulation is used in the glazing assemblies of other projects by Thomas Herzog (including the Youth Hostel in Windberg discussed in Chapter 2), his Prototype House and Studio in Bavaria is the first to use aerogel—a translucent silicone insulation.[17] Research with the European Commission in Brussels led to the development of this prototype house using aerogel panels. The aerogel is inserted between double-glazed panels in steel T-sections within timber supports. As a structural element with good thermal characteristics and fairly high daylight transmittance (45 percent), the aerogel panels suggest many new opportunities for glazing systems. Layla Dawson describes the benefits of this technology in *Design Review:* "The advantage of Aerogel as both insulator and translucent screen lies in its cellular structure. Its pore dimensions are smaller than the wavelength of solar radiation and too small to allow the free movement of air molecules which transmit heat . . . regardless of season and climate, an even temperature can be maintained across the interior of the room."[18] The elegant facade of the Prototype House combines translucent aerogel panels with clear windows that provide view and visual connection to the site. (See Figure 5.9.)

In addition to thermal benefits, gaps within glazing cavities can also provide structural opportunities. On the west facade of the Tokyo Church of Christ, Fumihiko Maki uses a 30-inch glazing cavity to create separate double-glazed systems on the exterior and interior of the wall. The exterior glazing uses large quantities of fritted glass in simple horizontal bands to control thermal gain and glare. Surrounding the frit glass and slicing through the lower portion of the facade are bands of clear glazing that admit a small amount of direct light to play against the surface of the interior glazing assembly. Soft, diffuse illumination is created in the sanctuary as light filters through a delicate fiberglass tissue placed between two panes of glass. The 30-inch cavity between the exte-

Figure 5.9 Exterior view of the Prototype House and Studio using aerogel glazing panels.
(Peter Bonfig)

Figure 5.10   West facade
of the Tokyo Church
of Christ.

(Dana Buntrock)

rior and interior glazing contains a Vieren-deel truss and return-air plenum that uses natural convection to provide hot air to ceiling ducts. The daylighting effect on the interior is reminiscent of a traditional shoji screen. It is also creates an ethereal and transcendent quality resulting from the changing shadows and play of light captured between the exterior and interior planes. The west sidelighting is complemented by illumination from two thin skylights that wash the interior of the south and north walls. Foster and Partners uses a simple variation on this theme at the Business Promotion Center in Duisburg, Germany, where computer-operated blinds are located within the glazing cavity. The envelope of the building consists of clear glazing on the exterior, a cavity with the

Figure 5.11   Interior of the Tokyo Church of Christ.

(Dana Buntrock)

blinds to modify direct sunlight and glare, and operable interior glazing. This three-dimensional system introduces dynamic elements that can be adjusted to meet varying daylighting and thermal needs. (See Figures 5.10 to 5.15.)

Glazing Assemblies with Integrated HVAC Systems

Several recent projects have used the glazing cavity as a space to integrate daylighting controls, passive heating, ventilation, and mechanical systems. The concept and physical characteristics of the building envelope are dramatically improved through such applications. The RWE AG Headquarters in Essen, Germany, by Ingenhoven, Overdiek and Partner uses a thermal buffer zone within the building envelope to regulate heat and light. A 20-inch thermal flue is created between a single pane of clear exterior glazing and an insulated interior glazing assembly. This buffer zone regulates heat loss and gain throughout the year. The inner glass wall can be opened to admit solar heat captured within the glazing cavity or to exhaust internal gains. The cavity also accommodates fresh-air inlets and outlets and horizontal blinds for shading. In contrast to a traditional static glazing assembly, this system is dynamic and changing. Occupants interact with the building envelope and its layers to adjust the quality of daylight, admit or control thermal gains, and regulate air. The circular building plan and location of all offices on the perimeter ensure daylighting and views for all employees. (See Figures 5.16 to 5.19.)

Sauerbruch Hutton Architects uses a

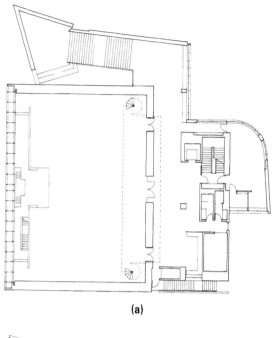

(a)

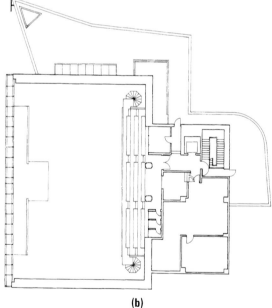

(b)

Figure 5.12 (a) Second- and (b) third-floor plan showing the sanctuary.

(Maki and Associates)

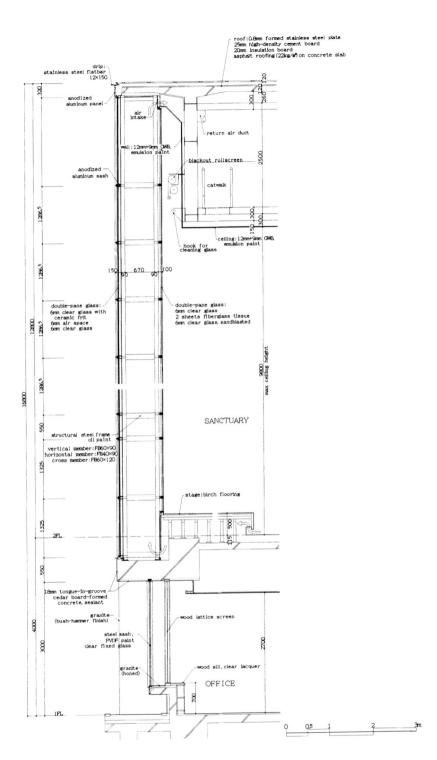

roof: 0.8mm formed stainless steel plate
25mm high-density cement board
20mm insulation board
asphalt roofing (22kg/m²) on concrete slab

drip:
stainless steel flatbar
12×150

anodized
aluminum panel

air
intake

return air duct

wall: 12mm+9mm GWB,
emulsion paint

blackout rollscreen

anodized
aluminum sash

catwalk

hook for
cleaning glass

ceiling: 12mm+9mm GWB,
emulsion paint

double-pane glass:
6mm clear glass with
ceramic frit
6mm air space
6mm clear glass

double-pane glass:
6mm clear glass
2 sheets fiberglass tissue
6mm clear glass, sandblasted

max ceiling height

SANCTUARY

structural steel frame
oil paint

vertical member: FB60×90
horizontal member: FB40×90
cross member: FB60×120

stage: birch flooring

2FL

18mm tongue-in-groove
cedar board-formed
concrete, sealant

granite
(bush-hammer finish)

steel sash,
PVDF paint
clear fixed glass

wood lattice screen

granite
(honed)

wood sill, clear lacquer

OFFICE

1FL

0 0.5 1   2   3m

Figure 5.13 Detail section of the west wall of the Tokyo Church of Christ.

(Maki and Associates)

Figure 5.14 Exterior of the Business Promotion Center in Duisburg.

(© Ralph Richter/architekturphoto)

similar integrated approach for the GSW Headquarters in Berlin. Oriented on a north-south axis, the thin profile of the building provides excellent daylight penetration in the office spaces. A circulation corridor on the east acts as a daylighting and thermal buffer zone and provides the fresh-air supply to the adjacent offices. The west facade uses a thermal flue with adjustable vertical louvers of perforated metal to control thermal gains and glare in the afternoon. Depending on the time of day and weather, the louvers can be opened to maximize daylight, partially

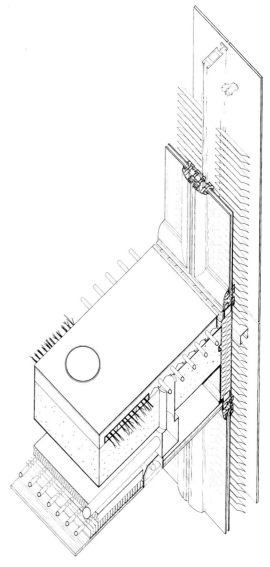

Figure 5.15 Axonometric detail of the building envelope at the Business Promotion Center in Duisburg.

(Foster and Partners)

closed to control sunlight, or completely closed to minimize gains (while still providing diffuse daylight through the perforations). During the overheated period, the stack effect exhausts heat from the building and facilitates natural ventilation. The flue is also

Figure 5.16 Exterior view of RWE AG Headquarters.

(Holger Knauf)

used to capture solar gains with a heat-recovery unit for redistribution to the offices. The skin of the building takes on a dynamic quality as occupants set the vertical louvers in varied positions to meet their particular luminous and thermal needs. (See Figures 5.20 to 5.26.)

Both of these projects challenge the perception of the building envelope as a static system. Operable glazing, dynamic shading, passive strategies, natural ventilation, and integrated mechanical systems provide opportunities to respond to varying environmental conditions. Occupants tune the envelope to respond to changing requirements for lighting, heating, and cooling. The three-dimensional and dynamic characteristics of the building envelope enable the building to more easily respond to changing environmental conditions. This approach is distinct from new glass technologies that focus only on the characteristics of the glazing itself as a means of environmental response. Dynamic systems present the occupants with a greater level of personal choice and interaction with the environment. Many of these approaches also challenge the concept of luminous and thermal comfort in office spaces and the role of user interaction. They tend to provide greater variability, increased involvement of occupants, and less-uniform control. Even the concept of adjustable blinds, which are essential and common in all the preceding examples, can be a

(a)

Figure 5.17 Detail of an exterior wall at the RWE AG Headquarters illustrating the glazing assembly under different conditions: (a) with no shading, (b) with louvered shading devices, and (c) with translucent shading device.

(Holger Knauf)

(b)

(c)

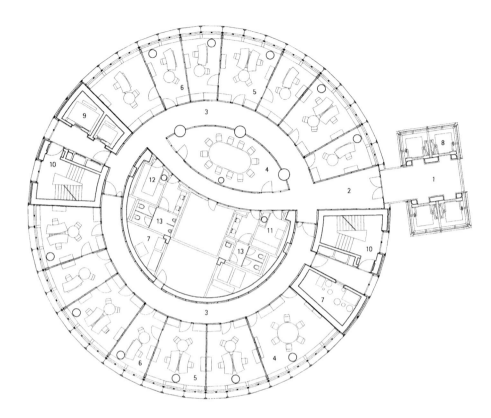

1   Liftlobby
2   Zugangsflur
3   Ringflur
4   Besprechungsraum
5   Büroraum 3 Achsen
6   Büroraum 2 Achsen
7   Technik
8   externe Liftgruppe
9   Feuerwehrlift
10 Fluchttreppenhaus
11 Büroservice
12 Teeküche
13 Toiletten

Figure 5.18   Typical plan of RWE AG Headquarters.

(Ingenhoven Overdiek Kahlen and Partner)

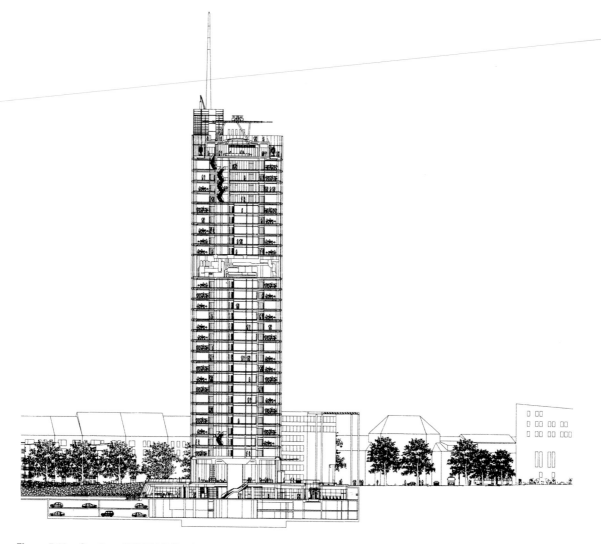

Figure 5.19 Section of RWE AG Headquarters.
(Ingenhoven Overdiek Kahlen and Partner)

Figure 5.20 Exterior rendering of the north and east facades of the GSW Headquarters.

(Lepkowski & Hillman Studios)

Figure 5.21 Exterior rendering of the north and west facades of the GSW Headquarters.

(Lepkowski & Hillman Studios)

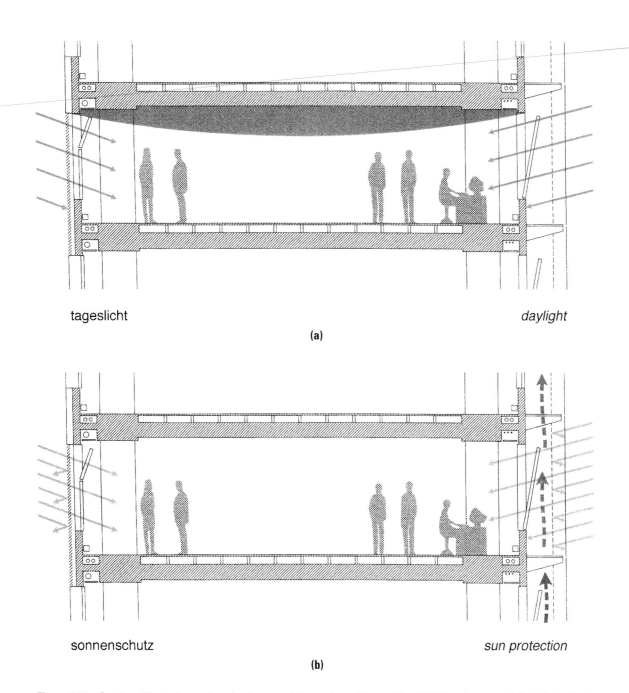

tageslicht   *daylight*

(a)

sonnenschutz   *sun protection*

(b)

Figure 5.22 Sections illustrating various luminous and thermal conditions at the GSW Headquarters: (a) daylight admission, and (b) sun protection.

(Sauerbruch Hutton Architects)

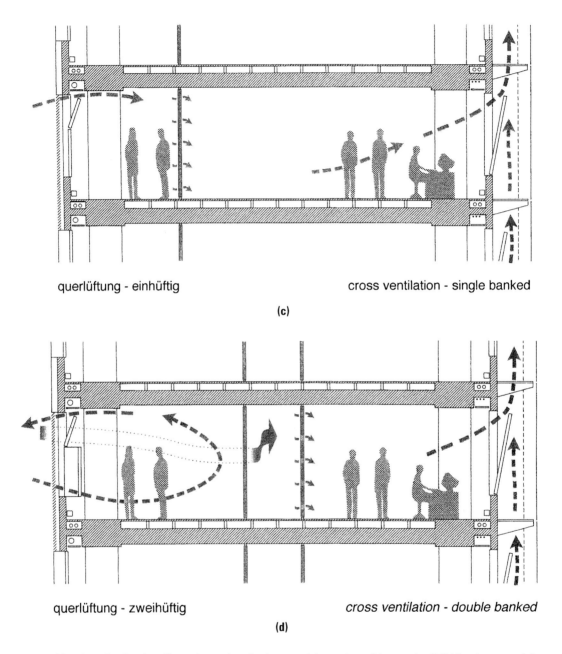

querlüftung - einhüftig   cross ventilation - single banked

(c)

querlüftung - zweihüftig   *cross ventilation - double banked*

(d)

Figure 5.22 (*Continued*)   Sections illustrating various luminous and thermal conditions at the GSW Headquarters: (c) cross ventilation with an open plan (or single-banked condition), and (d) cross ventilation with a central corridor (or double-banked condition).

(Sauerbruch Hutton Architects)

speichermasse - winter   *thermal mass - winter*

(e)

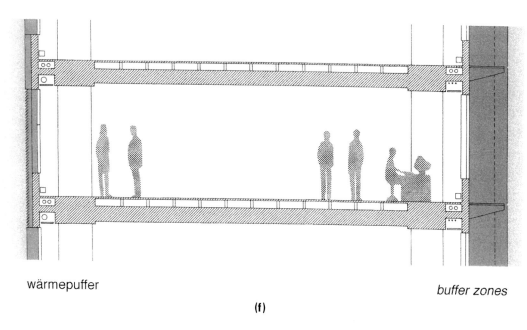

wärmepuffer   *buffer zones*

(f)

Figure 5.22 (*Continued*)   Sections illustrating various luminous and thermal conditions at the GSW Headquarters: (e) thermal mass in winter, and (f) buffer zones.

(Sauerbruch Hutton Architects)

Figure 5.23   Exterior of
the Carré d'Art in
the evening.
(James H. Morris)

Figure 5.24   Exterior detail of the Carré d'Art.
(James H. Morris)

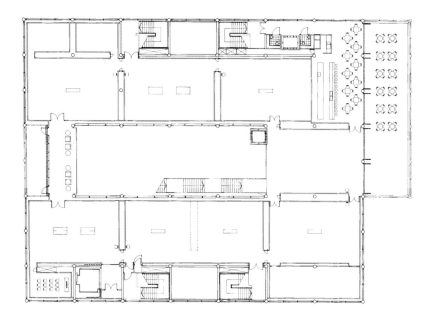

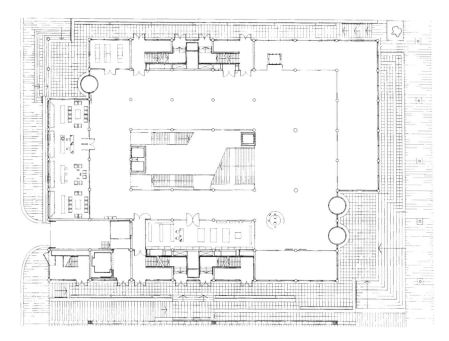

Figure 5.25a Plan of the upper gallery and café (top) and the ground floor at the Carré d'Art.

(Foster and Partners)

difficult strategy to achieve with some designers and clients. Who
will maintain and adjust the blinds? What if they are left in different positions? Will the facade look cluttered or unkempt? What
if they break? Yet it appears that some designers are putting
human comfort ahead of these important, but perhaps secondary
issues.

INTEGRATED GLAZING AND SHADING SYSTEMS

The integration of external and internal shading systems with new
glazing assemblies expands on the preceding examples to also
consider the daylighting opportunities outside and inside the
building envelope. These additional layers of daylighting and
thermal response extend the building envelope in ways that further enhance human interaction with the environment. As glazing
technologies have evolved during the past decade, so, too, have
shading devices. Marietta Millet and Fritz Griffin once challenged
designers to explore the aesthetic potential of shading devices, or
what they called a "shady aesthetic."[19] While this has been slow

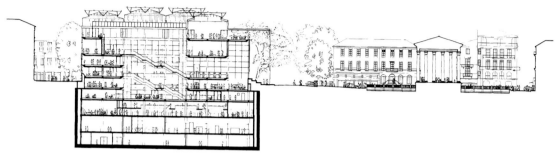

Figure 5.27 Section of the Carré d'Art.
(Foster and Partner)

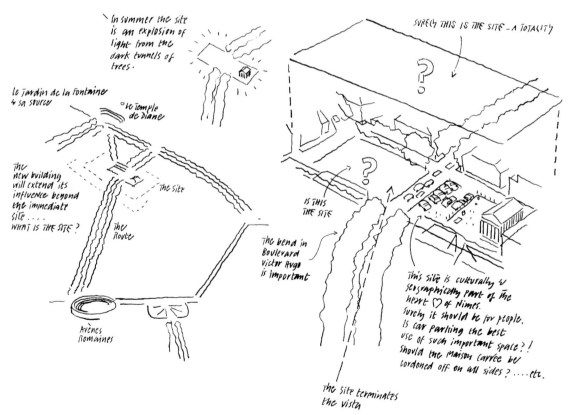

Figure 5.28 Sketch of contextual concepts of the Carré d'Art by Norman Foster.
(Foster and Partner)

in happening, shading devices are gaining popularity. Today you find them in many beautiful forms, shapes, and materials: from solar glass louvers, perforated metal, and wire mesh to translucent fabrics. The integration of new glass technologies, glazing assemblies, and shading technologies is redefining the opportunities and aesthetic characteristics of the building envelope.

Exterior and Interior Shading Systems

Figure 5.29 Sketch of site concepts of the Carré d'Art by Norman Foster.

(Foster and Partner)

Environmental response, daylighting control, and thermal comfort can be achieved when new glass technologies are combined with internal and external shading systems. An elegant and straightforward daylighting solution by Foster and Partners is found at the Carré d'Art in Nimes, France. High-performance transparent and

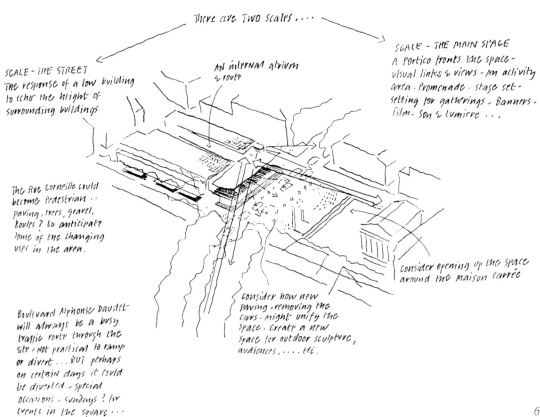

Figure 5.30 South facade of the Josef Gartner & Sons Headquarters.

(Josef Gartner & Sons)

translucent glazing assemblies are used in different areas to diffuse or admit sunlight as the daylighting requirements of the program dictate. Simple metal louvers are used in a variety of different ways to block and diffuse sunlight. Combined in a variety of configurations, the louvers respond to different luminous and thermal concerns. Horizontal louvers are used to create a shade portico and roof café; adjustable louvers are located beneath and above the skylights; and louvers are vertically positioned to control sunlight for sidelighting. Reconfiguring and reorienting the louvers provides shading solutions that respond to a variety of daylighting conditions, activities, and facade orientations. Although the louvers are altered in size or position to meet particular needs, there is an underlying repetition of form that gracefully unifies the parts into a larger whole. The simple louvered shading systems provide connections to the site, transparency, and flexibility that could not be met by glazing technologies alone. The shading and glazing technologies are used to augment architectural daylighting strategies that include a large atrium (with an elegant glazed staircase), abundant interior glazing for borrowed sidelighting, and skylights. (See Figures 5.27 to 5.33.)

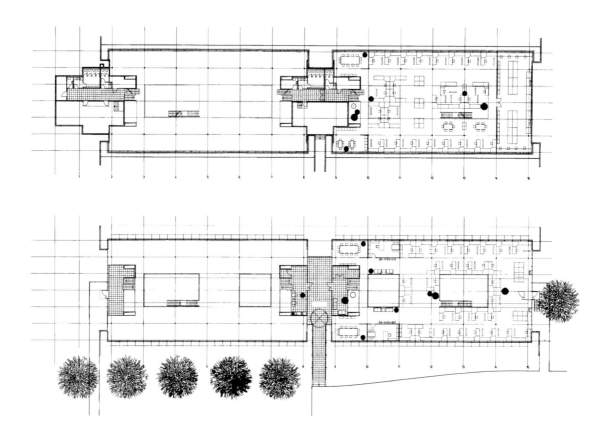

Figure 5.31   Plans of the
Josef Gartner & Sons
Headquarters.
(Josef Gartner & Sons)

Josef Gartner & Sons, a firm that designs curtain-wall systems, used its new office in Gundelfingen, Germany, as a demonstration of the company's holistic vision of the building envelope. Designed by Kurt Ackermann and Partner, the building integrates glazing and a variety of shading methods to create a sophisticated solution to luminous and thermal concerns. The two-story office is oriented on an east-west axis. Sidelighting is provided only on the north and south, eliminating problems with the low morning and afternoon sun. The apparent depth of the building is reduced with atria and centrally located skylights. The daylighting role of the envelope is made easier because the building was designed with good architectural daylighting strategies.

Exterior shading on the lower windows combines horizontally mounted aluminum louvers and vertically mounted glass louvers. The dual horizontal and vertical systems respond to the changing altitude and azimuth of the sun during various times of the year. Horizontal shading responds to high sun angles, while the adjustable heat-reflective glass louvers respond to low sun angles. Yet views of the site are maintained even when the glass louvers are in the closed position.

The Josef Gartner office uses a supplemental external blind to protect high clerestory windows. Interior fabric blinds enable occupants to further modify the quality and quantity of daylight in their personal work areas. The triple-glazed curtain wall is composed of operable windows with two layers of infrared reflecting film and argon gas. Light sensors and an environmental control system adjust the vertical glass louvers and the aluminum louvers mounted above the skylight. Although the building is transparent only on the north side and south sides, the high-performance glazing and shading systems maintain lighting quality, transparency and physical connections to the site throughout the interior. Energy-efficient ambient lighting with photocells and task lighting supplement daylighting when needed. Space planning and furnishings were selected to support the daylighting

Figure 5.32 Sections of the Josef Gartner & Sons Headquarters.

(Josef Gartner & Sons)

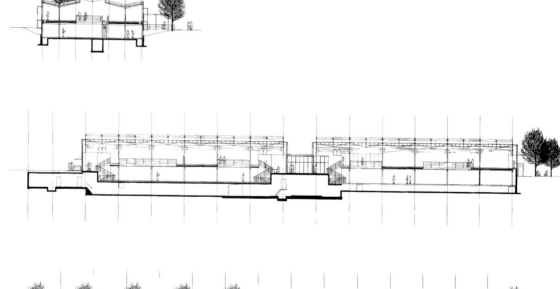

Figure 5.33 Detail of exterior shading at the Josef Gartner & Sons Headquarters.

(Josef Gartner & Sons)

design and maximize light distribution and penetration. These strategies form a comprehensive approach that combines lighting quality, energy efficiency, and aesthetics. The office is not only beautifully daylit, but also presents a pleasant environment that has varied lighting qualities, abundant views of the site and sky, and a high degree of occupant interaction and control of the luminous and thermal environments. The layering of horizontal and vertical louvers, interior and exterior systems, and fixed and adjustable shading provides diverse means of environmental response. The daylighting design meets the highest ecological, energy, and aesthetic standards. (See Figures 5.34 to 5.36.)

These last two examples take a distinctly three-dimensional and layered approach to the building envelope. This approach is biased toward greater interaction between the inside and outside, and potentially between the occupant and the environment. Whether the designer combines glass technologies and shading systems depends on the perceived benefits of flexibility, change, and user interaction. The daylighting technologies we have considered focus on glass technologies, the use of the glazing cavity, and combined glazing and shading systems. These solutions tend to become increasingly responsive to the environment as additional layers are added and greater variability and changeability are included in the systems. The more the occupants interact with the daylighting systems and technologies, the more likely they are to be aware of environmental forces, climate, and the places in which they live and work.

Technologies can take design to a new level of ecological response and connect users with the environment. We are in a period of rapid technological growth that challenges us to reconsider the relationship between ecological, architectural, and technological design decisions. In *Gray World, Green Heart,* landscape

Figure 5.34   View of an atrium and adjacent offices at the Josef Gartner & Sons Headquarters.

(Josef Gartner & Sons)

architect Robert Thayer cautions us about the risk of becoming ". . . as Leo Marx wrote in paraphrase of Thoreau, the 'tools of our tools.' "[20] As glazing and shading technologies as well as mechanical and environmental control systems continue to evolve, we need to pay attention to the lessons of the past and present. Just as the curtain wall is being reconsidered from a more explicitly ecological position, so, too, will be the role of technology in daylighting design. Technology is not the answer; it is only a means. Remember Aalto's point that a building is not a technological problem but rather an "archi-technological" problem. Ideally, there is no distinction between an architectural and technological approach; each approach should be so

Figure 5.35   Exterior view of the skylight and shading devices at the Josef Gartner & Sons Headquarters.

(Josef Gartner & Sons)

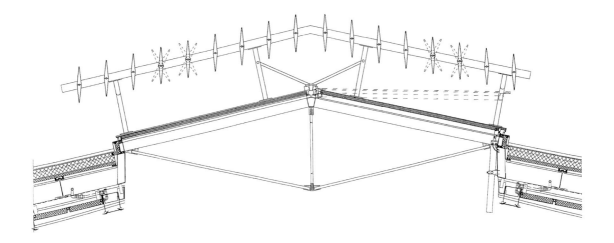

Figure 5.36 Section detail of the skylight and shading devices at the Josef Gartner & Sons Headquarters.

(Josef Gartner & Sons)

interwoven with the other that they become inseparable. This is true in daylighting designs that successfully combine architectural strategies and technologies for maximum ecological and experiential benefit. Yet this synthesis is not always achieved; there is a risk that designers will compromise architectural solutions at the expense of the new and latest technology—or even worse, use technology for its own sake rather than for its contribution to a larger whole. It is through architectural daylighting strategies, not technology, that the greatest ecological, luminous, and human meaning can be achieved.

ENDNOTES

1. Aarno Ruusuvuori, ed., *Alvar Aalto, 1898–1976* (Helsinki: Museum of Finnish Architecture, 1978), 113.
2. Pollution, resource consumption, water depletion, restricted food production, and numerous environmental concerns are cited as evidence of the problems resulting from technological developments. Postel argues that market forces, which often neglect environmental impacts, have driven technological developments. She suggests that initiatives such as environmental taxes, greater environmental regulation, and trade incentives could effect positive environmental change. Sandra Postel, "Carrying Capacity: The Earth's Bottom Line," *State of the World 1994,* ed. Lester Brown et al. (New York: W.W. Norton & Co., 1994), 13–19.

3. For an excellent discussion of the distinction between ecological sustainability and technological sustainability, see David Orr, "Two Meanings of Sustainability," *Ecological Literacy: Education and the Transition to a Postmodern World* (Albany: State University of New York Press, 1992), 23–40.

4. Lester Milbrath, *Envisioning a Sustainable Society: Learning Our Way Out* (Albany: State University of New York Press, 1989), 258.

5. The work, writing, and lectures of Alvar Aalto provide valuable insight into the integration of technology, culture, and architecture. Humanist and aesthetic concerns were prominent themes in his perceptions of technology. Goran Schildt, *Alvar Aalto: The Mature Years* (New York: Rizzoli, 1989), 272.

6. David Orr, 39.

7. Peter McCleary, "Some Characteristics of a New Concept of Technology," *Journal of Architectural Education* 42, no. 1 (fall 1988): 4.

8. Rapoport does not define "weak technology"; however, systems such as passive heating, passive cooling, and daylighting (which are not dependent on mechanical technologies) could be considered within this context. Amos Rapoport, *House, Form, and Culture* (Englewood Cliffs, N.J.: Prentice-Hall, 1969), 83.

9. David Rothenberg, *Hand's End: Technology and the Limits of Nature* (Berkeley, Calif.: University of California Press, 1993), 186.

10. Aarno Ruusuvuori, ed., 114.

11. Alexandra Tyng, *Beginnings: Louis I. Kahn's Philosophy of Architecture* (New York: John Wiley & Sons, 1984), 174.

12. Roger Stonehouse, "Dwelling with the Environment," paper presented at the *Architecture + Environment Conference*, California State University Polytechnic, Pomona, October 1994.

13. John Carmody, *Residential Windows: A Guide to New Technologies and Energy Performance* (New York: W.W. Norton, 1996), 110–111.

14. Designers need to remember that technology cannot solve all luminous and thermal concerns. Proper building and window orientation, attention to daylighting zoning, and shading remain important design considerations despite technological advances.

15. Günter Behnisch, "Plenary Chamber Complex in Bonn," firm literature from Behnisch & Partner (October 1994): 3.

16. Barbara Erwine provides a concise summary of current opportunities and constraints for new glazing technologies in the article "A View to the Future," *Lighting Design + Application* 26, no. 2 (February 1996): 34–39. See also John Carmody, *Residential Windows: A Guide to New Technologies and Energy Performance* (New York: W.W. Norton, 1996) and David Button and Brian Pye, eds., *Glass in Building* (Oxford: Butterworth Architecture, 1993).

17. The Environmental Energy Technologies Division at the Lawrence Berkeley National Laboratory provides an excellent overview of the history and technical characteristics of aerogel. For information, see "Aerogel: Energy-Efficient Material for Buildings," http://candle.lbl.gov/CBS/NEWSLETTER/ NL8/Aerogel.html, Internet.

18. Layla Dawson, "Light Spirited," *Design Review* 197, no. 1175 (January 1995): 21.

19. Fritz Griffin and Marietta Millet, "Shady Aesthetics," *Journal of Architectural Education* 37, no. 3 (spring–summer 1984): 43–60.

20. In *Gray World, Green Heart,* Robert Thayer draws on Leo Marx's concepts of the "machine in the garden" and expands Yi-Fu Tuan's concept of "topophilia" (love of place) by contrasting it with "technophilia" (love of technology) and "technophobia" (guilt, fear, or aversion of technology). His discussion provides insight into our cultural perspectives on technology (loves and fears) that can inform any type of design and planning of the built environment. Even with daylighting design, we need to be reminded of why we use technology, when is it most or least appropriate, and what can or cannot be resolved with its use. The answer to good daylighting is an integration of both technology and design. The challenge is to address daylighting concerns through thoughtful building design while augmenting performance with new technologies. For an intriguing discussion of our views on technology and nature, see Robert Thayer, *Gray World, Green Heart: Technology, Nature, and Sustainable Landscape* (New York: John Wiley & Sons, 1994).

HUMAN CONSIDERATIONS

Address Health and Well-Being

Health is connection and competence in terms of the whole, which has as its outer limits the earth, and as its inner limits, the heart.[1]

—LEONARD DUHL, M.D.

Our sense of health and well-being is influenced by a host of factors, some of which are related to the physical and psychological conditions of the body, spirit, and mind, while others are affected by the quality and characteristics of the natural and built environments. In *The Turning Point,* Fritjof Capra suggests that human health is integrally related to the environment: ". . . our experience of feeling healthy involves the feeling of physical, psychological and spiritual integrity, of a sense of balance among the various components of the organism and between the organism and its environment."[2] Daylight is one of many important environmental health factors. As a result, medical researchers continue to explore the tangible and intangible effects of sunlight on the human body and mind. Physiological conditions associated with insufficient daylight range from rickets, jaundice, and osteoporosis to more elusive conditions such as seasonal affective disorder (SAD). Other health issues directly or indirectly related to visual comfort and the qualities of light in the built environment include building-related illnesses (BRI) and sick building syndrome (SBS).

It is well documented that our sense of health and well-being is dependent on more than just our physical condition. Our emotions, attitudes, approaches to life, and the quality of the environment are also contributing factors. Whether it is to treat specific illnesses or to provide visual comfort, daylighting is essential in creating both healthy bodies and healing environments. While there are many facets of light and health, we will focus on three areas of concern: light and clinical therapy (phototherapy, chronotherapy, and chromotherapy); visual comfort (building-related illnesses and sick building syndrome); and light in healing environments (strategies and contributing factors). The relationships between health and quality of life (including social, environmental, and spiritual connections) will be addressed in Chapter 7.

LIGHT AND CLINICAL THERAPY

According the U.S. Environmental Protection Agency, the average American spends 90 percent of his or her time indoors.[3] With so many hours spent inside, it is alarming that research continues to reveal the hazards of indoor environments on human health. As we spend fewer hours outside, high-quality daylit environments play an increasingly important role in maintaining health and well-being. Most people know intuitively that appropriate quantities and qualities of daylight make them feel good, that they prefer a room with a window, and that views are important. We all know that a plant left in a dark room will die, yet many people (and often building owners) are not convinced that humans have the same biological need for daylight. For some, common sense and intuition are sufficient to suggest that there is a relationship between daylight and health; for others, more research findings and evidence are needed. Many of the early theories regarding the effects of light on human physiology began with intuitive speculations and commonsense observations about the physical luminous environment. These theories were later formally investigated and elaborated upon with scientific studies. The treatment of jaundice with light from the visible region of the spectrum is one such case. Although test-tube studies suggested a relationship between light and jaundice, it was a nurse in Great Britain who first observed this effect on humans. She found that newborns located adjacent to open windows were less likely to develop jaundice than infants placed farther from the windows. The nurse's suspicion was later confirmed with research by Dr. Jerold F. Lucy of the University of Vermont College of Medicine when he and his colleagues successfully used phototherapy to treat jaundice.[4]

There is a place for both intuitive and scientific inquiry in the design of healthy and healing environments. We need to trust our senses and feelings in response to the built environment; however, we also need to rigorously observe, test, and analyze the influences of the environment on human health. A brief overview of human biological responses to light will reveal that many lessons can be learned from scientific studies that challenge design thinking. Subsequently, we will consider how medical research in phototherapy, chronotherapy, and chromotherapy (light, time, and color) might help designers create healthier and more healing environments.

Phototherapy

Although seasonal affective disorder (SAD) is perhaps the most recent and commonly known illness that is treated with light or phototherapy, many other conditions have a much longer history. Rickets, a debilitating bone disease that causes physical deformities, was one of the first illnesses associated with sunlight. In the early 1900s scientists linked rickets to a deficiency of vitamin D. Although a form of vitamin D can be obtained from various foods (including fish and cod-liver oil), it is also a hormone produced by the skin. Exposure to sunlight sets off an elegant cycle that causes the skin to produce vitamin D, which increases the absorption of calcium in the intestine, which is then released to the skeleton to strengthen bones. Although rickets is a rare disease, it can still be found in children primarily between the ages of 6 and 24 months. Calcium, phosphorous, and vitamin D supplements can help minimize the risk of rickets; however, moderate exposure to sunlight is also important. Only 15 minutes of sunlight is needed on the hands and face to provide sufficient exposure for vitamin D production.[5]

Osteoporosis, or porous bones, is another disease directly associated with a vitamin D deficiency and, indirectly, with sunlight. The prevalence and debilitating effects of osteoporosis are profound. According to the National Osteoporosis Foundation, 10 million people are affected by the disease and as many as 18 million have low bone mass, which leads to over $14 billion in direct expenditures at hospitals and nursing homes.[6] Many factors increase the risk of osteoporosis, including gender, age, body size, and ethnicity. Diet, exercise, and calcium supplements are the primary strategies for minimizing the risk of what is often called a "silent disease" because it takes many years before symptoms may occur. Yet the therapeutic effects of sunlight should not be underestimated, for it facilitates the production of vitamin D and subsequently the absorption of calcium. Exposure to sunlight is a particular concern for people who are less physically mobile, as the National Osteoporosis Foundation explains: "Vitamin D plays an important role in calcium absorption and in bone health. It is synthesized in the skin through exposure to sunlight. While many people are able to obtain enough vitamin D naturally, studies show that vitamin D production decreases in the elderly, who are housebound, and during the winter."[7]

Jaundice has been treated with light for nearly four decades. The condition is common in newborns, though it normally disappears following the first or second week of life. Jaundice results when the liver does not filter bilirubin (which is produced when red blood cells die). It is estimated that over 50 percent of newborns have livers that are not fully developed at birth, and 2 percent of these newborns require phototherapy administered by a physician to overcome the ailment. Supplemental home treatment may include sunbaths; often 10 to 15 minutes twice per day in a sunny window is sufficient.[8]

It has become increasingly evident that humans also have a psychological need for light (which is integrally related to and influenced by physiological needs). Seasonal affective disorder (SAD) has received great attention since Dr. Norman Rosenthal and his colleagues first published the findings of their research in 1984.[9] Recent research has shown that other conditions also respond to phototherapy, including panic disorders, insomnia, depression, bulimia nervosa, alcohol dependence, and even dementia. The studies on SAD have had a profound impact on our understanding of the human biological response to light. SAD is characterized as a seasonal recurrence of depression that is frequently (but not always) associated with the fall and winter months. Contrary to clinical depression, which may result in weight loss and insomnia, the symptoms of SAD can include fatigue, lack of energy, increased sleep, carbohydrate craving, and weight gain. Most people experience some degree of mood and physiological changes that correspond to the seasons; however, people with SAD have symptoms that impair normal functioning.

Despite the proliferation of research during the past decade, there is still much to understand about the treatment and factors that influence SAD. Although it is generally believed that contributing factors include decreased light levels and shorter days in winter (which are exacerbated at higher latitudes), research studies show discrepancies. For example, according to the Mood Disorders Clinic at the University of British Columbia, there is a direct correlation between the frequency of SAD and geographic location: "In Florida, less than 1% of the general population have SAD, while in Alaska as many as 10% of people may suffer from winter depression."[10] Yet recent research cited by Dr. Raymond Lam of the Department of Psychiatry at the Vancouver Hospital and Health Science Center suggests that incidents of SAD may occur with similar frequency in Alaska, Switzerland, and Italy.[11] According to Dr. Lam, "One plausible explanation is a 'ceiling effect' with prevalence rates reaching a plateau above a certain latitude."[12] In addition, a recent study in Italy by Fraedda and associates challenges the assumption that SAD is a fall/winter phenomenon. Fraedda found that 9.7 percent of patients with mood disorders had seasonal patterns that were equally divided between spring/summer and fall/winter.[13] Yet, despite conflicting studies, SAD is still generally associated with the fall and winter seasons in temperate and northern latitudes when days are shorter and daylight is less abundant.

It is projected that as many as 60 to 80 percent of patients with SAD respond favorably to phototherapy.[14] Yet researchers are uncertain about why light therapy is effective and how it works. In addition to other possible factors, it is believed that light decreases levels of melatonin (a hormone that can act as a sedative), changes levels of serotonin and dopamine in the brain, and modifies the body's biological clock. Dr. Al Lewy and his colleagues at the National Institutes of Health first demonstrated that an illuminance level of 2500 lux (approximately 250 footcandles) suppressed the production of melatonin, while a lower level of 500 lux (50 footcandles) was ineffective.[15] In 1988, additional studies on phototherapy and melatonin by Drs. Al Lewy and George Brainard and their colleagues found that there is a direct relationship between light intensity and hormone levels.

While the administration of phototherapy has been standard-
ized (most physicians prescribe either an electric light box positioned close to the patient or a light visor worn like a hat), the
required amounts of light and exposure periods for the treatment
of SAD are still under debate. Some of the first studies used illuminance levels of 2500 lux, with exposure times as long as two
hours. Under these conditions, it was found that patient symptoms would begin to ease after several days, with significant
reductions after 7 to 10 days. Other studies have used levels
as high as 10,000 lux for shorter periods (30 minutes). Until
recently, it was believed that high illuminance levels (2500 to
10,000 lux, far in excess of typical indoor light levels) were
needed to offset the effects of SAD. However, a recent study by
Dr. Rosenthal and colleagues, which compared light visors at 400
lux (40 footcandles) and 6000 lux (600 footcandles), found that
lower light levels provide effective treatment, although relapse
was higher at 400 lux.[16] In addition, a multicenter light visor
study by Drs. Joffe, Moeul, Lam, and colleagues found no significant difference in the antidepressant efficacy at 60, 600, and
3500 lux.[17] Dr. Raymond Lam of the Department of Psychiatry at
Vancouver Hospital and Health Science Center speculates that the
proximity of the visor and the placebo effect may contribute to
the high level of response at low light levels. In addition, he suggests that illuminance may not be the most effective measure of
biologic response. Despite these concerns, Dr. Lam concludes:
"There is increasing evidence that even low illumination can
affect biologic parameters so that for some patients, light as low
as 100 lux [10 footcandles] may be therapeutically effective."[18]

The earlier studies used high illuminance levels that were most
effectively administered with electric light sources such as light
boxes or visors. Architectural daylighting was not feasible for
therapy because high light intensities would be difficult and often
unwanted in buildings due to heat gain and possible visual discomfort. Yet the recently revealed efficacy of lower light levels
suggests that daylighting could play a role in the treatment of
SAD and perhaps milder forms of seasonal and nonclinical
depression. Dr. Terman and colleagues at the Columbia University Medical Center studied the seasonal symptom patterns of
"healthy residents" (those who do not experience SAD) in New
York City. They found that 50 percent of respondents experience
mild signs of depression during the winter months, with symptoms that included modest weight gain, increased sleep, de-

creased social activity, and loss of energy.[19] These symptoms may sound familiar to many of us. Humans, like most animals, slow down and conserve energy during the winter months. Survival is dependent on resourcefulness, which includes the conservation of energy. Do we want to tamper with what appears to be a naturally occurring biological response? The desire to overcome the body's response to winter is evident in the tremendous number of people who make seasonal pilgrimages to sunny locations. Flight from the north is so extensive that Michigan, Wisconsin, Minnesota, and Canada residents are known as "snowbirds" because of their winter migration to popular destinations such as Florida, South Carolina, and Arizona. It appears that some people are more sensitive to the physiological and psychological effects of light. While most people would benefit from a winter junket to Cancún, we would probably also feel better if we spent more time outside and worked and lived in well-daylit spaces.

Is there a relationship between people who experience SAD (and nonclinical depression) and the characteristics of the luminous environments in which they live and work? Are there particular quantities and qualities of daylight that elicit favorable biological responses? How much daylight is needed to maintain human health and well-being? Are there health implications that relate to a person's proximity to a window? An innovative project by Dr. George Brainard and colleagues is exploring the human biological and behavioral impacts, and the related energy implications, of electric lighting systems in architecture.[20] Dr. Brainard points out potential conflicts between the amount of light needed for biologic response, current illuminance recommendations by the Illuminating Engineering Society of North America, and energy-efficiency design. He suggests that the low levels of illuminance recommended for some tasks are equivalent to biological darkness. Brainard explains that our challenge is to meet both energy and biological needs: "It would be unconscionable to suggest that we waste any of our valuable energy resources. We should all conserve energy and preserve the ecology of our environment. In the process, we also should be careful not to waste human productivity, health, and well-being. Ultimately we need to determine energy-efficient strategies for lighting that provide optimal visual stimulation as well as optimum biological stimulation."[21] When appropriately designed, daylighting is an obvious solution which saves energy while responding to human biological needs. This is particularly evident since recent research has confirmed the benefits of lower illuminance levels (which are more consistent with those that can be achieved by daylighting). The architectural implications of phototherapy are ripe for study. Although the research is pending, it is reasonable to suggest that the benefits of daylighting go beyond energy and natural resources to also embrace human health and well-being.

Chronotherapy

A related area of study is *chronobiology*—the investigation of biological rhythms or time-related cycles. Because light is one of the main determinants of biological rhythms, chronotherapy (a type of phototherapy) can be used to influence these cycles. The *circadian (24-hour) rhythm,* such as the human sleep-wake cycle, is perhaps the most commonly recognized biologic pattern. (The sleep-wake cycle is actually slightly longer than 24 hours when there are no time cues, suggesting that lunar cycles may be as important as solar cycles). The National Science Foundation (NSF) Center for Biological Timing reports that there other important cycles. *Infradian rhythms* (hibernation, migration, menstruation, and reproductive cycles) exceed 24 hours. *Ultradian rhythms* (90-minute sleep cycles and hormone rhythms) last less than 24 hours. *Tidal rhythms* correspond with the 24-hour 51-minute cycle of the moon. These rhythms cause the ebb and flow of the oceans, influence the activities and behaviors of organisms in the intertidal zone, and even affect cellular rhythms, hormone releases, and genetic activity.[22] Humans, plants, and animals—all of life—are influenced by biological rhythms. These cycles are *endogenous,* or produced from within, yet are influenced by social and environmental factors such as sunlight, noise, and other stimulants and depressants.

Some people experience brief sleep-wake cycles within the 24-hour circadian rhythm. For these people, the desire for a nap during midday can be overwhelming (most frequently between 2:00 and 5:00 P.M.). Surprisingly, it has been found that a nap has little effect on amount of sleep needed at night. According to Jurgen Aschoff, ". . . neither the duration of the main sleep nor the circadian cycle is affected by napping."[23] These short naps are often valuable for replenishing energy and creativity. Albert Einstein was a great believer in naps, and his work may be seen as a vindication of their benefits. We use sleep and naps to explore ideas and solve problems. When important decisions are pending, we often want to "sleep on it," to take some time to consciously and subconsciously process issues. Today you even hear about designated spaces for "power napping" in corporate environments (as though a mere nap is insufficient). Whether you need a nap or just a good night's sleep, it is well documented that disruption of circadian rhythms and sleep patterns can cause serious physiological and psychological stress and even illnesses.

Much of the research related to architectural design and daylighting has focused on the effects of shift work, jet lag, and insomnia. It may not be surprising to learn that many of the catastrophic accidents of the twentieth century occurred during the late shift, including disasters at Three Mile Island (4:00 A.M.), Chernobyl (1:23 A.M.), Bhopal (12:40 A.M.), and on the Exxon Valdez (12:04 A.M.).[24] According to the NSF Center for Biological Timing, "Researchers have found that 'the neural processes controlling alertness and sleep produce an increased sleep tendency and diminished capacity to functioning during certain early morning hours (circa 2–7 A.M.) and, to a lesser degree, during a period in the mid-afternoon (circa 2–5 P.M.), whether or not we have slept.' "[25] The potential for errors, accidents, and the loss of productivity is significant when we realize that 20 percent of U.S. employees work night shifts. In addition to increasing the likelihood of mishaps, shift work also contributes to health problems such as gastrointestinal and cardiovascular disease. A report by Dr. Eastman and colleagues from the Biological Rhythms Research Laboratory at Rush-Presbyterian–St. Luke's Medical Center in Chicago explains,

> The unhealthy symptoms and many deleterious consequences of shift work can be explained by a mismatch between the work-sleep schedule and the internal circadian rhythms. This mismatch occurs because the 24-h zeitgebers ["time givers," or external time cues], such as the natural light-dark cycle, keep the circadian rhythms from phase shifting to align with the night-work, day-sleep schedule. . . . Bright light field studies, in which subjects live at home, show that the use of artificial nocturnal bright light combined with enforced daytime day (sleep) periods can phase shift circadian rhythms despite exposure to the conflicting 24-h zeitgebers.[26]

Studies by the National Aeronautics and Space Administration (NASA) confirm that bright-light exposure can be used to alleviate circadian disruptions associated with shift work and jet lag. A study by the NASA Ames Research Center used naps rather than light therapy as a means of reducing the stress, fatigue, and risk of error experienced by airplane pilots with irregular work hours and frequent jet lag. The effect of scheduled rest for the flight crew was studied during a 12-day period when the crew flew long-distance routes. The NASA study concluded, ". . . there were significant positive effects on both performance and alertness as a result of the cockpit nap."[27]

Chronobiologists are also studying the relationship between biological cycles and insomnia. This is a particular problem among people over the age of 65, more than 50 percent of whom suffer from chronic sleep disturbances. An insomnia study by Dr. Campbell and colleagues at the Department of Psychiatry at Cornell University found that light therapy can be an effective alternative to prescription medication: "Exposure to bright light resulted in substantial changes in sleep quality. Waking time within sleep was reduced by an hour, and sleep efficiency improved from 77.5% to 90%, without altering time spent in bed. Increased sleep time was in the form of Stage 2 sleep, REM sleep [rapid eye movement sleep], and slow wave sleep. The effects were remarkably consistent across subjects."[28]

The preceding studies on shift work, jet lag, and insomnia reveal that humans have distinct sleep-wake cycles and circadian rhythms that can be reinforced or altered by light. They also illustrate that our internal, or endogenous, clock is influenced by environmental cues such as daylight, keeping our bodies tuned and our biological clocks set to correspond with circadian rhythms. Light can also be used to reset our internal clocks, as was shown in the studies of shift workers and people with insomnia. A variety of questions can be raised from the research. If light not only makes us feel better, but appears to set our biological clocks so we can sleep better, then is it possible that the office worker next to the window has a stronger circadian rhythm? Is it possible that this person gets more sleep and as a result performs more effectively the next day? Do people fortunate enough to work in well-daylit spaces benefit from a quiet and unacknowledged tuning of their circadian rhythms? Chronotherapy also raises the question of whether we might benefit from spaces of darkness as well as spaces of light in our built environments. The NASA cockpit-crew study showed the benefit of rest during work. While we might find humor in the concept of a "power nap," it could be that corporations are on the leading edge in providing a dark sleeping space adjacent to the boardroom.

When we look at the effect of full-spectrum electric lighting and daylighting in schools we find compelling health implications that may also be related to our biological rhythms. Although full-spectrum light is not necessary for the phototherapuetic treatment of SAD (the quantity of light and exposure period are critical), it appears that it still has other health benefits. A study conducted by the Policy and Planning Branch of Alberta Education in Canada found that students who were exposed to full-spectrum electric light benefit from higher attendance, more positive moods, less dental decay, and above-average growth in height.[29] Although a study using daylight as the full-spectrum light source has not been conducted, we can speculate that it may have similar (and perhaps additional) positive effects. A related study by Michael Nicklas and Gary Baily of Innovative Design evaluated the performance of students in daylit schools. These experiments were based on a theory that students would be more focused on their tasks in windowless classrooms. It should come as no surprise that Nicklas and Baily found that the opposite was true: "Students who attended daylit schools out-performed the students who were attending non-daylit schools by 5 to 14 percent, depending upon whether you consider short or long-term impacts. . . . When you consider the impact on student performance resulting from being within a daylit facility for multiple years, the impact is even greater."[30]

Because performance was the primary concern in the windowless-school study, we can only speculate on the relationship of daylight to health. We know intuitively that our own performance is related to many factors, including our ability to concentrate and focus, our interest level, and our sense of well-being. We know that a bad night's sleep (and for some, a day without a nap) can contribute to fatigue, stress, disorientation, and lack of concentration. We also know from research that there are relationships between performance and biological rhythms (NASA and Dr. Boulos et al.) as well as between full-spectrum light and physical health (Policy and Planning Branch, Alberta Education in Canada). What are the connections between health, chronotherapy, daylighting, and architecture? How important is it for us to be in tune with our biological rhythms? What role does the luminous environment play in this tuning? At this time there are no answers; there are only questions. The sooner we bring together researchers in chronobiology and architecture, the sooner we can understand whether we can or should tune our built environments to our biological rhythms.

Chromotherapy

A related area of study is *chromotherapy,* or the use of color for therapeutic benefit. The concept of chromotherapy is not new, as Dianne Ackerman explains in *A Natural History of the Senses:* "Ancient cultures (Greek, Egyptian, Chinese, Indian, and others) used color therapies of many sorts, prescribing colors for various distresses of the body and soul. Color can alarm, excite, calm, uplift."[31] Color theory is a vast and fascinating topic, which is explored in fields as varied as science, art, and architecture. Elusive and complex, color has the power to intrigue and mystify. Leonard Shlain, M.D., suggests in *Art & Physics* that color can even evoke fear and distrust:

> The tightly logical, left-brain attitude that has ruled Western culture for six hundred years has regarded color with a certain suspicion. It has generally been believed that people who responded to color rather than to line were not wholly trustworthy. Love of color was somehow instinctual and primitive, indicating a Dionysian cast to one's psyche rather than the restrained and Apollonian one appropriate for a proper man. Color precedes words and antedates civilization, connected as it is to the subterranean groundwaters of the archaic limbic system. Infants respond to brightly colored objects long before they learn words or even complex purposeful movements.[32]

Color can be described and studied in many ways, from a wavelength in physics to an emotional response in psychology to color theory in art. Indeed, the art and science of color have developed simultaneously. For example, shortly after Johann Wolfgang von Goethe completed his early-nineteenth-century work on the theory and phenomena of color, scientists Gustav Kirchhoff and Robert Bunsen studied spectrum analysis, and James Clerk Maxwell formulated the laws of electromagnetic fields. Meanwhile, artists such as van Gogh, Monet, Cézanne, and Gauguin used vibrant colors to evoke moods and emotions.

The anthroposophic works of Rudolf Steiner and his followers perhaps best illustrate the application of chromotherapy in architectural design. The anthroposophic concept of "living architecture" suggests that the built environment has patterns, rhythms, and energies that influence and shape human experience. According to Steiner, ". . . in coloring form we should feel: 'Now we are endowing form with soul.' We breathe soul into dead form when, through color, we make it living."[33] This anthroposophic notion is elaborated upon in Robert Logsdon's essay "The Human Side: Understanding the Application of Lazure Painting Techniques." "Through a building's structure, it has a body. Through its form, skin, and gesture, it has a life body. Through color, it is ensouled. Finally, through the presence and activities of human beings, it has spirit. Consciousness is given through human beings, yet all the elements of the building itself are influencing the consciousness of the people. As Leland Kaiser said, 'In designing buildings, we are designing consciousness.' First we give shape to the buildings, then they begin to shape us."[34]

Implicit in this approach to design is a belief that decisions concerning architectural form, materials, color, and light influence how we feel. The use of color, whether inherent to materials or applied, is one of many factors used by anthroposophic designers to bring architecture to life. Architect Erik Asmussen employs a variety of chomotherapeutic concepts at the Vidarkliniken (Vidar Clinic), which is an anthroposophic hospital in Järna, Sweden. At a recent Healthcare Design Conference, Professors Gary Coates and Susanne Siepl-Coates explained Asmussen's use of color:

> The choice of color in the patient rooms is an obvious example in which the building contributes directly to the healing of the patient. In anthroposophy, illnesses are in principle divided into two kinds: *sclerotic,* or illnesses that are considered to be cold in nature, and *inflammatory* illnesses, such as fevers. Depending on the type of illness, doctors prescribe either warm rose-colored or cool blue-violet-colored rooms for their patients. Color is never used for merely symbolic or decorative purposes; rather, it is intended to serve the process of healing and to support the functions occurring in the spaces in which it is applied.[35]

A rich choreography of color, light, and materials can create a comforting and healing environment. Asmussen, in the tradition of Steiner, uses a technique known as *lazure painting*. A luminous effect results from light transmitted through and reflected from many layers of translucent paint that are applied over a white base coat. An infinite number of colors can be achieved by layer-

Figure 6.1 View
of a warm-rose
room for patients with
inflammatory illnesses at
the Vidar Clinic.

(Max Plunger)

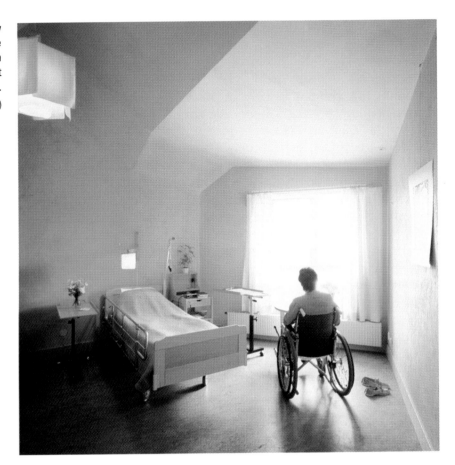

ing paint of different hue, value, and chroma. The interaction of color and light results in the beautiful and unique effects of lazure painting found in the healing environment of Vidar Clinic. As Gary Coates explains in his book *Erik Asmussen,*

> As in all of Asmussen's buildings for anthroposophical groups, the interior spaces in the clinic are painted by the "lazure" method, or veil painting. Colors in the patient rooms use vegetable dyes in a casein and beeswax medium. The corridors, which are painted in a warm yellow ocher, use paints made with mineral dyes. The rose-pink exterior color is made from artificial pigments. The result is a progression of color quality from hard to soft as one moves from outside to inside, with the colors of the most intimate and vulnerable spaces, the patient rooms, being the softest and most alive.[36]

(See Figures 6.1 and 6.2.)

In his essay "Environmental Design Technology: Using Color & Light as Medicine," lighting designer Craig Roeder describes the chromotherapeutic implications of color. For example, red vitalizes and is associated with hemoglobin and liver. Green is cooling, soothing, and calming; it is associated with the sympathetic nervous system, relieves tension, and lowers blood pressure. Blue is cold, electrical, and has contracting potencies associated with arteries, veins, and blood pressure; it is considered an anticarcinogen.[37] According to chromotherapy, there are healing associations with all primary and secondary colors (red, yellow, and blue, as well as orange, green, and violet). While the concept of chromotherapy is intriguing, its healing properties and effectiveness have yet to be fully understood and confirmed. Despite its experimental (if not alternative) approach to healing, a small but

Figure 6.2 View of a blue-violet room for patients with sclerotic illnesses at the Vidar Clinic.

(Max Plunger)

increasing number of health professionals and designers are investigating the therapeutic implications of color.

There is still much to study and much to learn about the effects of color on health. Yet even without a clear understanding of how color works, we can still experience its healing effects. As Florence Nightingale wrote in 1893: "People say the effect is only on the mind. It is no such thing. The effect is on the body too. Little as we know about the way in which we are affected by form, by color, and light, we do know this, that they have an actual physical effect. Variety of form and brilliancy of color in the objects presented to patients are actual means of recovery."[38] For now, knowing that color sets a stage, creates a mood, and shapes our experience in both tangible and intangible ways may be sufficient to prompt us to experiment with the joys, beauty, and healing effects of color in the built environment.

VISUAL COMFORT

Visual comfort has received much attention during the past several decades as the use of computers and video display terminals (VDTs) has proliferated. Less attention has been focused on the links between visual comfort and two recently occurring architectural health concerns—*sick building syndrome* (SBS) and *building-related illnesses* (BRI). Although SBS and BRI are primarily associated with indoor air quality (IAQ), there are also daylighting factors that can directly or indirectly contribute to each.

Sick Building Syndrome and Building-Related Illness

The United States Environmental Protection Agency (EPA) distinguishes between SBS and BRI in the following way:

> The term "sick building syndrome" (SBS) is used to describe a situation in which building occupants experience acute health and comfort effects that appear to be linked to time spent in a building, but no specific illness or cause can be identified. The complaints may be localized in a particular room or zone, or may be widespread throughout the building. In contrast, the term "building related illness" (BRI) is used when symptoms of diagnosable illness are identified and can be attributed directly to airborne building contaminants.[39]

A variety of factors influence the health of a building, including ventilation, building materials, temperature, humidity, moisture control, and lighting conditions. The primary culprit, however, is believed to be poor IAQ. According to the World Health Organization (WHO) ". . . up to 30 percent of new and remodeled buildings worldwide may be the subject of excessive complaints related to indoor air quality. . . ."[40] The EPA estimates that as many as 21 million Americans may be affected, resulting in lost productivity, medical problems, and damage to materials and equipment costing tens of billions of dollars per year (other sources estimate costs as great as $65 billion annually).[41]

The effects of BRI (asthma, legionellosis, fiberglass dermatitis, etc.) are caused by airborne contaminants. The causes of SBS are far more ambiguous. Early studies from the United Kingdom found a direct correlation between SBS symptoms and mechanical ventilation. Others argued that tighter buildings and lower ventilation rates, which resulted from the energy crisis of the 1970s, combined with an increased use of synthetic materials containing volatile organic compounds (VOCs) exacerbated air-quality problems. Although there is some disagreement on the history and causes of SBS, there is consensus that the main strategies to mitigate problems include removal, dilution, and filtration of pollutants. The American Society of Heating, Refrigerating, and Air Conditioning Engineers (ASHRAE) airflow standards have increased from 5 cubic feet per minute (cfm) in 1973 to 15 to 60 cfm in 1989 (depending upon occupant loads and activities). These rates are only recommendations, and local building codes may vary.

It also appears that SBS and BRI are more frequent in newer air-conditioned buildings. John C. Bruening, a writer specializing in issues of health and safety, states, "SBS has been linked with inadequate building ventilation because symptoms usually are more prevalent in air-conditioned buildings than in naturally ventilated buildings with operable windows."[42] Subsequently, daylighting, operable windows, and natural ventilation are indirectly related SBS. While it is not possible or even desirable to integrate daylighting and natural ventilation into all buildings, these strategies should be seriously considered for appropriate climates, occupant loads, activities, and sites where pollution is not worse outside the building. (Because few midsize or large buildings could be adequately or completely ventilated without mechanical systems, it is more likely that the natural and mechanical systems could be combined and used respectively during appropriate times of the year or day.) The use of environmental control systems, sensors, and window interlocks enables the regulation of mechanical ventilation when windows are open.

Although IAQ may be a primary factor contributing to SBS, researchers suggest that there may be a potpourri of other related issues. Some researchers and designers clearly identify lighting as an SBS factor. In *Lighting Design,* Carl Gardner and Barry Hannaford explain that, "Poor lighting can be a major, but unrecognized, cause of worker dissatisfaction and inefficiency. For example, it can cause workers to make more mistakes, or to take more time to read written material, and to work slower. Employees' health may even be affected; badly designed, poorly specified lighting can cause stress and is often associated with glare, eye strain, migraines and other features of what is known as 'sick building syndrome.' "[43] A recent study by Alan Hedge, associate professor of the College of Human Ecology at Cornell University, reinforces Gardner and Hannaford's perspective: "SBS complaints seem to be the result of the interaction of a multitude of environmental, occupational, and psychological factors, and they probably are not caused by poor indoor air quality alone."[44] Hedge found that the quality of the lighting environment correlates directly to the frequency of vision-related symptoms such as headache, eyestrain, and visual discomfort. The lack of user control over lighting conditions and light sources that cause high glare and flicker are related concerns. Yet the EPA considers lighting to be an indirect issue, or what they call an "SBS comfort and productivity factor," that can affect both the level of indoor pollutants and occupants' perception of air quality. EPA comfort and productivity factors include heat or glare from sunlight; glare from ceiling lights and computer monitors; and occupants' feelings about physical aspects of the workplace, including the availability of natural light, aesthetics, color, and style, as well as other issues.[45] Whether lighting is characterized as a direct or indirect factor for SBS is unimportant. The critical issue is that people are experiencing health problems associated with poor lighting conditions. Designers and owners have a responsibility to alleviate, if not eliminate, visual comfort problems.

Figure 6.3 Exterior view of the Commerzbank Headquarters.

(Ian Lambot)

Foster and Partners have considered many of these health issues and related ecological concerns in the design of the Commerzbank in Frankfurt, Germany. Rising to a height of 840 feet (259 meters), the project is considered to be the first ecological skyscraper. Similar to the system we saw at the RWE AG Headquarters in Essen by Ingenhoven, Overdiek and Partner, the Commerzbank uses a double-layered envelope to provide natural

Figure 6.4 View of an office overlooking a green space in the Commerzbank Headquarters.

(Ian Lambot)

ventilation and daylight from the ground level to the fiftieth floor. The envelope of the building incorporates exterior glazing, a vertical shaft for natural ventilation, and interior operable windows. The triangular plan includes three petal-shaped elements containing office spaces and a slender vertical atrium in the center. Nine four-story "sky gardens" spiral up the interior of the atrium to create pleasant community spaces and interior views while also improving indoor air quality. Interior windows in office spaces can be opened to the atrium. Services and vertical transportation are located in three corners of the triangular plan. The thin office spaces and

Figure 6.5 View of an office with operable windows in the Commerzbank Headquarters.

(Ian Lambot)

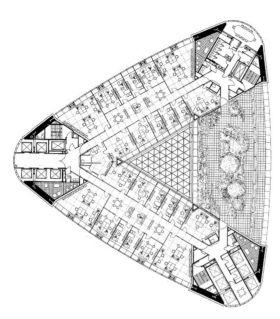

Figure 6.6 Typical floor plan of the Commerzbank.
(Foster and Partners)

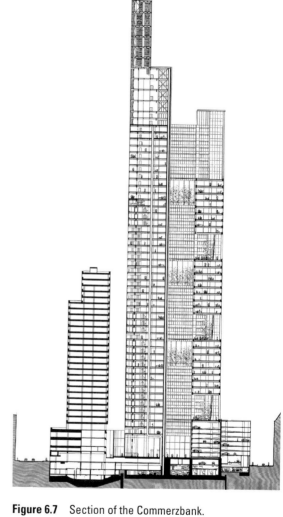

Figure 6.7 Section of the Commerzbank.
(Foster and Partners)

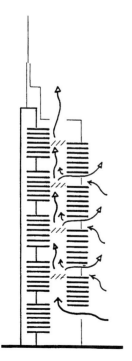

Figure 6.8 Sketch of the ventilation concept for the Commerzbank.
(Foster and Partners)

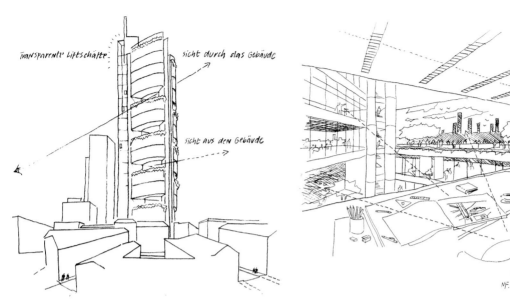

Figure 6.9   Exterior sketch of the Commerzbank.

(Foster and Partners)

Figure 6.10   Interior sketch of an office at the Commerz-bank.

(Foster and Partners)

interior atrium provide all workers with access to bilateral daylight, abundant views outside and inside, and access to natural ventilation. (See Figures 6.3 to 6.10.)

Computer Vision Syndrome and Other Health Issues

Buildings need to create a luminous environment that supports human activities without compromising design, aesthetic, and ecological objectives. The types of strategies and approaches used to ensure visual comfort are particular to specific activities. It would be impossible to summarize all of the various luminous concerns that might occur within the built environment. Instead, we will focus on several lighting issues related to health and visual comfort that can serve as points of departure for broader daylighting design considerations. (The *Lighting Handbook,* by the Illuminating Engineering Society of North America, provides an excellent overview of the relationship between various activities and recommended lighting qualities, quantities, and considerations.)[46]

Two related aspects of visual comfort concern the appropriate quality and quantity of light. Both of these factors can relate to stress, headaches, eyestrain, and general well-being. (It may not be surprising that eyestrain is the most common complaint associated with lighting.)[47] In our market-driven workplaces, increased productivity has been a primary motivating factor for improving visual comfort. Yet we have long known that the quantity of light is but one factor that influences productivity. A classic illustration of this point occurred in the early part of this century when a study at the Hawthorne Works of the Western Electric Company found increased productivity with both high and low levels of illumination. Dr. Elton Mayo and colleagues from Harvard University studied these unanticipated and baffling results. Interviews with employees revealed that the increased attention paid by the company and researchers during the studies was the primary contributing factor for increased productivity. The "Hawthorne effect" reminds us that the amount of light is but one factor in productivity. We also need to consider the psychological aspects of visual comfort. The quantity of light is perhaps the easiest issue to address in lighting design (although there are some potential conflicts concerning illuminance levels, health, and energy that will be considered later). The quality of the luminous environment is the more elusive and difficult aspect of visual comfort. To gain insight into both the quantitative and qualitative challenges of visual comfort, it is useful to explore the lighting implications of a recently defined condition known as *computer vision syndrome* (CVS).

The American Optometric Association defines CVS as a "complex of eye and vision problems related to near work which are experienced during or related to computer use," with symptoms ranging from headaches, eyestrain, blurred vision, and irritated eyes to backache, neckache, and double vision.[48] Many factors can contribute to CVS, including lighting, furniture and equipment ergonomics, poor work habits, existing vision disorders, as well as other environmental and physiological factors. Given the increased use of computers, it is not surprising that a large number of people are experiencing vision problems. According to Dr. Jeffrey Anshel, an ophthalmologist and principal of Corporate Vision Consulting, studies have shown that as many at 75 to 90 percent of VDT users experience visual symptoms. He estimates that over 10 million eye examinations are given annually in the

United States for vision problems related to VDT use.[49] One-third of these vision problems are attributed to environmental factors, of which lighting is an important consideration.

The most common qualitative lighting problems associated with VDT use include direct glare (from sunlight and lighting fixtures), reflected glare (from patterns of light and shadow projected off the computer screen), and veiling reflections (from specular surfaces). The most common solutions to such problems before the advent of VDT work spaces were to move the paper, reposition the light source, or change one's viewing position. These solutions are less feasible with computer work because the VDT is in a different position and orientation than was a desktop with paper. The situation is compounded by tasks such as reading and writing, during which we frequently shift our visual focus from one location to another. People frequently adopt unhealthy body positions and visual habits to overcome glare and lighting problems, leading to headaches, strain, and backaches. Poor lighting can also lead to decreased productivity. It is estimated that VDT-related errors cost employers $5 to $10 per square foot annually (versus a typical cost of $1 to $2 per square foot for good lighting).[50]

User control and flexibility are important factors for visual comfort. Occupants should be able to modify the amount of light, respond to changing qualities of light during the day, and control reflections from windows or skylights. These concerns can be addressed by window design, through space planning, and with furnishings and fixtures. Indirect lighting strategies (whether from daylighting, electric lighting, or both) are popular because they minimize the need for lighting control. Even so, window shades, blinds, or other types of treatments are often necessary to control glare and reflections. Daylighting should be integrated with electric lighting systems designed to optimize visual comfort. This is fairly easy today, because many new electric lighting fixtures have been developed specifically for VDT applications. Finally, excessive contrast should be avoided to minimize eyestrain due to varying illuminance levels. Adjustable task lighting can be used if supplemental lighting is needed at the workstation, and lighting control systems can help to balance contrast within the space.

Space planning, equipment, and work habits can also contribute to the perceived quality of daylighting and electric lighting. Furniture that can be easily moved, such as chairs on casters and lightweight adjustable surfaces, enables users to physically respond to lighting conditions. There are often seasonal daylighting issues that can be resolved by repositioning a desk, adjusting a surface, or reorienting a monitor (perpendicular to or at an appropriate angle from the window) to eliminate glare while maintaining adequate illumination for visual tasks. Equipment can also be fitted with screens and filters to reduce glare. Even small steps such as keeping screens and eyeglasses clean can reduce eyestrain.

The quantity of light required for computer use is a controversial issue. In computer rooms, the IESNA recommends a minimum of 5 footcandles for safety; however, they also recommend that illuminance levels not exceed 50 footcandles on the horizontal workplane (in order to do other tasks such as reading).[51] Given the problems associated with glare and reflections, the trend has been to decrease the amount of light in spaces with computers. It is not uncommon to enter a computer lab that is virtually in darkness, with workers or students emerging into the light at lunch and during breaks. The underlying concept is to control VDT glare with lower light levels; however, we should remember that chronobiological studies suggest this type of luminous environment is the biological equivalent of night. While we might control glare with low light levels, are we subjecting occupants to other unanticipated health risks? Computer users should not be banished to dark spaces, particularly those who might spend years or lifetimes in these conditions. The *amount* of light is not the problem, but rather the *quality* of light. If the quality of light is appropriate, illuminance levels can far exceed 50 footcandles. The challenge is to use appropriate daylighting and electric lighting strategies that integrate visual comfort, productivity, energy efficiency, and the various health-related benefits of sunlight.

The PowerGen Headquarters by Bennetts Associates explicitly tried to create a work environment that supported the health and well-being of the building occupants. While decreased energy and resource consumption were essential design concerns, neither was considered more important than the quality of the environment. Many of the design goals used for the project highlighted the importance of daylighting: providing diffuse and evenly distributed daylight, minimizing glare, increasing connections to the natural environment, promoting a sense of well-being, and reduc-

Figure 6.11   Interior atrium at the PowerGen Headquarters.

(Adam Jackaway)

Figure 6.12 View of offices from the atrium at the PowerGen Headquarters.

(Adam Jackaway)

ing electric lighting loads.[52] The central atrium at the heart of this linear building is the primary strategy used to provide bilateral illumination in the office spaces, to create more evenly distributed daylight, and to create a pleasant community space. Louvered exterior overhangs and adjustable interior perforated blinds help to reduce glare from the expansive south glazing. The intentional admission of direct sunlight is limited to areas adjacent to the stair towers in the atrium. This play of sunlight is a welcome contrast to the even, diffuse illumination in the office spaces. Interior blinds are used to control direct sunlight through the south facade during the winter months. Daylighting is particularly abundant on the upper two floors and within the atrium. As a result, electric lighting fixtures are dimmed to compensate for the daylight from the atrium and exterior. After completing a daylighting analysis of the building, Adam Jackaway and David Greene concluded that, "With a simple geometry and a modest budget, the designers have created a beautifully daylit office building. Daylight levels are good throughout, differing little from floor to floor. The building maintains a pleasantly light and open atmosphere. . . . Overall, the building is a joy to visit and, judging by occupant satisfaction . . . , it is a wonderful place to work."[53] (See Figures 6.11 to 6.14.)

Visual relief, variety, and interest in the luminous environment also influence health and well-being. Related concerns include providing views, locating people within close proximity of windows, and creating different qualities and characters of light within the building or space. Providing views is one of the simplest and most beneficial means of promoting well-being. Why are

Figure 6.13 Plan of PowerGen Headquarters.

(Adam Jackaway)

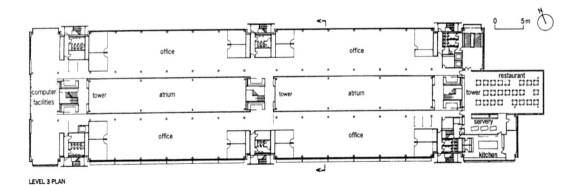

LEVEL 3 PLAN

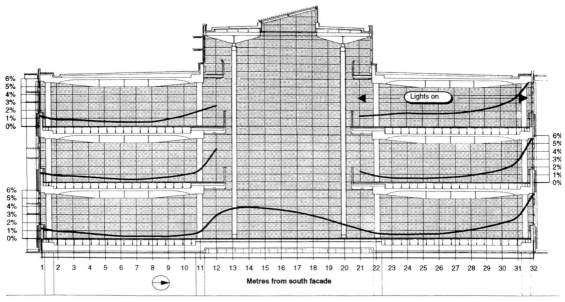

6%
5%
4%
3%
2%
1%
0%

Lights on

6%
5%
4%
3%
2%
1%
0%

6%
5%
4%
3%
2%
1%
0%

1 2 3 4 5 6 7 8 9 10 11 12 13 14 15 16 17 18 19 20 21 22 23 24 25 26 27 28 29 30 31 32

Metres from south facade

Daylight factor measurements by Adam Jackaway, Research in Building Group, University of Westminister

some types of spaces deemed unworthy of daylighting and views (operating rooms, auditoriums, theaters, control rooms, commercial kitchens, rest rooms, storage rooms, and mechanical spaces, to name a few)? Surgeon and writer Dr. Richard Selzer explains his thoughts on the lack of daylighting in contemporary operating rooms:

Figure 6.14 Section with daylight factor measurements of the PowerGen Headquarters.

(Adam Jackaway)

> Not long ago, operating rooms had windows. It was a boon and a blessing in spite of the occasional fly that managed to get in through screens and threaten our sterility. . . . For us who battled on, there was the benediction of the sky, the applause, and reproach of thunder, a divine consultation crackled in on the lightning. At night in emergency, there was the longevity of the stars to deflate a surgeon's ego. It did no patient a disservice to have heaven looking over his doctor's shoulder. I very much fear that having bricked up our windows, we have lost more than the breeze; we have severed a celestial connection.[54]

Windows remind us of our place within the cosmos, enable us to view the weather, and allow us to experience the changing qualities of light and time. Views can also reduce muscle strain by allowing the eyes to shift focus from the near field surrounding the work area to distant objects. Views can also help us physically heal. In a study of gallbladder-surgery patients, it was found that those with views of trees required less medication, had fewer complaints of headaches and nausea, had more positive comments in nurses' notes, and spent less time in the hospital than did patients with a view of a brick wall.[55] A similar study by Judith H. Heerwagen at the University of Washington found, ". . . that people in hospital intensive care units with windows recovered faster than a comparable group recovering in windowless ICUs."[56]

Ulrich's and Heerwagen's research suggests that there is a physiological relationship between views, health, and well-being. Several countries have recognized that views are more than an amenity, as Christine Johnson Coffin explains in her essay "Thick Buildings": "Europeans have taken a stronger stance on workplace windows. In Germany, windows are expected near workstations. In Finland, where at midwinter the few daylight hours occur entirely during the workday, daylighting is a legal requirement in workplaces. The Netherlands also requires windows in workplaces. Indeed, a further Dutch requirement prevents the use of mechanical air conditioning in new structures unless required by machinery or processes."[57] Daylighting should be viewed not as a "privilege," but as a "right" that ensures the physical and psychological well-being of occupants.

A final health consideration concerns the relationships between daylighting, operable windows, and natural ventilation. Although operable windows are rare in large buildings designed during the past several decades, there appears to be renewed interest in their use in commercial applications. The Audubon House in New York City, designed in 1891 by George Post and recently renovated by the Croxton Collaborative, is a large urban office building that includes operable windows and extensive use of daylighting. Workstations are organized around the perimeter of the building to provide daylighting, views to the city, and visual relief. A central atrium balances the sidelighting, provides indirect illumination to adjacent work spaces, and acts as a gathering point for public interaction. In other large buildings with significant wind loads, safety considerations, and poor acoustic and outdoor air quality, operable windows may be inappropriate. Yet a surprising number of new buildings are challenging our preconceptions about the use of operable windows. As we found at the Commerzbank by Foster & Partners, the RWE AG Headquarters, and the GSW Headquarters by Sauerbruch Hutton Architects, double envelopes with interior operable windows can solve problems associated with exterior operable windows (such as wind loads, noise, poor air quality, and safety). For additional information on these projects see Chapter 2.

HEALING ENVIRONMENTS

What distinguishes a pleasant environment from a healing environment? If we explore the difference between "curing" and "healing" we may gain insight into distinctions that can inform the design of the built environment. Dr. Leland Kaiser, Professor Emeritus of the University of Colorado, healthcare consultant, and author, explains: "Curing is scientific, technological, and focused on patients as bodies. Healing is spiritual, experiential, and focused on patients as people. Curing is high tech. Healing is high touch. Healing healthcare institutions integrate both these dimensions in the overall patient experience."[58] Kaiser points out that healing environments are personal; they enrich human experiences, enhance the senses, and let people know they are individuals. Tali Neumann, registered nurse and medical administrator at St. Luke's Episcopal Hospital in Houston, Texas, believes that healing environments make people "feel at home." While there are many definitions of *home,* Neumann refers to a person's sense of belonging, rootedness, and wholeness. This quality should not be misinterpreted to mean that the physical environment is necessarily homelike, but rather that its characteristics and features make people feel welcome, balanced, and at one with the world. According to Neumann (who has worked to implement healing characteristics in the design of healthcare facilities) environmental factors include color, light, texture and pattern, rhythm, balance and emphasis, scale and proportion, symbolism, spirituality, and a sense of community.[59] What can designers learn from healthcare professionals like Kaiser and Neumann? An important lesson may be that healing environments need not be limited to healthcare facilities per se, but that we could all benefit from more healing qualities at home, at work, and within our communities at large. The challenge is to find ways of translating concepts of healing environments into architectural form.

If we revisit architect Eric Asmussen's Vidar Clinic, we find

Figure 6.15 Exterior view of Vidar Clinic with the Baltic Sea in the distance.

(Max Plunger)

unprecedented care and attention paid to health and well-being. Asmussen's work embodies a design theory based on seven principles that provide a framework for creating humane and healing environments. The principles transcend scale and architectural topic—they can inform daylighting as easily as building construction, detailing, or site planning. Subsequently, Asmussen's design theories and principles are helpful in weaving issues of health and well-being into the larger architectural agenda. As previously mentioned, the clinic practices and continues research founded on the anthroposophic principles of Rudolf Steiner. Gary Coates and Susanne Siepl-Coates, who have spent years studying the work of Asmussen, explain the underlying concepts of the Vidar Clinic, "Anthroposophists' care is based on a view of the world in which the human being consists of body, soul, and spirit. . . . In anthroposophy, illness is not seen as a failing of body parts, but as an imbalance between a person's inner and outer world; between the person's physical body and the nonphysical aspects of the body, soul, and spirit. The goal of anthroposophic medicine is to reestablish this balance by engaging the patient in a conscious process of self-healing and spiritual growth."[60] Patients are actively involved in the process of healing and recuperation. Healthcare workers not only attend to needs of patients, but also to those of family and friends.

The seven underlying principles in the work of Asmussen are unity and function; polarity; metamorphosis; harmony with nature and site; the living wall; the dynamic equilibrium of spatial experience; and color luminosity and color perspective. As Gary Coates explains in his book *Erik Asmussen*, the principles should not be viewed as a checklist but rather as a way of understanding design thinking, which at Vidar Clinic results in the creation of a healing environment. Although there are many features to study at the Vidar Clinic, we will focus on the healing lessons and implications of Asmussen's anthroposophic principles as revealed in the daylighting experience in the hospital. (The facility includes an anthroposophic hospital, outpatient clinic, and staff and visitor housing.) Sited in the rolling hills and farmland outside Järna, Sweden, and near the Baltic Sea, the hospital is surrounded by nature and community. The two-story linear building is oriented on a north-south axis. The patient rooms and dayrooms are located in the north and south wings on either side of the centrally located community spaces and outdoor courtyard. Community spaces include mineral and herbal baths and massage rooms in the basement; the entry, administration offices, pharmacy, dining hall, and café on the first floor; and various types of therapy rooms on the upper floor. Staff housing and the out-

Figure 6.16 Site plan of the Vidar Clinic.

(Drawings by Susanne Siepl-Coates; previously published in *Erik Asmussen, Architect* by Gary J. Coates, Byggförlaget, Stockholm, 1997)

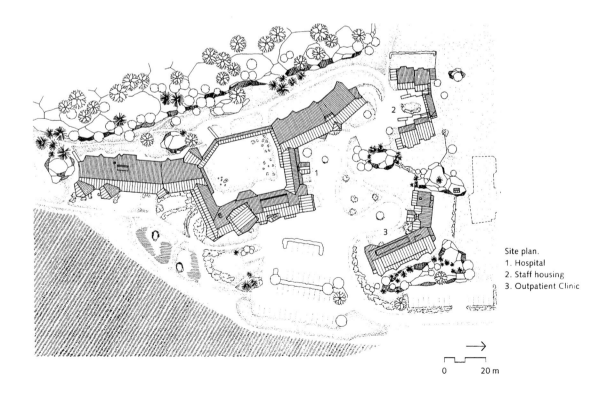

Site plan.
1. Hospital
2. Staff housing
3. Outpatient Clinic

0   20 m

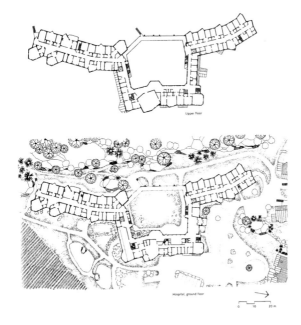

Figure 6.17 Ground-level and upper-floor plans of the Vidar Clinic.

(Drawings by Susanne Siepl-Coates; previously published in *Erik Asmussen, Architect* by Gary J. Coates, Byggförlaget, Stockholm, 1997)

patient clinic are located in separate buildings to the north.

Surrounded by agricultural fields to the east, granite rock outcroppings and trees to the west and south, and the Baltic Sea to the north, the landscape is a critical component of the design and the healing experience. Because the building form, scale, proportions, materials, and colors are more residential than institutional; the building could easily be mistaken for multifamily housing, or perhaps a monastery or retreat center. The building has welcoming and comforting qualities that are reinforced by the low, horizontal building form, articulated roof, varied fenestration and window forms, and warm rose-colored stucco plaster. Asmussen's seven design principles will be used to understand how one might translate health and well-being into design thinking, to explore the place of daylighting within this framework, and to question how this approach to design challenges standard architectural practice. (See Figures 6.15 to 6.18.)

The first principle, "unity of form and function," suggests that form is the vehicle through which function is realized. Function is broadly interpreted to include physical, psychological, social, cultural, and spiritual considerations and activities. As Coates explains, "Asmussen tries to shape his buildings so that they express the inner spirit of the life they contain while supporting in a practical way all the activities that occur within them."[61] For daylighting, this principle suggests that we explore programmatic issues (how light is used, for whom, for what tasks, and to achieve what qualities) from a much broader and more diverse perspective. At the Vidar Clinic this principle is reflected in the way that daylighting is used not only to meet lighting requirements for particular tasks, but also to create rich, luminous qualities, connect patients with nature, and support healing and therapeutic approaches. For example, the daylighting in the patients' rooms was designed to provide views from the patient's

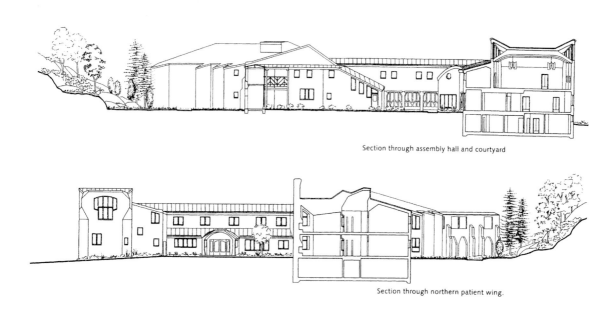

Section through assembly hall and courtyard

Section through northern patient wing.

perspective, ambient illumination, and chromotherapeutic healing. In contrast, the daylighting in the dayroom (Figure 6.19) is used to differentiate areas within the space, to connect with different aspects of the landscape (through views of the sky and site and the admission of site sounds and smells), and to provide different qualities of illumination and social interaction. The three zones within the dayroom have distinct luminous qualities and characteristics. A large clerestory window captures the sky and brings light deep within the space to define the entry and main community space. The second zone is marked by a pool of light from a single window in an alcove that frames a select view to the south and creates a more intimate personal space. Finally, the sunroom is an outwardly focused area that is filled with changing qualities of light. Large sliding windows extend the room into the landscape and connect occupants to the healing properties of nature. The variety of luminous qualities enables patients to find a place within this space with varied qualities and degrees of connection to the community and landscape.

Asmussen's second principle, "polarity," views contrast and opposition not as separate forces that are at odds with each other,

Figure 6.18 Sections through the assembly hall and patient wing.

(Drawings by Susanne Siepl-Coates; previously published in *Erik Asmussen, Architect* by Gary J. Coates, Byggförlaget, Stockholm, 1997)

Figure 6.19 Exterior view of the west facade showing the upper-level dayroom at the Vidar Clinic.

(Max Plunger)

but rather as extremes along a continuum. It emphasizes the notion of interconnections rather than separations. Seemingly disparate architectural expressions and experiences are woven together to enhance human experience and awaken the senses. This principle is evident as one moves through the building or within a single room. Distinct luminous experiences combine to reinforce different types of healing relationships. For example, the lower-level massage rooms and mineral baths have high windows that enhance the experience of being recessed into the earth. The light filtered from above creates a quiet, calming, therapeutic experience that is inwardly focused and connected with the earth. On the first floor, the community space has large glazed doors that admit abundant sunlight in the afternoon and provide physical connection with the gardens. The dynamic and interactive qualities of the light and space reinforce community connections in the hospital cafeteria, café (Figure 6.20), foyer, and adjacent public spaces. In contrast, the assembly room (Figure 6.21) on the upper level has clerestory windows that frame views of the sky to the east and west. The vertical and expansive space is emphasized by the changing qualities of toplighting in the morning and afternoon and is filled with vibrant and dynamic light to support and energize community gatherings. As Siepl-Coates and Coates explain: "The room appears filled by an invisible energy that cannot be contained. The walls swell outward slightly in the middle of the room, and the ceiling pushes upward at its edges, letting daylight stream in through large, clerestory windows."[62] These contrasting experiences are manifested as you move vertically through the building. Yet a variety of luminous experiences

Figure 6.20 View of the hospital cafeteria.

(Max Plunger)

Figure 6.21 View of the
assembly room.
(Max Plunger)

can also be found as you move horizontally through the building and even within a single space. For example, the corridors (Figure 6.22) expand to create small alcoves marked by pockets of daylight in which people can rest and visit. This experience is contrasted by lower illuminance levels, shadows, and electric lighting along the corridor path.

The third principle, "metamorphosis," reflects the transformations of form as found in nature and the unity of parts within a whole. Coates explains, ". . . metamorphosis is an immaterial pattern of relationships that gives unity to parts that are spatially separate and morphologically different."[63] Although there are many exam-

Figure 6.22 View of a corridor at the Vidar Clinic.
(Max Plunger)

ples of metamorphosis at the Vidar Clinic, a daylighting manifestation is reflected in the design of the facades and window detailing. A hierarchy is created as window sizes, forms, and details are varied to reflect the different types of activities behind the facade. The window forms are distinct yet related. For example, rectangular windows of similar width but varying height are used singularly, in groups of two or three, or in multiple clusters depending on whether daylight is needed for small or large rooms. Large keyhole-shaped windows mark special spaces such as the sculpture-therapy room (Figure 6.23). Glazed doors adjacent to the courtyard have the same proportions as nearby windows. The glazed doors also incorporate branchlike mullions that are repeated in the windows of the dayrooms and on the handrails of the arcade. Even the canted corners and lintel above the door are reminiscent of beveled posts on the adjacent stair. Such references between the forms, materials, colors, and details in virtually all aspects of the building contribute to a complexity and richness within the spaces while maintaining an underlying order and unity.

The fourth principle, "harmony with nature and site," suggests that buildings should have a relationship to the environment that is specific to the location, microclimate, and ecological context. There are no generic solutions, only particular responses. The built environment should support, maintain, and even enhance nature and the site. The Vidar Clinic responds to and interacts with the site and nature in many ways. For example, each facade of the building is treated differently to capture and frame particular views of the landscape and qualities of light. The overall building massing extends out into the landscape through thin linear patient wings and also gathers the landscape inside through the courtyard and arcade. The thin form of the building provides access to daylight and views throughout. Windows were carefully designed from the patients' point of view to ensure a healing

Figure 6.23 View of the sculpture-therapy room at the Vidar Clinic.

(Max Plunger)

connection to the site and nature. Corridors periodically open into alcoves to extend space outside and to provide views of the fields and woods, while clerestory windows gather light for the inner portions of the building and connect with the sky. Public spaces open to the courtyard to draw the site and gardens into the interior of the building (Figure 6.24). Therapy rooms frame particular views of the earth, horizon, or sky. Varying degrees of separation or connection create different types of relationships with the site and nature that depend on the types of activities, users, and healing intentions.

Asmussen's fifth principle, "the living wall," suggests that architecture is alive and dynamic, responding to both the occupants and the environment. This concept is expressed in the writing of Rudolf Steiner: "Every wall opens itself, so to speak, through the artistic motifs, to the whole wide world, and one

Figure 6.24 Exterior view of the garden adjacent to the community space at the Vidar Clinic.

(Max Plunger)

enters this building with the consciousness that one is not in a building but in the world: the walls are transparent."[64] Steiner is not suggesting that the walls are literally transparent, but rather that a building can hold or enclose the occupant while still creating a sense of connection to the world. At the Vidar Clinic, the walls mediate between internal and external forces, between the patients and the environment. The courtyard (which is surrounded by common spaces in the central portion of the building, the north and south patient wings, and the western arcade) captures a piece of the site for gardening and community gathering. It serves as a transitional space between the inside and the landscape beyond. The thin western arcade (Figure 6.25) can be used for circulation between patient wings or as a shaded, protected, yet semipublic sitting area. Being neither inside nor outside, the arcade creates a transition between the privacy of the patient rooms and the community and nature at large. With its protective wall on the outside and delicate handrails on the inside, the arcade gestures inward to the courtyard and hospital community. The sheltering roof and large windows cut into the thick outer wall provide protection while still connecting to the site, forest, and granite outcroppings beyond. In contrast, the lower level of the arcade has large arched openings that frame the landscape and provide physical access to the daylight, site, and surrounding forest. The walls of the building, which contain large windows and doors to facilitate an exchange between inside and outside, surround the north, east, and south sides of the courtyard. Variable elements such as shades, drapes, and operable windows are also expressions of the living wall. Asmussen addresses this concept in other compelling ways, but the underlying concept is that the wall (and subsequently the daylight, window, and window treatments) is not static, but rather something dynamic that responds to life within and outside the building.

The sixth principle, "dynamic equilibrium of spatial experience," suggests that contrasting experiences such as up/down, in/out, expansion/contraction, and earth/sky should be juxtaposed yet unified. The concept suggests that while complexity and variety are important, juxtaposition is essential. If we go up, somewhere else we come down. If we experience expansion of space, it is juxtaposed with contraction. If we connect to the earth, somewhere we connect to the sky. For every action there is an equal and opposite reaction. It captures movement and balance. The luminous journey through the building and its varied

Figure 6.25 Exterior view of the garden and west arcade at the Vidar Clinic.
(Max Plunger)

sequence of spaces, colors, and qualities of light may best represent this concept. Throughout the hospital, one finds a juxtaposition of balance and counterpoints. Patterns of light are placed next to places of shadow. Windows direct the eyes upward or outward. There are specially framed views as well as expansive vistas. Soft indirect daylight contrasts with dynamic sunlight. Exuberant high levels of illumination are contrasted with quiet and reserved low levels of illumination. Uniform and irregular distributions of light create dynamic and calm spaces. Daylight interacts with cool and warm colors. Although there are contrasting experiences, there is always a counterpoint that maintains balance and equilibrium.

Finally, the principle of "color luminosity and color perspective" explores the interaction between color, light, and perspective.

The stunning depth of color and light at Vidar Clinic is achieved through the use of the lazure painting method described in the discussion of chromotherapy earlier in this chapter (see Figures 6.1 and 6.2). The particularly luminous and three-dimensional effect results from the interaction of light transmitted through and reflected from thin layers of translucent color. Robert Logsdon compares the color and luminous effect of this painting technique to inherent qualities in nature: "The 'aliveness' of the surface, resulting from the transparent interplay of color, relates to colors found in nature, where monotone does not exist. Monotone is tiring. Variety is enlivening. Nature is dominated by transparent and translucent elements. Think of the sky, the air, the water, clouds, leaves, flowers, feathers of birds, wings of insects and the skin of humans and animals; even slices of wood or stone allow light to pass through."[65] The vibrancy and luminosity of lazure painting—whether reminiscent of nature or simply beautiful in its own right—creates a richness and liveliness that cannot be achieved with opaque paint. Unlike most traditional healthcare facilities, there are no achromatic spaces at Vidar Clinic. Color is choreographed throughout the building to support both the activities and the healing processes.

The seven principles that inform the work of Erik Asmussen suggest the breadth and depth to which issues of health and well-being can be integrated with architectural design. At the Vidar Clinic we find unprecedented attention to human experience and a far broader interpretation of healing and healthful architecture than is commonly found in good, if not outstanding, architectural design. Siepl-Coates and Coates suggest that, "In Asmussen's work, we're looking at a different stream of science, medicine, and architecture."[66] Yet one could also argue that Asmussen's work simply expresses design excellence in which health is integral and not separate from design. Asmussen challenges us to consider health within the language of architectural form, materials, color, and light.

The creation of healing environments will ultimately require an integration of human and technological concerns, as Dr. Leland Kaiser suggested ("Curing is scientific, technological, and focused on patients as bodies. Healing is spiritual, experiential, and focused on patients as people"). As Robert Logsdon explains: "Today we have the advantage of more scientific knowledge, but too often we lose sight of the soul's need for truth, beauty, and goodness. Our goal must be to unite these elements of healing in architecture and in the healing professions."[67] Whether we are considering the use of daylight to treat medical conditions, to reinforce biological needs, to provide visual comfort, or to create healing environments, we must remember that daylighting should always be tailored to the needs of the individual. As David Wyon of the National Swedish Institute for Building Research reminds us: "A healthy building must provide what each individual user of the building requires of it . . . insight, information, and influence."[68] The role of daylighting in healing architecture should not be limited to healthcare facilities, but rather should be found in all architecture. Although daylighting is just one of many architectural issues, its effects on the body, spirit, and mind make it a profoundly important design consideration. Daylight is essential not only to human health and well-being, but also, as Thich Nhat Hanh reminds us, to human survival:

> We have to remember that our body is not limited to what lies within the boundary of our skin. Our body is much more immense. We know that if our heart stops beating, the flow of our life will stop, but we do not take the time to notice that many things outside of our bodies are equally essential for our survival. . . . If the sun were to stop shining, the flow of our life would stop. The sun is our second heart, our heart outside of our body.[69]

ENDNOTES

1. Carol Venolia, *Healing Environments* (Berkeley, Calif.: Celestial Arts, 1988), 7.
2. Fritjof Capra, *The Turning Point: Science, Society, and the Rising Culture* (New York: Simon & Schuster, 1982), quoted in Russell Leslie, "Listening to Lighting's Music," *Lighting Design and Applications* 31, no. 3 (March 1991): 8.
3. U.S. Environmental Protection Agency, Office of Air and Radiation, *Targeting Indoor Air Pollution,* EPA Document #400-R-92-012 (March 1993), 1.
4. Richard Smith, "Light and Health: A Broad Overview," *Lighting Design + Application* 26, no. 2 (February 1986): 38.
5. Ibid., 37.
6. Osteoporosis and Related Bone Diseases National Resource Center, National Osteoporosis Foundation, Washington, D.C.: http:www.osteo.org, Internet.

7. Ibid.

8. *Physician's Desk Reference,* Family Guide Encyclopedia of Medical Care, http://www.healthsquare.com/hspage2.htm, Internet.

9. N. E. Rosenthal et al., "Seasonal Affective Disorder. A Description of the Syndrome and Preliminary Findings with Light Therapy," *Archives of General Psychiatry* 41 (1984): 72–80, in PhotoTherapeutics References, http://www.phothera.com/ptref.htm, Internet.

10. University of British Columbia/Vancouver Hospital and Health Sciences Center Mood Disorders Clinic, "Information about Seasonal Affective Disorder (SAD)," http://www.psychiatry.ubc.ca/mood/md_sad.html, Internet, 1.

11. Dr. Raymond Lam, Department of Psychiatry, Vancouver Hospital and Health Sciences Center, "Seasonal Affective Disorder," *Current Opinion in Psychiatry,* January 1994, http://www.mentalhealt . . . k/p40-sad.html#Head_10, Internet, 2.

12. Ibid.

13. G. L. Faedda et al., "Seasonal Mood Disorders: Patterns of Seasonal Recurrence in Mania and Depression," *Archives of General Psychiatry* 50 (1993): 17–23, quoted in Dr. Raymond Lam, 2.

14. University of British Columbia/Vancouver Hospital and Health Sciences Center Mood Disorders Clinic. A related study at the Harkness Eye Institute, Columbia Presbyterian Medical Center in New York City, concluded that light therapy resulted in about 75 percent clinical remissions. For a discussion of the study see P. F. Gallin et al., "Ophthalmologic Examination of Patients with Seasonal Affective Disorder, before and after Bright Light Therapy," *American Journal of Ophthalmology* 119, no. 2 (Feb. 1995): 202–210, in Photo Therapeutics References, http://www.phothera.com/ptref.htm, Internet.

15. A. J. Lewy et al., "Light Suppresses Melatonin Secretion in Humans," *Science* 21 (1980): 1267–1269, quoted in 1980, cited in George C. Brainard, "The Future Is Now: Implications of the Effect of Light on Hormones, Brain & Behavior, *Journal of Healthcare Design* 7, http://www.healthdesign.org/library/jounal/journal1/j77.htm, Internet, 3.

16. N. E. Rosenthal et al., "A Multicenter Study of the Light Visor for Seasonal Affective Disorder: No Difference in Efficacy

Found Between Two Different Intensities," *Neuropsychopharmacology* 8, no. 2 (Feb. 1993): 151–160, in Photo-Therapeutics References, http://www.phothera.com/ptref.htm, Internet.

17. R. T. Joffe et al., "Light Visor Treatment for Seasonal Affective Disorder: A Multicenter Study," *Psychiatry Research* 46, no. 1 (Jan. 1993): 29–39, in PhotoTherapeutics References, http://www.phothera.com/ptref.htm, Internet.

18. Raymond Lam, 3.

19. Terman et al., "Seasonal Symptom Patterns in New York: Patients and Population," in *Seasonal Affective Disorder,* C. Thompson and T. Silverstone, eds. (London: Clinical Neuroscience Publishers, 1989), 77–95, quoted in George Brainard, "The Future Is Now: Implications of the Effect of Light on Hormones, Brain, & Behavior," *Journal of Healthcare Design,* vol. 7: 4.

20. George Brainard et al., "Architectural Lighting: Balancing Biological Effects with Utility Costs," *The Biologic Effects of Light,* M. R. Holick and E. G. Jung, eds. (New York: Walter de Gruyter & Co., 1994), 169–185.

21. George Brainard, "The Future Is Now: Implications of the Effect of Light on Hormones, Brain, & Behavior," *Journal of Healthcare Design,* vol. 7, http:www.healthdesign.org., Internet, 9.

22. National Science Foundation Center for Biological Timing, http://www.cbt.virginia.edu/tutorial/REFERENCES.html., Internet. This website provides an excellent overview of chronobiology and current research efforts throughout the world.

23. Jurgen Aschoff, "Naps as Integral Parts of the Wake Time within the Human Sleep-Wake Cycle," *Journal of Biological Rhythms* 9 (1994): 145–155, quoted in National Science Foundation Center for Biological Timing.

24. National Science Foundation Center for Biological Timing and George Brainard, "The Future Is Now: Implications of the Effect of Light on Hormones, Brain, & Behavior," 6.

25. Merrill Mitler et al., "Catastrophes, Sleep, and Public Policy: Consensus Report," *Sleep* 11 (1988): 100–109, quoted in National Science Foundation Center for Biological Timing.

26. C. I. Eastman et al., "Light Treatment for Sleep Disorders: Consensus Report, VI. Shift Work," *Journal of Biological Rhythms* 10, no. 2 (June 1995): 157–164.

27. Mark R. Rosenking et al., "Crew Factors in Flight Operations IX: Effects of Planned Cockpit Rest on Crew Performance and Alertness in Long-Haul Operations," *NASA Technical Memorandum No. 108839* (Moffett Field, Calif.: Ames Research Center, 1994), quoted in National Science Foundation Center for Biological Timing.

28. S. S. Campbell et al., "Light Treatment for Sleep Disorders, Consensus Report, III. Alerting and Activating Effects," *Journal of Biological Rhythms* 10, no. 2 (June 1995): 129–132, in PhotoTherapeutics References, http://www.phothera.com/ptref.htm, Internet.

29. Hathaway, Hargreaves, Thompson, and Novitsky, *A Study into the Effects of Light on Children of Elementary School Age—A Case of Daylight Robbery* (Policy and Planning Branch, Planning and Information Services Division, Alberta Education, January 1992), quoted in Michael H. Nicklas and Gary B. Bailey, "Analysis of the Performance of Students in Daylit Schools," *Proceedings of the 21st National Passive Solar Conference* (Boulder, Colo.: American Solar Energy Society, 1996), 133.

30. Ibid., 137.

31. Diane Ackerman, *A Natural History of the Senses* (New York: Vintage Books, 1990), 255.

32. Leonard Shlain, *Art & Physics: Parallel Vision in Space, Time & Light* (New York: William Morrow & Co., 1991), 171.

33. Gary J. Coates, *Erik Asmussen, Architect* (Stockholm: Byggförlaget, 1997), 198.

34. Robert M. Logsdon, "The Human Side: Understanding the Application of Lazure Painting Techniques," *Journal of Healthcare Design,* vol. 7, http://www.healthdesign.org/library/journal/journal7/j728.htm, Internet, 7.

35. Gary J. Coates and Susanne Siepl-Coates, "New Design Technologies: Healing Architecture—A Case Study of the Vidarkliniken," *Journal of Healthcare Design,* vol. 8, http://www.healthdesign.org/library/journal/journal8/j817.htm, Internet, 7.

36. Gary Coates, 130–131.

37. According to lighting designer Craig Roeder, the chromotherapeutic applications of color include the following: red vitalizes and is associated with hemoglobin and liver; orange is associated with muscle spasms or cramps, is calcium-building, enhances body metabolism, and strengthens lungs;

yellow is stimulating and cleansing and is associated with nerves, the brain, and motor stimulation; green is cooling, soothing, and calming, is associated with the sympathetic nervous system, relieves tension, and lowers blood pressure; blue is cold, electrical, has contracting potencies associated with arteries, veins, and blood pressure, and is an anticarcinogenic; purple is the color of anger, divinity, and royalty and is associated with the spleen, blood purification, heart, and motor nerves. For additional information see Craig Roeder, "Environmental Design Technology: Using Color & Light as Medicine," *Journal of Healthcare Design,* vol. 8, http://www .healthdesign.org/library/journal/journal8/j821.htm., Internet, 5–6.

38. Tali Neumann, "Design Trends: Creating a Healing Health-care Environment, *Journal of Healthcare Design,* vol. 7, http://www.healthdesign.org/library/journal/journal7/j712 .htm, Internet, 4.

39. The United States Environmental Protection Agency, Office of Radiation and Indoor Air (6607J), *Indoor Air Facts No. 4* (revised) (Washington, D.C.: EPA Office of Air and Radiation, April 1991), 1.

40. Ibid.

41. U.S. Environmental Protection Agency, Office of Air and Radiation (6601), *Targeting Indoor Air Pollution:* 3.

42. John Bruening, *See the Light: Good Lighting Balances Sources,* http://www.meadhatcher.com., Internet, 2.

43. Carl Gardner and Barry Hannaford, *Lighting Design* (N.Y.: John Wiley & Sons, 1993), 185.

44. Alan Hedge, *Indoor Air Quality and 'Sick' Building Syndrome in Offices,* Mead-Hatcher, Inc., Ergonomic Articles, http:// www.meadhatcher.com/sick.html, Internet, 4.

45. The United States Environmental Protection Agency, Office of Air and Radiation, Indoor Environments Division, *An Office Building Occupant's Guide to Indoor Air Quality,* EPA-402-K-97-003 (Washington, D.C.: October 1997), 7–8.

46. Mark S. Rae, ed., *Lighting Handbook* (New York: Illuminating Engineering Society of North America, 1995).

47. Dr. Jeffrey Anshel, Computer Vision Syndrome: Causes & Cures," *Managing Office Technology,* July 1997, http://www .meadhatcher.com., Internet, 4.

48. Ibid., 1.

49. Ibid.
50. L. Lamarre, "Lighting the Office Environment," *Electric Power Research Journal,* Electric Power Research Institute (October 1996): 16–39, quoted in David Breeding, *Surveying Office Illumination,* nttp://www.meadhatcher.com, Internet, 2.
51. Mark S. Rae, ed., 535, 538.
52. Adam Jackaway and David Greene, "PowerGen in the Light of Day," *The Architects' Journal* (14 March 1996): 46.
53. Ibid., 47
54. Bernie S. Siegel, "Healthcare Design in the Next Century," *Journal of Healthcare Design,* vol. 7, http://www.healthdesign.org/library/journal/journal7/j72.htm, Internet, 1–2.
55. Tali Neumann, 6.
56. Jacqueline Vischer, "The Psychology of Daylighting," *Architecture* 76, no. 1 (June 1987): 110.
57. Christine Johnson Coffin, "Thick Buildings," *Places* 9, no. 3 (winter 1995): 71.
58. Robin Orr, "Design Quality: Designing for the Human Side of Healthcare," *Journal of Healthcare Design,* vol. 6, http://www.healthdesign.org/library/journal/journal6/j620.htm, Internet.
59. Tali Neumann, 4–13.
60. Gary J. Coates and Susanne Siepl-Coates, 5.
61. Gary Coates, 186.
62. Gary J. Coates and Susanne Siepl-Coates, 8.
63. Gary Coates, 190.
64. Ibid., 196.
65. Robert M. Logsdon, 2.
66. Gary J. Coates and Susanne Siepl-Coates, 2.
67. Robert M. Logsdon, 2.
68. D. P. Wyon, "The Ergonomics of Healthy Buildings: Overcoming Barriers to Productivity," *IAQ '91* (Washington, D.C.: ASHRAE, 1991), 449.
69. Thich Nhat Hanh, "Love in Action," in *The Soul of Nature,* edited by M. Tobias (New York: Penguin Books, 1996), 131.

Chapter 7

Consider Quality of Life

Ecology is the mysterious work of providing home for the soul, one that is felt in the very depths of the heart. . . . Once we have the imagination that sees home in such a profound and far-reaching sense, protection of that environment will follow, for ecology is a state of mind, an attitude, and a posture that begins at the very place you find yourself this minute, and extends to places you will never see in your lifetime. . . .[1]

—THOMAS MOORE

Despite many technical and scientific advances, we have a limited understanding of how daylighting affects us. Alvar Aalto reminds us that human experiences, even those that are intangible, should not be overlooked: "In recent decades, architecture has often been compared with science, and some have tried to make its methods more scientific, even to transform it into pure science. But architecture is not a science. It is still the same great synthetic process, a conglomeration of thousands of significant human functions, and it will stay that way. Its essence can never become purely analytical. Architectural study always involves a moment of art and instinct. Its purpose is still to bring the world of matter into harmony with human life."[2]

Quantitative standards (such as recommended footcandles, daylight factors, or contrast ratios) are but one measure of successful daylighting design. Even these seemingly tangible criteria change with time and insight. For example, the illuminance levels recommended by the Illuminating Engineering Society of North America (IESNA) have decreased over the past 50 years as lighting designers have begun to understand that the quality of light is as important as the quantity. Some would even argue that qualitative issues should take precedence, as Christopher Day suggests in *Places of the Soul:* ". . . failure to nourish the soul is experienced also as a failure to provide the right physical environment, even though the instruments say otherwise. The qualities of environment are more important than their quantity."[3] Christopher Day implies that the challenge of architectural design is to create meaningful human experiences. It is not enough for architecture to support the human body; it must also support the human spirit.

Quality of life is a subjective concept; what constitutes "quality" will differ from person to person. In *Envisioning a Sustainable Society,* Lester Milbrath, professor of sociology and political science at State University of New York (SUNY) in Buffalo, provides the following thoughts: "Quality in living is experienced only by individuals and is *necessarily* subjective. Objective conditions may contribute to or detract from the experience of quality but human reactions are not automatic to physical conditions; the experience occurs only subjectively. . . . Quality is not a constant state but a variable ranging from high quality to low quality. . . ." Milbrath goes on to explain that "people generally experience a high quality of life when they have a sense of long-term happiness, physical well-being, completeness or fullness of life, and anticipation of life's unfolding drama (hope and confidence)."[4]

Happiness, well-being, completeness, fullness, and hope are as difficult to quantify as they are to translate into architecture and daylighting design. We have all had luminous experiences that either supported or undermined our sense of happiness, well-being, hope, and even confidence. Consider the quality-of-life implications of a simple office window. How would your quality of life be affected if your office window overlooked a public square, a garden, a loading dock, or a brick wall? How would you be affected if the window were operable, nonoperable, broken, or boarded up? Would it matter if the window were clear, translucent, or transparent? Would you care if it had blinds or good thermal characteristics? What if the window were located high above your head or low to the floor? What if there were no window in your office? We know intuitively that daylighting can make architecture more meaningful, pleasant, reassuring, supportive, and healthy in all senses of the word. The challenge is to determine how these ends can be achieved.

Our relationships between each other and our environment are fundamental to a high quality of life. As Roslyn Lindheim explains in "New Design Parameters for Healthy Places," various types of connections are essential for humans: "Studies of people who get sick most often and most seriously indicate that the people in these groups are in some way 'out of connection' and lack meaningful social and natural connectedness."[5] Lester Milbrath suggests that these connections are not only beneficial to humans, but also to the larger ecological community of which we are part: "Almost without exception, humans need to belong to a community where they are valued and loved. This gives them a sense of security and identity. In return, they empathize with and extend compassion to others in their community; this feeling often extends to all the creatures in the biocommunity."[6] Quality of life has ecological implications. Thomas Moore suggests this in slightly different terms when he says "ecology is the work of providing home for the soul. . . . Once we have the imagination that sees home in such a profound and far-reaching sense, protection of that environment will follow. . . ." Quality of life implies connections to other people, the natural environment, and for some, the sacred and spiritual in daily life. This chapter will consider how daylighting can be a means of supporting social, environmental, and even spiritual connections to enhance quality of life.

SOCIAL CONNECTIONS

In her essay "New Design Parameters for Healthy Places," Roslyn Lindheim discusses seven factors that contribute to people's sense of connectedness.[7] The first three environmental design factors—social connectedness; hierarchy, self-esteem, and meaning; and participation and control—also provide an excellent framework for reconsidering the social implications of daylighting. They will be used as a point of departure for the following discussion. First, we will consider how daylighting encourages us to meet and gather in different ways, how daylighting can shape and influence our social connectedness. Next, we will address how daylighting supports or undermines social hierarchies and power structures. Finally, we will investigate how daylighting either encourages or discourages people to participate in and interact with their social, built, and natural environments.

Human Contact

People gather in places with distinct qualities of light. In a warm climate, people might pause under the dappled light of a tree-lined plaza; in a cold climate, they might sit in a pool of warm sunlight from a south-facing window. If you watch any public space, you will find people migrating to different locations as the sun and shade move during the course of a day. Daylight obviously influences our movement through space, but can it also shape our social interactions? Can daylighting encourage people to pause, sit, talk, gather, or interact in different ways? If so, what characteristics and qualities of light encourage different types of social interaction?

Just as we need shelter, food, and water, we also need human contact and social interactions. In *Places of the Soul,* architect Christopher Day argues that: "To quite a large extent *how* people meet is supported or hindered by the environment."[8] Consider what types of places and particularly what "places of light" you are drawn to for different types of social interactions. Which places of light support a quiet conversation, a lively debate, learning, reflection, or a celebration? Which places of light support small or large groups? Professor J. Stephen Weeks of the Univer-

Figure 7.1 Reading carrels at Exeter Library.

(J. Stephen Weeks)

sity of Minnesota distinguishes between "the place for one, the few, and the many." This is a useful hierarchy for understanding the relationship between scale, social activity, and potential characteristics of the physical environment.

At times, we desire a place for "one," which may be a solitary refuge for reflection, concentration, introspection, or observation (perhaps a place to watch people while still feeling part of a larger community). The place of light for one is an intimate experience. It can be found in the reading carrels designed by Louis Kahn at the Exeter Library. Each study area is defined by a personal space of light within a public realm. On the other hand, it may be within the quiet shadows of the thin vertical space between the book stacks at Exeter, where a person searches these narrow chasms in solitude. At other times, we come together as a "few" in more communal activities—to interact, to talk, to visit, or to play. These places of light might contain pockets or pools of light and shadow that gather and hold several people. The low horizontal windows in Tadao Ando's Soseikan Tea House wash the floor surface

Figure 7.2   Interior rendering of the Soseikan Tea House.

to define a space of light for the master of the tea ceremony and the seated participants. Light is concentrated along the low horizontal surface of the floor where people are seated, while shadow envelops the ceremony. Finally, we gather as a larger community of "many" to celebrate, to debate, or to share a public experience. Public places of light unify and draw people together. The expansive west glazing in the reception area/gallery of Frank Gehry's Weisman Art Museum defines a volume of light that surrounds the visitors and provides visual connections to the Mississippi River, Minneapolis skyline, and larger community. The administrative space above the reception area has an interior wall just inside the west facade. This double layer creates a thin vertical slot on the interior of the west facade. Patterns of light and

Figure 7.3   West facade of the Weisman Art Museum.

(Rosemary D. Dolata)

Figure 7.4   Reception
area behind the west
facade of the Weisman
Art Museum.

(Rosemary D. Dolata)

Figure 7.5 View of the slot behind the west facade of the Weisman Art Museum.

(Rosemary D. Dolata)

shadow, changing color, and views of the sky can be seen within the slot from both the upper and lower levels. Direct sunlight, high quantities of illumination, and a wide distribution unify the space and people within. (See Figures 7.1 to 7.5.)

Alexandra Tyng explains:

> Kahn described the room as a living entity created by people. Because it is alive, it is sensitive to what goes on inside it. The form idea of each room should be so clearly stated that the room automatically implies its use. One's own room is a personal space in which one can be alone to think, whereas a large room is a space for collective events, for communication between people. Moreover, since the room is alive, it can adjust itself to the moment. Kahn suggested that, if a personal conversation took place inside a large room, the walls would move inward to form a more intimate space.[9]

As we discussed in Chapter 4, the Newton Library in Surrey, British Columbia, designed by Patkau Architects, creates a variety of luminous experiences that correspond with different types of social connections. Sited in a suburban area south of Vancouver that has no town center, the library provides a place for people to gather, to interact, and to build community. The rectilinear mass of the library contains an information area, library stacks, and public reading areas. Smaller, more intimate spaces periodi-

Figure 7.6 View of the south reading carrels at the Newton Library.

(James Dow)

cally project out of the building mass to provide intimate spaces for staff, small groups, and individuals. A central circulation spine slices through the building to define a northern and southern zone. Support and staff spaces as well as periodicals and computer stations are located to the north. The public reading areas, book stacks, and small reading niches are located to the south. The roof gestures upward on either side of the circulation spine to gather daylight from the north and south. An expansive two-story curtain wall on the north is punctured by the mass of the smaller offices and support spaces (which contain more-discreet windows at the corners of the rooms). The large northern curtain wall admits abundant indirect daylight, which contrasts with the smaller windows, shading devices, and controlled admission of light on the south.

Different areas of the library have distinct moods and characters of light. The periodical area in the northwest corner of the building has an open, spacious, and extroverted quality of light created by a two-story curtain wall that visually connects the inside to the outside and admits high quantities of illumination. The soft indirect northern light defines a volume of space for a community of people. In contrast, the south side of the library has two distinctly different experiences of light. A series of niches protrude from the south facade to capture intimate volumes of light for individuals and small groups. In the small niches, the window, desk, and structure are gracefully integrated to define a personal space of light. A perforated ventilation grille is inserted into the view window (with the sill placed at desk height). External shading devices provide solar control as needed. Two larger niches for small groups are located at the west and east ends of the south facade.

In contrast to the small windows in the individual niches, the glazing in the group areas extends from floor to ceiling. The large windows spanning from floor to ceiling admit high illuminance levels and create a strong connection between inside and outside. Adjustable task lighting provides supplemental illumination in both types of niches. The area immediately behind the reading niches, which contains the book stacks and large public reading tables, has yet another quality of light. In this area, south clerestory windows bring soft ambient illumination deep into the space. Interior blinds can be adjusted to control the quantity and

Figure 7.7 View of the north reading area at the Newton Library.

(James Dow)

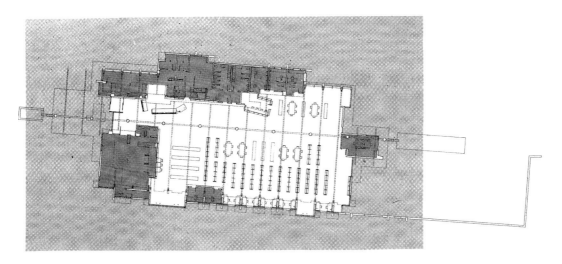

Floor Plan

1	circulation desk	8	adults' library workroom
2	multipurpose room	9	adults' librarian
3	circulation workroom	10	chief librarian
4	shipping/receiving	11	computer room
5	janitor's room	12	children's librarian
6	circulation supervisor	13	children's library workroom
7	staff room	14	seminar room

Figure 7.8   Plan of the Newton Library.

(Patkau Architects)

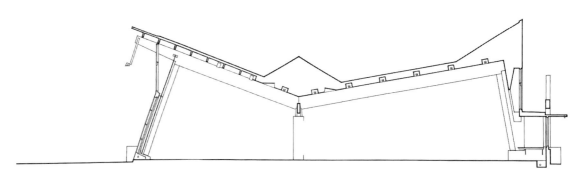

Figure 7.9   Section of the Newton Library.

(Patkau Architects)

quality of daylight or sunlight. Finally, the windows on the south-west corner and west facade admit sidelighting to a multipurpose room and entry. Small view windows frame the landscape, while floor-to-ceiling windows minimize the distinction between the inside and outside. Although daylighting is just one aspect of the design that supports social connections, it illustrates that window sizes, forms, and detailing can help create unique places of light in which the individual comes together with the community. As Doug Aberly explains in his essay "Inventing the Sustainable City": "To survive, humans must have shelter. To *flourish* humans need community—a physical stage upon which all the drama of our kind can be played."[10] (See Figures 7.6 to 7.9.)

Hierarchy and Power

In his essay "An Outline for an Ecological Politics," Murray Bookchin explores the social implications of hierarchy and power from an ecological perspective:

> Over the centuries social conflicts have fostered the development of hier-archies and classes based on domination and exploitation in which the great majority of human beings have been as ruthlessly abused as the nat-ural world itself. Social ecology carefully focuses this social history and reveals that the very *idea* of dominating nature stems from the domination of human by human. . . . Thus, social ecologists understand that until we undertake the project of liberating human beings from domination and hierarchy—economic exploitation and class rule, as orthodox socialists would have it—our chances of saving the wild areas of the planet and wildlife are remote at best.[11]

For better or worse, we live in a society that is, to a great extent, hierarchically structured and governed by force and power. Is there a way in which power (and the resulting hierarchies) can be reconsidered and restructured to build communities and foster social connections?

How might these issues be related to daylighting design? Roslyn Lindheim reminds us that daylight can be equated with power: "The design of the built environment constantly reminds us of our position in every hierarchy. The size and quality of space have always been indicators of social status, whether it is the size of a house, the exclusiveness of a neighborhood, or the proximity to a window in an office building. . . . The location of the secretarial office is routinely predictable: the boss occupies the outer office with the windows and views; the support staff is clustered in the interior."[12] Daylight can be a status symbol associated with prestige. The rent for an apartment is often influenced by access to light and views—with the most expensive spaces typically having the best access to both. In office buildings with open plans, the people with seniority typically get the seat by the window. Ask any architecture student who gets the desk with the view and you find it is usually the fastest and strongest. When given the choice, most people would select a window seat, yet power often determines who has the greatest access to daylight.

The political implications of light are reflected in the value our society places on access to daylight. As Fuller Moore explains in *Concepts and Practice of Architectural Daylighting,* this concern has been reflected in zoning regulations throughout history: "The ancient Greeks and Romans mandated minimum lighting standards for their cities. The British Law of Ancient Lights (which dates to 1189) and its later embodiment into statue law, The Prescription Act of 1832, provided that if a window enjoyed uninterrupted access to daylight for a twenty-year period, right to that access became permanent."[13] In cities such as Seattle and San Francisco, recent zoning regulations use height restrictions to prevent new construction from infringing on daylighting access and views for existing buildings. Other countries approach the problem of daylight access from the inside. In European countries such as Germany, Finland, Sweden, and Denmark it is expected that employees will be located near windows; some even mandate that the position of a workstation be no farther than 6 to 7 meters (approximately 20 feet) from a window.[14] Though we may rarely consider who gets access to daylight, the inequities in its distribution influence our well-being and perceptions of ourselves within the larger community. The question to consider is how daylighting design can create environments that build community, encourage interaction rather than separation, foster social connections, and subsequently enhance our quality of life.

Several precedents from preceding chapters are useful in reconsidering the hierarchical implications of daylight, particularly in the work environment. The SEI Headquarters by Meyer, Scherer & Rockcastle; the Allopro Administration Building by Jürgen Hansen and Ralf Petersen; and the GSW Headquarters by Sauerbruch Hutton Architects ensure that all employees have access to daylight regardless of their job title. Strategies which minimize a hierarchical approach to daylight include placing workstations close to window walls, planning for daylight access, providing flexible furnishings, and using thin building plans and sections.

In contrast, as we saw in Chapter 3, the SEI Headquarters uses an open-office plan, in which all employees share the same space and have the same access to daylight. The width of the space is designed to ensure that no employee is farther than 32 feet from the window wall. Flexible furnishing and an easily accessible power/data system allow employees to easily reconfigure teams. SEI, a financial services company, also has challenged the typical office hierarchy. First, there are no secretaries—everyone does his or her own work, from faxing a letter to making a plane reservation. No one has a private office; even Al West, the chairman of SEI, is located in the same space as other employees (and yes, he has to do his own secretarial work). All employees have identical desks, no special furnishings for upper management. Great attention was given to the furniture design, comprising a variety of tables, desks, and electronic components that enable teams to be easily reconfigured. SEI values collaboration and found that flexible space, abundant ambient daylight, and flexible furniture were the best ways to facilitate teamwork. Jeff Scherer, from Meyer, Scherer & Rockcastle, explains several ways that SEI redefines hierarchy through the built environment. All workplace relationships are established by the core team; individuals fine-tune their own space; and workstations are essentially identical. He also explains that the simplicity and flexibility of the spaces enable complexity, the exchange of ideas (rather than protection of turf), and renewal (rather than repetition).[15] As corporations explore new work models and tear down old hierarchies, the physical and social structure of the workplace will need to respond to new and unanticipated changes. The following comment by SEI Chairman Al West applies as much to the social environment as to the physical environment: "Tear it down in ten years because it will not be right in that period of time. Based on the feeling that we are in the midst of a major transition in the way we work and the certainty that we are bound to be wrong."[16] The challenge is to provide conditions that support the changing social structure of work while creating architecture that is enduring and built to last.

The role of daylighting in learning environments is also being reconsidered. We need only look at the windowless schools of the 1960s and 1970s to see how the exclusion of daylight was perceived as a way to control and exert power over students' behavior. This desire to control student behavior, mandated from the top down, had negative effects on students and teachers. Fortunately, we find an increasing number of projects such as the Seabird Island School by Patkau Architects and the Durant Middle School by Innovative Design (both of which were discussed earlier) that illustrate the contributions of daylight in creating supportive and productive learning environments.

The increased attention to daylight in building types such as offices, schools, and medical facilities is representative of a growing concern about the effect of light on the quality of our built environments. The warrens of office cubicles, windows remotely located, and nonoperable windows, as well as the black-box schools of past decades, are being reconsidered to ensure that the needs of the individual and the community are recognized through architectural design. In *Places of the Soul,* Christopher Day speculates on the importance of acknowledging the individual in architectural design: ". . . I doubt if anything contributes so much to social malaise as anonymity—the feeling that you know nobody and nobody cares whether they know you."[17] Daylight and views have been perceived by some designers or clients as superfluous, unnecessary, or as a means of control over the occupants. Windowless environments (whether in offices, schools, hospitals, jails, or other building types) only contribute to dissatisfaction and a loss of individuality and self-control. We can only hope that the daylighting lessons from the past and the promise of new precedents will help to create environments that support the individual as well as the community.

Participation and Influence

Our ability to influence, modify, and interact with our environment also contributes to a higher quality of life. In *Lessons for Students in Architecture,* Herman Hertzberger states: "Architecture should offer an incentive to its users to influence it wherever possible, not merely to reinforce its identity, but more especially to enhance and affirm the identity of the users."[18] When we interact with architecture, it is often in response to changing activities, tasks, or environmental conditions. Our ability to change or mod-

Figure 7.10   View of the curtain wall in a typical office at RWE AG Headquarters.

(Holger Knauf)

ify the physical environment has effects on our relationships with each other, the natural environment, and the building itself. Even a simple adjustment to a window blind influences a variety of factors such as privacy, views, and the quality of luminous and thermal comfort. Allowing users to participate and interact with architecture has social and environmental implications. For example, each person has his or her own luminous and thermal preferences and comfort zones, yet we often share spaces with other individuals (each of whom also has individual preferences). Can or should spaces be designed to allow the individual to modify his or her luminous or thermal environment without infringing on the comfort of others? Can daylighting be designed to provide comfort for an individual as well as a community? Alvar Aalto reminds us of the challenge and importance of reconciling both the needs of the individual and the needs of the community: "Regardless of which social system prevails in the world or its parts, a softening human touch is needed to mold societies, cities, buildings, and even the smallest machine-made objects into something positive to the human psyche, without bringing individual freedom and the common good into conflict. . . . Architecture must be deeply rooted in place and circumstance; it requires a delicate sense of form; it must support man's emotional life."[19]

Figure 7.11 Detail view of control panels in an office at RWE AG Headquarters.

(Holger Knauf)

If we return to the RWE AG Headquarters in Essen, Germany, and the offices for Josef Gartner & Sons in Gundelfingen, Germany, we find daylighting strategies that support both the "individual freedom and the common good" to which Aalto alludes. (See Chapter 5 for a discussion of the daylighting technology used in these projects.) Both buildings have a technological aesthetic that may at first appear cold, if not harsh. Yet within this aesthetic lie humanizing elements which enable occupants to control their environment in ways that are rarely found in office buildings. At the RWE AG Headquarters, the design of the building envelope and its integration with the mechanical systems allow an unusual degree of occupant interaction. The envelope comprises a single pane of fixed glazing, a 20-inch buffer space with adjustable blinds, and interior sliding-glass doors (which can be opened to admit natural ventilation or thermal gains). Although a physical connection to the environment is limited by the fixed exterior glazing, a high degree of interaction between the occupants and the outside has been retained through the admission of abundant daylight, views, and natural ventilation. Control panels within each office allow occupants to adjust the blinds, electric lighting, ventilation louvers, and temperature within each office. When visiting the building, architect Mary Pepchinski observed the following: "On a typical office floor, occupants were using the controls to set rooms to different temperatures. The movable facade panels were easily unlocked and slid open with a crank. When open, however, wind noise was extremely loud. The natural-ventilation scheme appeared to deliver air that was both cool and fresh. The offices were very bright thanks to the floor-to-ceiling glazing, which also provided spectacular views over the city."[20] The offices are located along the perimeter of the building to ensure maximum daylight, natural ventilation, and views for all employees. Rather

Figure 7.12   Exterior view of the rooftop terrace and adjacent conference room at RWE AG Headquarters.

(Holger Knauf)

than the large, open plans so common in many office buildings, the RWE AG Headquarters is divided into small private and semi-private offices. These offices, coupled with easily accessible control systems, allow occupants to modify the luminous and thermal environment to meet their own needs without compromising the needs of others. Amenities that improve the quality of the work environment include a ground-level cafeteria and garden as well as a rooftop terrace overlooking the city. The rooftop conference room is filled with light and views of the sky. (See Figures 7.10 to 7.12.)

The office for Josef Gartner & Sons is much smaller in scale and consequently provides greater connection to the natural environment. The long, linear, two-story building is oriented to maximize solar access and control. In contrast to the private offices at the RWE AG Headquarters, the open offices at Josef Gartner & Sons are located along the perimeter of the building and adjacent to a centrally located atrium. Visual and physical connections to the environment are maximized for all employees. Although a computerized building-management system regulates overall luminous and thermal systems, occupants can fine-tune their environments. External and internal operable shading enables occupants to modify their views, illuminance levels, the quality of light, and luminous and thermal comfort. Operable windows enable occupants to adjust natural ventilation at their desks and to admit the sounds and smells of the site. Task lighting can be adjusted based on the available daylight and seasonal considerations. All employees have the ability to modify daylighting, ventilation, thermal gains, and electric lighting. (See Figures 7.13 and 7.14.)

Despite their different approaches, both of these buildings strive to provide individuals with the ability to influence the built environment. While the strategies may seem commonsense and straightforward, they stand in contrast to the approaches found in generations of workplaces which have provided few, if any, opportunities for human participation and influence. Seemingly insignificant design decisions such as the use of operable windows, dynamic shading devices, and adjustable task lighting can make a significant difference in the ability of an individual to participate in his or her environment. We would all benefit by heeding the words of

Figure 7.13 Interior view of an office area showing shading devices at Josef Gartner & Sons.

(Josef Gartner & Sons)

Figure 7.14 Exterior view of office with shading devices at Josef Gartner & Sons.

(Josef Gartner & Sons)

cellist Pablo Casals, who reminds us: "To live is not enough, we must take part."[21]

ENVIRONMENTAL CONNECTIONS

Human existence is moderated, defined, and perceived through the senses. Our understanding of life's richness and diversity is captured through the subtle complexities of touch, vision, hearing, smell, and taste. We understand a place by touching the surfaces, seeing the colors and qualities of light, and hearing the sounds which fill the spaces. We hear the gentle movement of wind in the trees; we smell a coming rainstorm long before it arrives; and we see the brilliance of reflected light on new-fallen snow. John Rader Platt, professor of physics at the University of Chicago, argues that our very survival is dependent on the stimulation of the senses: "The needs of man, if life is to survive, are usually said to be four—air, water, food, and in the severe climates, protection. But it is becoming clear today that the human organism has another absolute necessity. . . . This fifth need is the need for novelty—the need, throughout our waking life, for continuous variety in the external stimulation of our eyes, ears, sense organs, and all our nervous network."[22] The quality of our environmental experiences is defined by a multitude of sensuous stimuli related to the physical environment: brightness, color, texture, the properties of materials, temperature, and so forth. Sight, sound, touch, and vision each act as a threshold through which we gather information concerning our built and natural environments. Our senses allow us to feel, to experience life, to explore who we are, and to understand where we live. Michael Hough believes that: "Understanding place begins with feeling. Names conjure up a kaleidoscope of distinct unique sensory images; random, disconnected smells, sounds, and sights crowd our memories."[23]

Our aesthetic judgments (what we perceive to be beautiful, pleasing, or harmonious) are also linked to the senses. Yi-Fu Tuan explains in *Passing Strange and Wonderful,* ". . . the pervasive role of the aesthetic is suggested by its root meaning of 'feeling'— not just any kind of feeling, but 'shaped' feeling and sensitive perception. And it is suggested even more by its opposite, anesthetic, 'lack of feeling'—the condition of living death. The more attuned to the beauties of the world, the more we come to life and take joy in it."[24] One could argue that, to a great extent, a high quality of life involves aesthetic experiences that engage the natural and built environments through our perceptions and through the "feelings" made manifest by the five senses.

Some argue that vision is the most important sense in daylighting design, for it enables us to perceive our environment, to judge depth, distance, color, and to read textures and materials. Yet touch and hearing are also related to daylighting design, for windows admit the warmth of the sun, the feel of the wind, and the sounds of the site—all of which are experienced by different senses within the body. Diane Ackerman argues that our senses also connect us to a larger ecological whole: "Our several senses, which feel so personal and impromptu, and seem at times to divorce us from other people, reach far beyond us. They're an extension of the genetic chain that connects us to everyone who has ever lived; they bind us to other people and to animals, across time and country and happenstance. They bridge the personal and the impersonal, the one private soul with its many relatives, the individual with the universe, all of life on Earth."[25]

Figure 7.15 Exterior view of the south facade of the house at Bingie Point.

(Max Dupain)

Figure 7.16 Exterior view of the north facade of the house at Bingie Point.

(Max Dupain)

Two residential projects by Glenn Murcutt reveal how the relationship between our senses and daylighting design can foster a more comprehensive understanding of ourselves, the world in which we live, and as Diane Ackerman suggests, perhaps our larger ecological context. The two projects, the Bingie Point and Paddington Houses, were designed for the same client. Bingie Point is a rural site, while Paddington is an urban location, yet both projects create opportunities for the occupants to engage the environment through the senses. Vision, touch, and hearing (and their relationships to daylighting and thermal and acoustic design) foster environmental connections through the architecture. The projects also demonstrate that both rural and urban environments can provide compelling sensuous experiences that are deeply informed by the environment and the natural forces that shape our daily lives.

Rural Environments

The house at Bingie Point is one of the most familiar and elegant of Murcutt's designs. The structure was designed as a family vacation retreat in an isolated region of the Pacific coast to the south of Sydney. The landscape is stark and exposed to the coastal climate. The ocean, a small lake, grass tussocks, and exposed rock define the immediate environs, while the horizon and expansive vistas dominate the landscape. The concept for the house was to capture the qualitative experiences of camping on the site. According to Murcutt, ". . . My clients had often camped on this land before they came into possession of it in '75 and had in this way come to love its topography and contact with natural elements. They did not want an urban or suburban home, nor a farm. They . . . had in mind instead a space that would retain the atmosphere of their camping experiences."[26] Murcutt was able to achieve

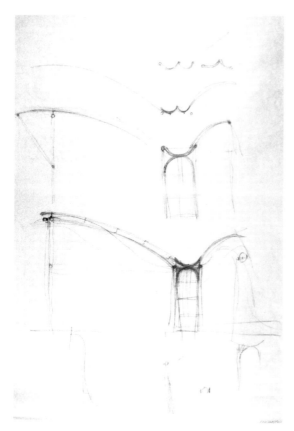

Figure 7.17 Conceptual sketch of the house at Bingie Point by Glenn Murcutt.

(Glenn Murcutt, from the collection of the Mitchell Library, State Library of New South Wales)

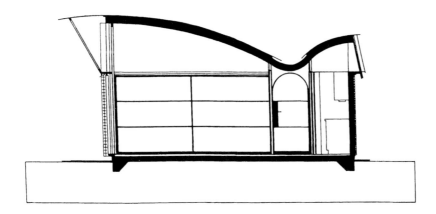

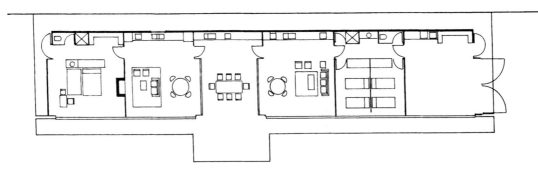

this goal through architectonic strategies that awaken the senses to the landscape and environmental forces. The linear house is sited on an east-west axis to take advantage of northern views over a small lake and the coast beyond. The massing is essentially an articulated lean-to, solid to the cold and harsh south winds and open to the warmth of the northern sunshine—an elaboration on the simplest of camping structures. The expansive glazing on the north side of the structure enables the owners to open the building to coastal breezes and the warmth of the northern sun, to see expansive vistas beyond the lake, and to hear the roll of the ocean and the music of the wind. The simple act of siting was instrumental in establishing the preliminary relationship between the senses and the environment.

The house is a single horizontal gesture upon an immense landscape. It is organized as a series of simple linear pavilions, a tripartite scheme in both plan and section. The three primary

Figure 7.18 Floor plan and section of the house at Bingie Point.

(Joe Ford)

spaces (the children's living areas, sheltered terrace, and parents' living areas) are arranged from east to west. In section, there are alternating rhythms of solid and void—of open and enclosed. The building is also divided into a tripartite scheme from north to south, with living spaces to the north, followed by a circulation spine and, finally, services to the south. Within this seemingly simple organization lie rich responses to the senses and the natural environment.

Vision and light enable us to perceive our environment—in a single glance we can estimate the size and weight of a surface or object, and even guess its temperature. Yet light goes beyond the perceptual realm: it also triggers an understanding of diurnal cycles; it connects us to the rhythms of the seasons; and it affects our emotions. As Diane Ackerman explains in *A Natural History of the Senses:* "Even people who have been blind since birth are greatly affected by light, because, although we need light to see, light also influences us in other subtle ways. It affects our moods, it rallies our hormones, it triggers our circadian rhythms."[27] Light and vision enrich our basic comprehension of natural forces and the workings of the environment: the time and mood of the day, the changing of seasons, and the beauty and complexities of sunlight and shadows. The house integrates a variety of visual sensations to create diverse luminous experiences. The form of the building is a simple rectilinear structure enclosed by a gently curving roof. Murcutt explains: ". . . [I] wanted the roof to suggest flight and to be very light, and to be able to open or close the walls to vary the intensity of light within as desired."[28] The geometric box and curving roof introduce a sensuous experience, which is subtly and elusively related to both vision and touch. The flowing roof form creates a compression of space along the circulation corridor and an expansion of space along the building perimeters. Even the interior partitions have clerestories beneath the ceiling plane, enhancing the visual effect of the roof plane as a very light, hovering structure—expressing Murcutt's desire to capture the quality of flight. The free-form roof quietly reminds one of the winged inhabitants who share the site and the life and energy of this coastal region while also creating varied luminous experiences on the north and south sides of the building.

The curved roof and clerestories over the south wall allow diffuse light to reflect off the convex ceiling to the service area below. High partition clerestories bring soft borrowed light from the northern rooms into the corridor and service areas on the south. The borrowed light and partition clerestories enhance the sense of spaciousness in the building and visually unite the interior and exterior. "The high clerestory . . . takes in the sky, so that one is always aware of the weather from inside the building and [is] woken by the morning light."[29] In contrast to the soft indirect light on the south side of the building, there is a dynamic play of sunlight on the north. An exterior horizontal shading device on the north facade creates rhythms of light and shadow that change with the hours and seasons. Complex patterns draw attention to different elements within the architecture—light creeps up wall planes, slips across the floors, and climbs over furniture. The play of light and shadow can be adjusted or eliminated by altering the shading louvers. Different types and qualities of views are carefully framed throughout the building, including broad vistas in the living areas, a framed hillside to the north, and focused axial perspectives through the building from the entries on the east and west. The daylighting strategies and the building form create visually exciting environments with complex textures and rhythms.

The sense of touch may be more subtle than vision, but touch reinforces what the eyes see and further defines the three-dimensional qualities of our environment. Touch registers weight, temperature, texture, and pressure—as well as pleasure. Our sense of touch and our comprehension of the built and natural environments are intricately linked to luminous and thermal design. The relationship between the sense of touch and vision is found in the luminous and thermal zoning of the house at Bingie Point. The living spaces are clustered to the north for solar gain (because of its Southern Hemisphere location), followed by buffer spaces on the south to moderate the cool southerly winds. The north facade is entirely glazed with operable exterior horizontal shades to control heat gain during the summer and early fall. A roof overhang prevents solar penetration on the north for several months around the time of the equinox while allowing sunlight to warm the living areas during the heating seasons.[30] The south facade is a heavy masonry wall clad in corrugated iron—the only opening is a small view window from the parents' living room. Murcutt described the south wall as ". . . the building's overcoat, (it) has a brick internal lining, retaining the heat in the winter and keeping the building cool in summer."[31] In addition to careful thermal zoning, the organization of the building creates a variety of sensuous experiences by layering interior and exterior spaces and developing transitions to the landscape. The centrally located terrace is an intermediary space providing sheltered contact with the site and climate. The roofed terrace, protected on three sides and open to the north, creates alternating interior and exterior spaces where one can feel the wind, sense the temperature changes, and observe the weather. Large sliding-glass doors surround the terrace and allow the living spaces to be literally opened to the site, sun, and wind.

Murcutt has also provided ventilation in both the north-south and the east-west orientations. From the east and west, doors can be opened to allow cross ventilation, and the north facade has a series of glass jalousies that can be manipulated to vary the amount and direction of airflow. On the south facade, an operable ventilation slot is located below the clerestory. Ventilation openings in all orientations allow the body to feel the subtle movements of the breeze and to be refreshed regardless of wind direction. The users can control the ventilation and feel the changes of weather throughout the day and seasons. To retain heat, the south wall and the internal partitions are made of heavy masonry. Concrete floor slabs are overlaid with ceramic tiles that vary in temperature depending on the seasons and the solar availability.

Our sense of hearing is often ignored or underestimated (unless sounds are troublesome, too loud or too quiet, or in some way unpleasant), yet sound plays a fundamental role in defining materials, volumes, distances, and movements in space. Our sense of hearing and its interactions with the built and natural environments help shape our world and give it meaning. The experience of sound at the house at Bingie Point directly results from the daylighting and thermal designs and the approach to the building envelope and windows. A delightful aspect of the architecture is that the users hear the natural environment. The openness of the house and its orientation toward the small lake and coastline allow sounds of the site and wildlife to filter through the building layers, connecting the inside to the outside. In addition, the plan organization, with its separation of parents and children, provides both physical and acoustic privacy. The interior finishes are largely reverberant, creating an acoustically live interior, which contrasts with the absorbent free-field condition of the outdoors. Opening the building to the site alters interior acoustics

Figure 7.20   View of the terrace at the house at Bingie Point.

(Max Dupain)

when desired. In addition, the sounds of rain on the corrugated iron roof remind the users of the source of the water supply, which is given special treatment through prominent rain gutters and an underground cistern. Throughout the house one is reminded of the many forces acting upon the site—the rhythm of the rain, the pounding of the ocean, the cry of the gulls, the gentle movement of the wind in the tussock grass. The strength of Murcutt's project lies in its melding of sensory experiences. The exterior shading devices, jalousie windows, clerestories, sliding-glass terrace doors, and ventilation panels all serve multiple sensory functions. The thermal and luminous environments make the user conscious of the power and beauty of this rural coastal site, of its uniqueness and its abundance of sensory experiences. The users can alter and fine-tune the environment, but equally important, they can see, feel, and touch the environment through the architecture. (See Figures 7.15 to 7.20.)

Urban Environments

Given the potential sensory overload of urban environments, one might assume that there are fewer opportunities to engage the senses in urban architecture. Murcutt's Paddington House, near Sydney, Australia, challenges this assumption. The nineteenth-century home is located on a site that slopes steeply to the northeast, creating a single-story facade at the street level and a two-story facade in the rear of the house. The original street facade remains largely intact, with major alterations focusing on the interior and rear of the building. In section, the house has three primary spaces in a split-level scheme: a large living and kitchen area at the rear garden level, a midlevel entry and guest bedroom at street grade, and a master bedroom above the living room and garden. Working within the confines of an existing envelope, Murcutt made alterations that introduce new sensuous and environmental experiences.

Despite the dense urban fabric and site constraints, the massing and configuration of the Paddington House create diverse luminous environments. Built on a hillside, the split-level design opens the interior to northeast light. The primary living spaces are oriented toward the rear of the house to face the morning and midday sun. Since the northeast sun can cause unwanted heat gain and glare, the user can control and alter the transparent skin

Figure 7.21   Exterior view of the Paddington House.

(Reiner Blunck)

through deep overhangs, awnings, and blinds to create desired lighting conditions. Large retractable blinds are fixed above pivoting glass doors in the living room, and a bedroom balcony shades the clerestory windows. An ingenious removable awning made of interwoven strips of fabric, with small holes left in the weave to give a dappled light, provides additional protection from the sun.[32] A skylight, located on the entry level between the master bedroom and the guest room, allows light to enter deep into the interior. The light filters through horizontal louvers at the base of the skylight, entering each of the bedrooms through clerestories located above interior partition walls. In addition, soft filtered light enters the living room through the floor slot. Upstairs, in the master bedroom, the roof overhang is designed to allow light to penetrate deeply during the winter and to provide shade during

Figure 7.22 Floor plans and section of the Paddington House.

(Joe Ford)

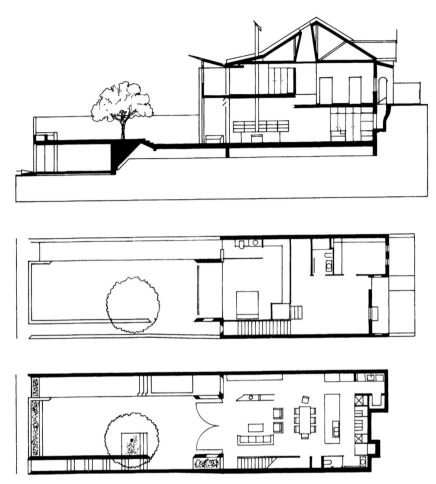

the summer. The quality of light changes constantly throughout the day and the seasons, with direct and indirect light alternating as the sun changes its relative position.

Carefully placed windows, finwalls, and view slots create controlled views, privacy, and an expansive sense of space at the Paddington House. Rory Spence describes these experiential effects:

> ... the blade walls ... provide privacy and enclosure for the transitional space between living room and terrace and for the bedroom balcony. Setting these blade walls in from the boundaries allows diagonal views from the upper level, while not obstructing similar views from adjacent houses.

> The angle of the balcony roof also has other functions. Its reversal of the traditional verandah roof form . . . opens up the view of the opposite hillside and sky from the interior, giving a sense of spatial expansiveness which counteracts any claustrophobia induced by the dense urban character of the neighborhood.[33]

In addition to the distant views captured on the upper levels, intimate garden views from the lower level provide visual relief and increase awareness of diurnal and seasonal changes.

This house is divided into distinct thermal and luminous environments. The lower living room, facing northeast, captures the warm midday sun during the winter months and can be shaded in the summer by extending the terrace awning. Pivoting glass walls in the living room open the building to the landscape, sun, wind, and sounds of the site. The midlevel entry is thermally and visually connected to the lower living room by a 20-inch slot. The elevated bedroom allows warm air to rise through the slot to the upper floors during the winter and breezes to flow throughout the house in the summer. The master bedroom has a northeast-facing balcony to mediate the amount of heat and light entering the room. Each zone within the house interacts thermally and luminously with the others. The upper-bedroom balcony provides heat and light for both the bedroom and the living room below, and the slot between living room and entry provides indirect illumination, ventilation, and heat transfer for multiple zones.

There are also a variety of luminous and thermal environments outside of the Paddington House. Two levels of terraces move outward from the living room. The first terrace is immediately adjacent to the house and is partially enclosed by the bedroom balcony. This terrace has an adjustable awning that creates a cool, shaded enclosure with a dappled quality of light. The second terrace is located several steps above the living-room grade. It is a large outdoor room defined by low walls and plantings, which is open to the sun and weather. The third outdoor space is a small, partially enclosed balcony off the master bedroom, defined by vertical finwalls and a large roof overhang. Each of these outdoor rooms provides different sensuous experiences that range from open, sun-drenched spaces to cool, shaded oases.

Even in this urban location, Murcutt opens the house to the sounds of the site. The building welcomes sounds of the site at the rear of the house while maintaining an appropriately closed street facade to filter urban noise. The house itself is an acoustic barrier for the garden and blocks noise to the windows, which are predominantly located on the rear facade. The users, as well as birds and animals, find acoustic shelter on the garden side. A slender reflecting pool masks unwanted noise by recycling rainwater captured from the roof. The water cascades from the reflecting pool down a series of steps to a smaller basin adjacent to a low living-room window. The sounds of moving water create a gentle acoustic background. Within the house, areas are zoned to provide acoustic relief for the private guest room and master bedroom, while allowing a free movement of sound between the more public living room and entry. (See Figures 7.21 to 7.24.)

Murcutt's works reveal that architecture is a filter between our senses and the world in which we live. As a filter, architecture

Figure 7.23 Interior view of the entry level of the Paddington House.

(Reiner Blunck)

Figure 7.24 View of the interior of the Paddington House from the lower-level garden.

(Reiner Blunck)

moderates and defines our sense of luminous, thermal, and acoustic comfort, pleasure, and well-being. The Bingie Point and Paddington Houses are inherently responsive to the environment, inviting interactions between the users, climate, and site. The projects illustrate that regardless of location, architecture can enhance the senses and foster environmental connections. Murcutt's work reminds us that architecture of the senses invites us to touch our environment (with our eyes and with our bodies) and provides variety and contrast—through different textures, colors, and temperatures. Architecture of the senses captures the dynamic qualities of light; it defines the mood of the day, the changing of the seasons, and the beauty and complexities of sunlight and shadow. It allows the wind to carry scents and to comfort our bodies. It lets us know that we're alive. Architecture of the senses allows us to see the world, to touch the seasons, and to welcome in the sounds and resonance of life. It reminds us that we live in a dynamic and constantly changing world, a living organism much like our own bodies. Architecture of the senses nurtures our awareness of the world and fosters a greater understanding of our kinship with all of life.

SPIRITUAL CONNECTIONS

Throughout history, people have linked issues of spirituality and sacredness with ecology and nature. In the last century, John Burroughs wrote: "Nature-love as Emerson knew it, and as Wordsworth knew it . . . has distinctly a religious value. . . . The forms and creeds of religion change, but the sentiment of religion—the wonder and reverence and love we feel in the presence of the inscrutable universe—persist."[34] Henryk Skolimowski, professor of ecological philosophy at the University of Lodz, Poland, more recently wrote:

> To understand fully the intricacies of ecological interconnections is to treat ecological habitats reverentially. . . . Reverence therefore emerges as a deeper understanding of ecology, of the earth, and of ourselves. . . . The true work for ecology is not only through campaigns to save this or that threatened habitat (though this is important too) but also in creating an attitude of mind within which the ecological and the spiritual are one. Ecology is about the well-being of bio-habitats existing outside of man. Yet probed with a sufficient depth, *ecology is about the state of the human soul.* . . .[35]

Spirituality is yet another way that people try to grasp, reconcile, understand, or perhaps merely acknowledge the mystery and interconnections of life. Skolimowski suggests, ". . . it can only be confirmed in our innermost intuition when we are individually united with this ultimate oneness for which there is no word. Only in the silence of our unfathomable souls can we intuit the quintessential unity of all things spiritual."[36] These thoughts suggest that human reverence, care, and appreciation of nature are inherently spiritual. Eliot Porter echoes this sentiment in his interpretation of Henry David Thoreau's writings: "One cannot even begin to 'love Nature' in any profitable sense until one has achieved an empathy, a sense of oneness and of participation.

'Appreciation' means an identification, a sort of mystical experience, religion in the most fundamental sense of the terms."[37] Some argue that it is only by changing our attitudes and gaining a reverence for life that we may hope to resolve current ecological dilemmas. Recycling programs, protests, environmental actions, and legislation will do little until humans understand the sacredness of the earth.

Throughout history, we find rich examples of transcendent or spiritual qualities in architectural daylighting. Gothic architecture, more than perhaps any other style, explicitly used daylighting for its spiritual effects. In *Passing Strange and Wonderful,* Yi-Fu Tuan describes the mystery and power of Gothic light:

> The cathedral, though built of stone, was an embodiment of motion in music, and also of cyclical manifestations of God's work such as "the regular movements of time and the seasons . . . , the rhythms of nature, [and] the motions and humours of biological life." . . . In the words of Otto von Sims, "The Gothic wall seems to be porous: light filters through it, permeating it, merging with it, transfiguring it. The stained-glass windows of the Gothic are structurally and aesthetically not openings in the wall to admit light, but transparent walls. The Gothic may be described as transparent, diaphanous architecture . . . a continuous sphere of light."[38]

Regardless of the architectural style or period, daylight has always been an essential medium for transforming architecture into sacred space. Yet sacred space should not be limited to our temples, chapels, synagogues, and mosques. If ecology and spirituality are indeed linked, if our reverence for life will foster ecological awareness and care for the environment, then we should start by making ecological and spiritual connections in the spaces we inhabit every day.

The role of the sacred in secular spaces (at home, at work, and in our communities) is often overlooked—if not neglected. Arthur Aminotte, a Lakota teacher, writer, and artist, challenges the concept that sacred space can even be created within architecture: "The Lakota sacred traditions have remained institutionalized as 'organized religion.' Today, they formally and consciously reject permanent sacred architecture as suitable or as having any lasting significance. . . . Rather, by not being in a structure, one is in the sacred temple—*templum*—which is the world itself, with the actual dirt of the earth as the floor and the vast blue dome of the actual sky as the ceiling."[39] Somewhere between our designated sacred spaces and the open sky and earth are the places we inhabit on a daily basis. These are the places that will most likely open our eyes to the sacred and ecological significance of the world in which we live. In his talks to architecture students, Louis Kahn said: "I think every building must have a sacred place."[40] Can the spiritual and sacred aspects of daylighting be used in everyday places to enhance the ecological awareness of the human spirit and soul?[41] What types of luminous phenomena awaken ecological values and foster respect and reverence for the environment and for all of life?

Since it opened in 1987, the Internationale Nederlanden Bank (ING) Headquarters has been acclaimed for its sensitive approach to the health and well-being of its occupants as well as for its energy efficiency. (See Figures 7.25 and 7.26.) Yet less attention has been paid to the ways in which this 538,000-square-foot office complex also captures qualities of spirituality and sacredness in the least likely of places—the work environment. In an

Figure 7.25 Exterior view of the ING Headquarters.

(Alberts & von Huut)

interview with *Design Book Review,* architect Anton Alberts (from the design firm Alberts & von Huut) explains the relationship between ecological design, human considerations, and spirituality at ING: ". . . I say truly ecological buildings are organic, which is a special way of including social and physical phenomena. Otherwise you only work on the material level. . . . You need more, you need art, spiritual ideas, human development—you need beauty, it's a basic functional human need. Then, inspired by beauty people might consider their spiritual problems and develop a new kind of philosophy."[42] The ING Headquarters is based on the anthroposophical design principles of Rudolf Steiner, which use ". . . organic volumes and forms to elicit humane spaces with a spiritual sensibility."[43] The works and teachings of Steiner, perhaps more than any other architect, explicitly link ecology and spirituality. Architect Kenneth Bayes explains Steiner's views on this relationship: "Architectural creation, suggested Steiner, is the answer the human soul gives in order to regain a relationship, while on earth, with the cosmos. . . ."[44] Steiner frames ecological inquiries within a spiritual context: "Only if we know upon what laws and fundamental spiritual impulses our work must be grounded, only if what we do is in harmony with the evolutionary forces operating in mankind as a whole—only then will achievement be within our reach."[45]

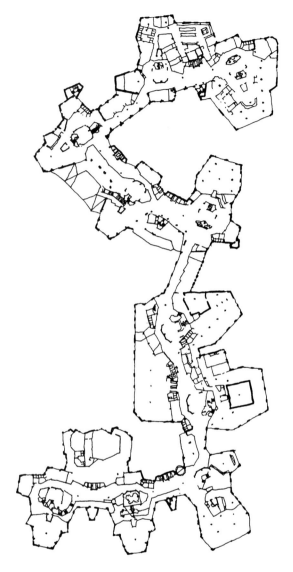

Figure 7.26 Plan of the ING Headquarters.
(Joe Ford)

The ING Headquarters comprises a thin serpentine plan with 10 vertical office towers (of varying heights) linked together by a linear street which expands and contracts to accommodate gardens, water features, courtyards, restaurants, services, and gathering spaces. This large program is reduced to several smaller

Figure 7.27   View of a garden at the ING Headquarters.

(Alberts & von Huut)

Figure 7.28
View of an atrium in the ING Headquarters.
(Alberts & von Huut)

buildings to create human-scale spaces and a sense of community. Each tower is punctured by a central atrium filled with daylight, plants, artwork, and an open stair. Offices on upper levels have internal windows that overlook the activities within the atria and gather borrowed daylight. The top of each atrium includes artwork designed by Judith Gor and Joost van Santen. Their installations are fabricated of specular surfaces that animate the vertical spaces with a changing play of light. The thinness of the serpentine plan, vertical towers, and atria provide daylighting throughout the building and within the offices. Occupants are located no farther than 20 feet (6 meters) from a window. While the highly articulated office plan can make the arrangement of furnishings difficult, it ensures access to views and daylight from multiple orientations. Deeply recessed windows, motorized external shading, internal blinds, and operable windows control luminous and thermal comfort.

English, Japanese, and Finnish gardens are tucked into curves along the outside of the building. Garden pathways, seating, and eating areas encourage employees to use the outside spaces throughout the day. Water elements, which are brought to life by the movement of the sun and changing sky conditions, provide a visual and acoustic counterpoint to the many different plants within the gardens. Windows and glazed doors provide a variety of visual and physical connections to the gardens as one moves along the internal street which links the office towers. In addition, many of the upper offices have garden views. The physical connection to the gardens, abundant views, and large, numerous windows enhance awareness of the seasons, changing qualities of light, and weather. (See Figures 7.27 to 7.30.)

Figure 7.29 Detail of artwork in an atrium at the ING Headquarters.

(Alberts & von Huut)

Architects Albert and von Huut use organic forms in section and plan to create spaces of varied size, shape, and height. As a result, different types and qualities of light are found throughout the building. Direct sidelighting from the bridge along the inter-

Figure 7.30
View of an office at the
ING Headquarters.

(Alberts & von Huut)

nal street is contrasted by the diffuse toplighting of a vertical atrium or a framed vista from an upper office. Materials, colors, and detailing further distinguish particular places within a larger whole. The ING building is a visual feast; perhaps too sumptuous at times, but a welcome departure from typical office environments. The integration of daylight, varied spatial experiences, craft, textures, materials, artwork, and the landscape creates a unique human experience at the ING Headquarters.

While some architectural critics have faulted the building for its design abundance, Anton Alberts is not concerned. As he explained in a recent interview: "I don't design for architects, I build for people."[46] Alberts and von Huut clearly see a relationship between ecology, spirituality, and daylighting at the ING Headquarters. In the tradition of Rudolf Steiner, the architects view function (and program) as pragmatic, poetic, and spiritual. Kenneth Bayes explains Steiner's anthroposophic concept of function: " 'Function' is the purpose of a building and the way it serves the people using it. It has often been taken in the narrow sense of providing space of a kind which allows physical activities to take place efficiently. But people have other needs, too—of soul and spirit. True functionalism takes notice of these and results in architecture which satisfies the whole man. One might say that Steiner added 'spiritual functionalism.' "[47]

Steiner, Kahn, and Alberts argue that through the human experience of aesthetics and beauty, larger ecological, cosmological, and spiritual sensitivities are awakened. Each suggests in his own way that ecological inquiries can and should be framed within the context of human experience. In reconsidering the ecological opportunities of daylighting, we need to expand our understanding of the roles of environmental, social, and spiritual connections. It is not enough merely to sustain our bodies—it is the social, cultural, and spiritual aspects of daylighting that sustain the human spirit and make life worth living. As feminist and philosopher Simone de Beauvoir explains: "Life is occupied in both perpetuating itself and in surpassing itself; if all it does is maintain itself, then living is only not dying."[48] The meaning and quality of our lives are directly related to our care for each other and the world in which we live. As Thomas Moore suggests, it is perhaps our social, environmental, and spiritual connections that will ultimately lead to respect for the earth: "Ecology is a sensibility, not a political position. . . . Soulful education in ecology involves an evocation of home that may start on the surface as responsibility and the pragmatics of living, but must go deeper in order to satisfy the soul. . . . Relatedness, whether among people, things, or places, requires story and memory which ultimately lead to value and reverence. . . ."[49]

ENDNOTES

1. Thomas Moore, "Ecology: Sacred Homemaking," in *The Soul of Nature: Celebrating the Spirit of the Earth,* edited by Michael Tobias (New York: Penguin Books, 1996), 137.
2. Göran Schildt, *Alvar Aalto: The Mature Years* (New York: Rizzoli International Publications, 1989), 273.
3. Christopher Day, *Places of the Soul* (Northamptonshire, England: Thorsons Publishing Group, 1990), 56.
4. Lester Milbrath, *Envisioning a Sustainable Society: Learning Our Way Out* (New York: SUNY Press, 1989), 68–69. Lester Milbrath provides an excellent overview of the ecological and sociological implications of sustainable design. He vividly explains the many forces that have led us to the current debate on sustainable design and provides insight into how we might move forward in the future.

5. Roslyn Lindheim, "New Design Parameters for Healthy Places," *Places* 2, no. 4 (1985): 17–27.

6. Ibid., 79.

7. In the essay *New Design Parameters for Healthy Places,* Roslyn Lindheim describes the following issues as essential in the creation of built environments that are supportive and positive for humans: social connectedness; self-esteem and meaning (as related to hierarchy); participation and control; connection to the natural order; contact with nature; connection to the life cycle; and connection to place.

8. Christopher Day, 162.

9. Alexandra Tyng, *Beginnings: Louis I. Kahn's Philosophy of Architecture* (New York: John Wiley & Sons, 1984), 81.

10. Doug Aberley, ed., *Futures by Design* (Philadelphia: New Society Publishers, 1994), 60.

11. Murray Bookchin argues that it is impossible to separate social and ecological issues: "We should never lose sight of the fact that the project of human liberation is always an ecological project as well, just as, conversely, the project of defending the Earth has also become a social project." For discussion of his views on the politics of ecology, see Murray Bookchin, "An Outline for an Ecological Politics," *Futures by Design,* ed. Doug Aberley (Philadelphia: New Society Publishers, 1994), 43–49.

12. Roslyn Lindheim, 21.

13. Fuller Moore, *Concepts and Practice of Architectural Daylighting* (New York: Van Nostrand Reinhold Company, 1985), 52–53.

14. Christine Johnson Coffin makes a compelling argument for the design of "thin buildings," which through their form and massing maximize daylighting, natural ventilation, and a strong relationship to the outside. For a discussion of the problems inherent to thick buildings, see Christine Johnson Coffin, "Thick Buildings," *Places* 9, no. 3 (winter 1995): 71.

15. Jeff Sherer, *Changing Workplace: Flexible for the Mobile Worker,* firm literature from Meyer, Scherer & Rockcastle (Minneapolis, Minn.).

16. Ibid.

17. Christopher Day, 162.

18. Stuart Brand, *How Buildings Learn* (New York: Penguin Books, 1994), 71, quoting from *Lessons for Students in*

Architecture by Herman Hertzberger (Rotterdam: Utgeverji 010, 1991), 148.

19. Göran Schildt, 168–169.
20. Mary Pepchinski provides an excellent overview of the occupant's perspective of the RWE AG Headquarters in Essen, Germany. Her insights and observations suggest new ways of considering office design. See Mary Pepchinski, "RWE AG Hochhaus Essen, Germany," *Architectural Record* 185, no. 6 (June 1997): 151.
21. Bill Willers, ed., *Learning to Listen to the Land* (Washington, D.C.: Island Press, 1991), 195.
22. Stuart Ewen, "Waste a Lot, Want a Lot," in *Learning to Listen to the Land,* edited by Bill Willers (Washington, D.C.: Island Press, 1991), 184.
23. Michael Hough, *Out of Place: Restoring Identity to the Regional Landscape* (New Haven: Yale University Press, 1990), 5.
24. Yi-Fu Tuan provides a compelling discussion about the experiences of the human senses and their relationships to our understanding and perceptions of the built and natural environments. Yi-Fu Tuan, *Passing Strange and Wonderful: Aesthetics, Nature, and Culture* (Washington, D.C.: Island Press, 1993), 1.
25. Diane Ackerman, *A Natural History of the Senses* (New York: Vintage Books, 1991), 308.
26. Manolo de Giorgi, "Glenn Murcutt: House at Moruya (NSW), Australia," *Domus,* no. 691 (February 1988): 68.
27. Diane Ackerman, 249.
28. Manolo de Giorgi, 70.
29. Rory Spence, "At Bingie Point," *Architectural Review* 179, no. 1068 (February 1986): 70–71.
30. Rory Spence, 71.
31. Ibid., 70.
32. Rory Spence, "Nature in the City," *Architectural Review* 189, no. 1134 (August 1991): 48.
33. Ibid.: 41–42.
34. John Burroughs in *The Soul of the World,* edited by Phil Cousineau (San Francisco: HarperCollins, 1993).
35. Henryk Skolimowski, *A Sacred Place to Dwell: Living with Reverence upon the Earth* (Rockport, Mass: Element Books Ltd., 1993), 6–7.

36. Ibid., 3.

37. Henry David Thoreau, *In Wildness Is the Preservation of the World,* selections and photographs by Eliot Porter (San Francisco: Sierra Club, 1962), 15.

38. Yi-Fu Tuan, *Passing Strange and Wonderful,* 137–141

39. T. C. McLuhan, *The Way of the Earth* (New York: Simon & Schuster, 1994), 408.

40. Louis Kahn, *Louis I. Kahn: Talks with Students* (Houston, Tex., 1969), 49.

41. Tenzin Gyatso, fourteenth Dalai Lama of Tibet, uses natural and luminous metaphors to differentiate between the human spirit and the soul: "I call the high and light aspects of my being *spirit* and the dark and heavy aspects *soul.* Soul is at home in the deep, shaded valleys. . . . Spirit is a land of high, white peaks and glittering jewel-like lakes and flowers." Tenzin Gyatso, in *The Soul of the World,* edited by Phil Cousineau (San Francisco: HarperCollins, 1993).

42. Anton Alberts acknowledges the influences of Gaudí, van de Velde, and Steiner in his work. "Dialogue: Anton Alberts," *Design Book Review,* no. 20 (spring 1991): 13.

43. William Browning, "Knock on Brick," *Progressive Architecture* 74, no. 3 (February 1993): 80.

44. Kenneth Bayes, *Living Architecture* (Anthroposophic Press, New York, 1994), 18.

45. Kenneth Bayes, 102.

46. *Design Book Review,* 13–14.

47. Kenneth Bayes, 59.

48. Duane Elgin, *Voluntary Simplicity: Toward a Way of Life That Is Outwardly Simple, Inwardly Rich,* rev. ed. (New York: William Morrow and Co., 1993), 36.

49. Thomas Moore, 140.

8

Learn from Nature

The crisis of sustainability and the problems of educa-
tion are in large measure a crisis of knowledge. But is
the problem, as is commonly believed, that we do not
know enough? Or that we know too much? . . . Or per-
haps it is that we have forgotten other ways of knowing
that lie in the realm of vision, intuition, revelation,
empathy, or even common sense?[1]

—DAVID W. ORR

In *Voluntary Simplicity,* Duane Elgin discusses the importance of being mindful of the world in which we live, the decisions we make, and the actions we take. He suggests that a sustainable future is dependent on education and learning from many of life's lessons that go unnoticed: "A witnessing or reflective consciousness has profound relevance for humanity's evolution toward a sustainable society. . . . Unless we expand our interior learning to match our technological advances, we will be destined to act to the detriment of ourselves and the rest of life on the planet."[2] Elgin believes that self-reflection is a process of education that ". . . expands our range of choice and allows us to respond to situations with greater flexibility and creativity. . . . And with learning comes increasing skillfulness of action. . . . Just as the faculty of human intellect had to be developed by entire cultures in order to support the emergence of the industrial revolution, so, too, must we now begin to develop the faculty of consciousness if we are to build a sustainable future."[3] By making our thinking and design processes visible, we can build our ecological literacy (whether through education and communication during design or through the expression of ideas in built form). In

Gray World, Green Heart, landscape architect Robert Thayer argues for "transparency" and "visual ecology" as requisites for sustainable design. Thayer states,

> Transparency—the ability to see into and understand the inner workings of a landscape—is an absolutely essential ingredient to sustainability. . . . It can be argued that as humans we have a *right* to know where we are, how we are connected, and *how* we are *doing.* . . . The biofeedback of experience between habitat and organism which guides environmental behavior is a cornerstone of ecology. In transparent landscapes, a *visual ecology,* where we are able to assess the conditions affecting us and make cogent environmental decisions, is both possible and necessary.[4]

Although Thayer is discussing landscape architecture, his concepts can be overlaid on daylighting and sustainable design in general. "Visual ecology" concerns our ability to see, to read, and to learn from our natural and built environments. We will consider how daylighting can be a means of achieving a visual ecology to inform and enhance our ecological literacy. First, we will explore the lessons we can learn from ecological processes. Next, we will consider how these processes can inform designs and thereby enhance our ecological literacy. Finally, we will examine ways in which movement through light can be used to educate people about buildings and surrounding ecosystems.

ECOLOGICAL PROCESSES

Fundamental shifts in thinking have occurred throughout history, redefining who we are and clarifying our place within the natural system. One such shift occurred when Nicolaus Copernicus showed that the sun was the center of the solar system. Our perception of the universe and ourselves was indelibly altered. How was Copernicus able to go beyond the thinking of his time, to find new ways of thinking and seeing? Surgeon Leonard Shlain explains in *Art & Physics:*

> Copernicus introduced a radical solution to the age-old mystery of the planets, which derived from what is essentially an artist's perspectivist question. He asked himself, "How would the orbits of the planets appear if viewed from the vantage of the sun instead of from the earth?" In his flash of insight, belief in the previous system was doomed. The hub of the solar

system *was* the sun, he realized. Copernicus, stepping outside the existing model of the solar system and looking back on it from an imaginary outside perspectivist point of view, was able to rearrange the planets and the sun in an entirely new way. . . .[5]

From Copernicus we learn that new models and ways of thinking often challenge accepted ways of thinking and require us to observe the world from a different perspective. What shifts in perception and thinking are necessary in moving toward a more sustainable future? How might we see design in a new light that challenges our accepted models of thinking, making, and doing? We might begin by better understanding the lessons we can learn from nature. The underlying concepts of ecological processes can and should inform how we think about design.

Seemingly disparate disciplines have contributed to our understanding of ecological processes and the underlying principles of ecology. As bioregionalist Doug Aberley explains in *Futures by Design,* "Ecology itself was formally created by Ernst Haeckel (1834–1919), for whom the belief that humans and nature were inextricably linked became the centerpiece of a unified philosophy, science, arts, theology, and politics."[6] The ecological design theories within the architectural profession have built on the works of many others. The influences of different disciplines and such diverse voices as Patrick Geddes, Ernst Haeckel, Henry David Thoreau, Ralph Waldo Emerson, Eugene and Howard Odum, Aldo Leopold, Gregory Bateson, James Lovelock, Margaret Mead, Wendell Berry, and many others can be traced through the works of ecological design proponents. Over the decades and centuries, many advocates of ecological design have contributed to the growing body of knowledge and practice that forms the foundation of current ecological design thinking. Frank Lloyd Wright, Rudolf Steiner, Buckminster Fuller, Malcolm Wells, Paolo Soleri, Ian McHarg, John Tillman Lyle, Wes Jackson, Amory and Hunter Lovins, John Todd and Nancy Jack Todd, Christopher Alexander, David Orr, Sim Van der Ryn, and William McDonough are but a few of these advocates. Underlying the works of these and other ecological theorists and designers is a belief that natural processes inform design thinking, that there are fundamental ecological principles, and that the natural laws hold important lessons for the design professions.

Ecological design theories should be based on concepts and

principles derived from nature. It is therefore essential to clarify the characteristics of natural processes and how they might inform design thinking. In *Overshoot: The Ecological Basis of Revolutionary Change,* William Catton Jr. speculates that we need to pay attention to "the processes that matter."[7] As Catton explains, ". . . what has happened to the American dream, and what is happening to human life all over the world, can be understood as ecological *succession* (and related processes). Members of the human species failed to heed clear omens of our own predicament because we did not know they were precedents. We had not yet learned what processes matter most. . . . We can still learn an important lesson by belatedly seeing that the precedents *were* precedents."[8] As Catton suggests, our challenge is to determine which processes matter and how these can inform the ways we think and what we do. Many people in the design professions have taken on the difficult task of trying to prioritize and clarify the underlying principles of ecological processes and design. Recent works on this topic include Ken Yeang's *Design with Nature,* Nancy Jack Todd and John Todd's *Bioshelters, Ocean Arks, City Farming,* Sim Van der Ryn and Stuart Cowan's *Ecological Design,* and William Catton's *Overshoot.* Sim Van der Ryn and Stuart Cowan suggest that patterns of nature are difficult to characterize: "These patterns, honed by life and time, cannot be easily enumerated. There is no end to the work of discerning them or to the work of translating them into designs that are both effective and culturally appropriate."[9] Catton argues that in order to learn from ecological processes, designers need a working knowledge of concepts such as the web of life, photosynthesis, symbiosis, antibiosis, competition, niche diversification, and biotic community.

Ecological design must work within the context of natural systems and processes. Although ecological concepts and processes may seem distant from architecture, the design professions do have a legacy of individuals who have attempted to translate ecological processes into something meaningful and useful for design. While many influential ecological design theories have been formulated through the decades and centuries, this discussion will focus on recent trends and representative theories that followed the influential social, political, and ecological movements of the 1960s and 1970s. The works of Malcolm Wells, Nancy Jack Todd and John Todd, William McDonough, John Tillman Lyle, and Sim Van der Ryn and Stuart Cowan continue to influence the evolution of ecological thought and practice. The following review of their ecological design theories will explore ways in which ecological processes have been interpreted through design at the end of the twentieth century. Each theory will be summarized and reconsidered within the context of daylighting design.

Malcolm Wells: A Wilderness-Based Checklist

We will begin with a modest book by Malcolm Wells entitled *Gentle Architecture.*[10] Although Malcolm Wells may be most recognized for his work in underground and earth-sheltered design, his thoughtful writings explore broader ecological issues. Wells uses wilderness as a compelling model for design. Howard Zahniser, director of the Wilderness Society, wrote the legal definition of wilderness (for the Wilderness Act): "A wilderness, in contrast with those areas where man and his own works dominate the landscape, is hereby recognized as an area where the Earth and its community of life are untrammeled by man, where man himself is a visitor who does not remain."[11] Wells explores the definition of wilderness and the design lessons that we might learn from it:

> . . . I see in the wilderness model the only way of saving the cities. Remember that what we call wilderness, or nature, is a community. . . . Wilderness has a flexible sort of stability over long period of time. Wilderness lives—thrives, in fact—by using only the energy that shines upon it or blows through it each year. The inhabitants of wilderness are all fully employed. It produces its own food without sapping, as cities do, half a continent to feed its largest communities. And it recycles everything. . . . In short, wilderness works. It had a billion-year head start over what we call civilization, a billion years to find the best way to survive here.[12]

Using wilderness as a guide, Wells developed what is essentially the first ecological design rating system. He drew explicitly on the lessons of natural systems and ecological processes, including concepts such as self-regulation, integration, diversity, photosynthesis, and renewability. Though his principles address broad design issues, many of Wells's underlying concepts can be interpreted to apply to daylighting. The wilderness-based checklist and related daylighting concepts are summarized in Table 8.1.[13]

Table 8.1   Malcolm Wells: A Wilderness-Based Checklist

Malcolm Wells, wilderness-based checklist	Related daylighting concepts
1. Creates pure air	1. Combine daylighting and natural ventilation
2. Creates pure water	2. Integrate daylighting and biological waste treatment systems
3. Stores rainwater	3. N/A
4. Produces its own food	4. Include conservatories, greenhouses, and sunspaces
5. Creates rich soil	5. N/A
6. Uses solar energy	6. Couple daylighting with passive solar design
7. Stores solar energy	7. Couple daylighting with passive solar design
8. Creates silence	8. N/A
9. Consumes its own wastes	9. Integrate daylighting with biological waste treatment systems
10. Maintains itself	10. Use daylighting to minimize the need for mechanical lighting, heating, and cooling
11. Matches nature's pace	11. Use daylighting to enhance awareness of natural cycles, seasons, and time of day
12. Provides wildlife habitat	12. N/A
13. Provides human habitat	13. Use daylighting to create meaningful and healthy spaces for people
14. Moderates climate and weather	14. Use daylighting strategies that are appropriate for the climate, site, and region
15. . . . and is beautiful	15. Explore the aesthetic and experiential opportunities of daylighting

John Todd and Nancy Jack Todd: Nine Precepts for Ecology as the Basis for Design

Tomorrow Is Our Permanent Address, published in 1980 by John Todd and Nancy Jack Todd, describes their investigations and experimentations with ecological engineering. This book was followed in 1984 by *Bioshelters, Ocean Arks, City Farming: Ecology as the Basis for Design* and in 1995 by *From EcoCities to Living Machines: Principles of Ecological Design.* Each of these books explores ways of using ecological models as a basis for design and technology. In *Bioshelters, Ocean Arks, City Farming,* Nancy Jack Todd and John Todd outline nine ecological design precepts. The precepts can be translated or applied to virtually any phase, scale, or topical issue related to design (e.g., different scales such as the site, building, or component design, as well as different topics such as water, waste, natural resources, energy). The precepts are also interdisciplinary; they apply equally well to architectural design, engineering, industrial design, manufacturing, agriculture, and so forth. John Todd and Nancy Jack Todd illustrate that it is possible to use ecological processes as an underlying frame-

Table 8.2 John Todd and Nancy Jack Todd: Nine Precepts for Ecology as the Basis for Design

John Todd and Nancy Jack Todd, precepts for ecology as the basis for design	Related daylighting concepts
1. The living world is a matrix for all design	1. Explore the daylighting lessons that can be learned from ecological processes
2. Design should follow, not oppose, the laws of life	2. Respond to solar phenomena and diurnal and seasonal patterns
3. Biological equity must determine design	3. Provide daylighting to all occupants; consider the political implications of light
4. Design must reflect bioregionality	4. Respond to climate, weather, environmental forces, site, and place
5. Projects should be based on renewable energy sources	5. Integrate daylighting, electric lighting, and passive systems
6. Design should be sustainable through the integration of living systems	6. Integrate daylighting with solar aquatic waste treatment systems and greenhouses
7. Design should be coevolutionary with the natural world	7. Explore the relationship between daylighting technologies and natural systems; design daylighting to be flexible and adaptable
8. Building and design should help to heal the planet	8. Create healthy and healing places of light; minimize the consumption of natural resources and related environmental impacts
9. Design should follow a sacred ecology	9. Consider how daylighting can reveal the interconnection between humans and the natural world

work for virtually all aspects of design. The nine precepts and related daylighting interpretations are summarized in Table 8.2.[14]

William McDonough: The Hannover Principles

The Hannover Principles, published in 1992 by William McDonough, served as design guidelines for the World's Fair 2000 in Hannover, Germany. The principles are intended to evolve and change over time, as McDonough explains: "The Hannover Principles should be seen as a living document committed to transformation and growth in the understanding of our interdependence with nature, in order that they may adapt as our knowledge of the world evolves."[15] A variety of factors, including content and timing, have made the Hannover Principles among the most widely distributed ecological design concepts. The role of people in creating change is made explicit in McDonough's use of action-oriented terms: *insist on, recognize, respect, accept responsibility, create, do not burden, rely on, understand, practice humility, seek constant improvement, encourage,* and so on. The Hannover Prin-

Table 8.3 William McDonough: The Hannover Principles

William McDonough, Hannover Principles	Related daylighting concepts
1. Insist on rights of humanity and nature to coexist in a healthy, supportive, diverse and sustainable condition	1. Consider the physiological and psychological implications of light as well as broader issues of health and well-being
2. Recognize interdependence. . . . Expand design considerations to recognize even distant effects	2. Use daylighting to reduce waste and resource consumption, promote health and well-being, and create beauty
3. Respect relationships between spirit and matter. . . .	3. Use daylighting to improve quality of life; consider the spiritual implications of light
4. Accept responsibility for the consequences of design decisions upon human well-being, the viability of natural systems and their right to coexist	4. Use daylighting to enhance the relationship between inside and outside; respond to climate, weather, and place
5. Create safe objects of long-term value. . . . Do not burden future generations . . . due to the careless creation of products, processes, or standards	5. Develop low-maintenance daylighting and electric lighting designs; use durable and dependable lighting components
6. Eliminate the concept of waste; evaluate and optimize the full life cycle of products and processes	6. Develop energy-efficient design; use daylighting to reduce electric lighting; use daylighting to do more with less; design for adaptability and flexibility
7. Rely on natural energy flows. . . .	7. Integrate daylighting with passive solar strategies, solar aquatic waste treatment systems, and greenhouses
8. Understand the limitations of design. . . . Treat nature as a model and mentor, not as an inconvenience to be evaded or controlled	8. Develop daylighting to respond to environmental forces, site, and solar phenomena; consider how ecological processes can inform daylighting
9. Seek constant improvement by the sharing of knowledge. . . .	9. Share daylighting design knowledge with others; educate clients and users

ciples can be viewed as a call to action. Drawing on the body of ecological design thinking, McDonough frames the issues from a moral and ethical perspective. Table 8.3 summarizes the Hannover Principles and related daylighting design concepts.[16]

John Tillman Lyle: Strategies for Regenerative Design

John Tillman Lyle published *Regenerative Design for Sustainable Development* in 1994. As a summary of the process, concepts, and strategies used for the design and construction of the Center for Regenerative Studies at the California State Polytechnic University in Pomona, it provides a vivid account of the opportunities and challenges involved in applying ecological design concepts. To understand Lyle's design strategies, it is useful to clarify the concept of regenerative design. Lyle suggests that,

> ... in order to be sustainable, the supply system for energy and materials must be continually self-renewing, or regenerative, in their operation. That is, sustainability requires ongoing regeneration. . . . *Regenerative design means replacing the present linear system of throughput flows with cyclical flows at sources, consumption centers, and sinks. . . . A regenerative system provides for continuous replacement, through its own functional processes, of the energy and materials used in its operation. . . . Regeneration has to do with rebirth of life itself, thus with hope for the future. . . .*[17]

Lyle challenges us to reconsider virtually all human activities— how we live on the land, the types of shelter we design, how we grow and consume food, create waste, use water, and so forth. Lyle's 12 strategies for regenerative design focus on systems and technologies that reduce energy consumption, waste, and natural resources. Although the strategies are broadly stated, they are aimed at particular ecological concerns and possible design solutions. Regenerative technology is an important aspect of the tangible solutions that are sought by Lyle. Although Lyle discusses broad planning, land use, and agricultural concerns, the underlying concepts can be reinterpreted for daylighting design. An emphasis on energy, resource consumption, waste, and systems integration is revealed when the regenerative design strategies are reconsidered within the context of daylighting design. Health, quality of life, and broader human considerations are implicit, rather than explicit concerns (e.g., humans indirectly benefit from clean water, unpolluted air, and reduced environmental impact). The 12 strategies for regenerative design and related daylighting implications are summarized in Table 8.4.[18]

Sim Van der Ryn and Stuart Cowan: Second-Generation Ecological Design

Our final example includes the ecological principles of Sim Van der Ryn and Stuart Cowan, which were published in 1995 in *Ecological Design*. Van der Ryn and Cowan define ecological design as ". . . any form of design that minimizes environmentally destructive impacts by integrating itself with living processes."[19] Ecolog-

Table 8.4   John Tillman Lyle: Strategies for Regenerative Design

John Tillman Lyle, strategies for regenerative design	Related daylighting concepts
1. Letting nature do the work	1. Integrate daylighting and passive systems to minimize dependency on fossil fuels
2. Considering nature as both model and context	2. Consider how ecological processes inform daylighting design
3. Aggregating, not isolating	3. Integrate daylighting with heating, cooling, and mechanical systems
4. Seeking optimum levels for multiple functions, not the maximum or minimum for any one	4. Use daylighting to achieve multiple goals (illumination, ventilation, thermal gains, electricity generation, etc.)
5. Matching technology to need	5. Use daylighting for illumination; select appropriate lighting technologies based on program, activities, and scale
6. Using information to replace power. . . . Given adequate information, we can achieve precise fits between system and function. . . .	6. Design daylighting to respond to program and function
7. Providing multiple pathways. In most cases, regenerative technologies are relatively small in scale and suited to specific applications under particular conditions . . . (i.e., combining photovoltaic and wind)	7. Create lighting diversity in the luminous environment; use bilateral and multilateral strategies; provide flexibility and adaptability
8. Seeking common solutions to disparate problems	8. Consider daylighting from multiple perspectives: environmental, architectural, and human factors
9. Managing storage as a key to sustainability	9. Link daylighting to passive solar strategies
10. Shaping form to guide flow	10. Shape the form of the building massing, plan, and section to maximize daylighting
11. Shaping form to manifest process	11. Use form, materials, and systems to express daylighting concepts
12. Prioritizing for sustainability	12. Make daylighting a priority

ical or natural processes are critical to what Van der Ryn and Cowan characterize as principles of "second-generation" ecological design. They explain that second-generation ecological design represents a movement toward the standardization of ecological practice: "The first generation of ecological design was based on small-scale experiments with living lightly in place. Many of the technologies and ideas of this generation, such as alternative building materials, renewable energy, organic foods, conservation, and recycling, have been widely adopted in piecemeal fashion. We now stand at the threshold of a second generation of ecological design. This second generation is not an alternative to dominant technology and design; it is the best path for their necessary evolution."[20] In five concise principles, Van der Ryn and

Table 8.5   Sim Van der Ryn and Stuart Cowan: Second-Generation Ecological Design

Sim Van der Ryn and Stuart Cowan, second-generation ecological design	Related daylighting concepts
1. Solutions grow from place	1. Develop daylighting design in response to environmental forces, site, and place
2. Accounting informs design	2. Consider the relationship between daylighting, energy, and natural resources; address systems integration; consider life-cycle and environmental costs
3. Design with nature	3. Draw on the lessons of natural processes (adaptation, evolution, self-maintenance, etc.); respond to natural forces; consider the relationship between daylighting and the health of the environment and occupants
4. Everyone is a designer	4. Develop a collaborative, interdisciplinary approach to daylighting design; involve clients, occupants, maintenance staff
5. Make nature visible	5. Use daylighting to reveal natural forces, enhance a sense of place, connect with the environment, illustrate patterns of energy consumption

Cowan are able to define essential ecological processes and interpret them so they are meaningful for the design. Van der Ryn and Cowan describe them as "five common-sense principles."[21] The importance of a "common-sense" approach to ecological design should not be underestimated. The principles are succinct yet richly complex, and each is framed broadly enough to use for various design considerations (e.g., construction, environmental technology, landscape design). The five principles and related daylighting implications are summarized in Table 8.5.[22]

The preceding theories and related ecological principles, precepts, and strategies illustrate varied ways of translating ecological processes for design. Although the theories vary in format, content, and tone, they all illustrate the importance of drawing on the lessons of nature. (See Table 8.6.) By reinterpreting these works to apply to daylighting design, we can expand our ways of thinking about daylighting so that it is viewed more broadly and

Table 8.6 Comparison of Ecological Concepts and Principles

Malcolm Wells: a wilderness-based checklist	John Todd and Nancy Jack Todd: nine precepts for ecology as the basis for design	William McDonough: The Hannover Principles	John Tillman Lyle: design strategies for regenerative design	Sim Van der Ryn and Stuart Cowan: second-generation ecological design
1. Creates pure air	1. The living world is a matrix for all design	1. Insist on rights of humanity and nature to coexist in a healthy, supportive, diverse, and sustainable condition	1. Letting nature do the work	1. Solutions grow from place
2. Creates pure water	2. Design should follow, not oppose, the laws of life		2. Considering nature as both model and context	2. Accounting informs design
3. Stores rainwater		2. Recognize interdependence. . . .		3. Design with nature
4. Produces its own food	3. Biological equity must determine design		3. Aggregating, not isolating	4. Everyone is a designer
5. Creates rich soil		3. Respect relationships between spirit and matter. . . .		5. Make nature visible
6. Uses solar energy	4. Design must reflect bioregionality		4. Seeking optimum levels for multiple functions, not the maximum or minimum for any one	
7. Stores solar energy		4. Accept responsibility for the consequences of design decisions. . . .		
8. Creates silence	5. Projects should be based on renewable energy sources		5. Matching technology to need	
9. Consumes its own wastes		5. Create safe objects of long-term value. . . .		
10. Maintains itself	6. Design should be sustainable through the integration of living systems	6. Eliminate the concept of waste. . . .	6. Using information to replace power	
11. Matches nature's pace		7. Rely on natural energy flows. . . .	7. Providing multiple pathways	
12. Provides wildlife habitat	7. Design should be coevolutionary with the natural world		8. Seeking common solutions to disparate problems	
13. Provides human habitat	8. Building and design should help to heal the planet	8. Understand the limitations of design. . . .		
14. Moderates climate and weather			9. Managing storage as a key to sustainability	
15. . . . and is beautiful	9. Design should follow a sacred ecology	9. Seek constant improvement by the sharing of knowledge. . . .	10. Shaping form to guide flow	
			11. Shaping form to manifest process	
			12. Prioritizing for sustainability	

comprehensively within the context of ecological processes. When we compare the propositions of the various authors, we find recurring concepts that are particularly relevant for daylighting:

- Use nature as a model.
- Consider bioregions.
- Design for coevolution and flexibility.
- Use renewable energy sources and natural energy flows.
- Minimize waste.
- Seek self-maintaining and -regulating systems.
- Promote health and healing.

These concepts are equally relevant for urban planning, landscape design, interior design, building construction, and other design considerations. A broad net is cast by ecological design; the concepts are expansive and inclusive. Principles often transcend disciplines, topics, design phases, and building scales. Most important, we find that ecological processes can inform many aspects of design. The wisdom of nature, and our efforts to respect its processes, will most clearly lead us toward a more sustainable future.

ECOLOGICAL LITERACY

Architectural design requires a process that helps to organize issues, questions, decisions, and, ultimately, actions that will lead to the realization of ideas through the built form. The typical design process includes project initiation, various phases of design, design documentation, construction, and finally occupation. Within each of these phases, various aspects of daylighting design need to be considered, from large-scale planning and programming concepts to the final resolution of construction details. The challenge is to reconsider the design process so that appropriate daylighting issues are addressed at various phases of design (and during operations) while also revisiting broader ecological concepts within each design phase. It is most important that the design team develop its own process for integrating issues of daylighting. The daylighting design process needs to be made explicit and visible so that designers, clients, owners, and occupants can more easily understand the role and opportunities of daylighting as well as the implications of various design decisions. The involvement of the design team typically diminishes soon after the building is occupied. The design process should therefore include an ecological timeline that extends well into the future. In this way, the ecological criteria used in the design process will not only influence the designers but will also educate the users of the building.

A building has processes that occur over time and throughout its life. The most obvious of these include lighting, heating, and cooling the building to make it comfortable and livable for the occupants. (Although they will not be addressed here, there are also social and cultural processes that influence how we use and interact in the building over time.) We know from building precedents discussed in preceding chapters that form, materials, and details can express ideas about the design and operation of lighting, heating, and cooling. Yet even if operational processes are expressed through architectural form and design, what lessons do they reveal? What do the processes of the building operation—or how it functions in time—teach us about the environment and our relationship to it? In preceding chapters, we have found that visible aspects of the daylighting design (form, materials, or detailing) can teach many different lessons. The expression of daylighting tells about the programmatic aspects of operations—how we use light, why it is needed, and when. It can help us understand where we live and the particular qualities of place, climate, and site. Daylighting can remind us of how we use energy and natural resources (or how we might reduce and minimize the use of each). We have also seen that daylighting can reveal concepts about time, change, and evolutionary processes. Daylighting can even help us understand the biological processes of health and well-being. Preceding chapters show us diverse ways in which daylighting can influence and shape many types of processes. It is through the operations or life of the building—and our interaction with it through time—that we learn about environmental, architectural, and human biological processes. We learn about ourselves and the environment as we respond to changing patterns of sunlight, make seasonal modifications to an interior blind, adjust a window to admit sun or air, feel the rhythms of the seasons outside our window, or see electric lighting controls respond to the moods of the sky.

The Real Goods Solar Living Center in Hopland, California, by Sim Van der Ryn of the Ecological Design Institute is particularly expressive in revealing the operational processes of daylighting for educational purposes. The building integrates daylighting with passive heating and cooling to teach visitors and occupants about ecological design and the environment. As architect David Arkin, of Arkin Tilt Architects, explains: "We are providing an 'Operator's Manual' to the Real Goods store staff to teach them how to properly tune the building for comfort, i.e., when to open or close the clerestories, etc. This could have all been automated, but we hope to let the staff interact with the building to afford them the opportunity to learn about their environment."[23] Many visual cues in the form of the building draw attention to various aspects of the daylighting, including an expressive telescoping footprint, curved roof forms with south-facing clerestory windows, and a variety of shading devices. The form itself awakens occupants to the processes of admitting and gathering the sun and wind for

Figure 8.1   View of south facade and gardens at the Real Goods Solar Living Center.

(Marietta Millet)

Figure 8.2 South trellis and shading devices on the south facade of the Real Goods Solar Living Center.

(Margot Kally McDonald)

illumination, heating, and cooling. The building seems to reach out and gather light through its large, expressive layers of shading, reminding visitors of seasonal and climatic changes. The design of the envelope includes operable windows, adjustable awnings, lightshelves, light-colored interior finishes, and transparency of the south facade—visual indicators that teach occupants about the processes of lighting, heating, and cooling the building. Equally important, the form and detailing of the building give the sun and wind a visual and physical presence that become tools for teaching about energy, resource conservation, environmental concerns, and related issues of human responsibilities and actions.

The "rainbow sundial calendar" and the "noon line calendar" are art installations used to educate occupants of Real Goods about solar and luminous phenomena. A skylight with four flat prisms and an oculus projects an image of the sun (a disc of white light) along a line that marks true north-south. Solar noon is indi-

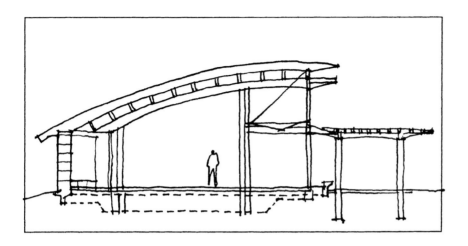

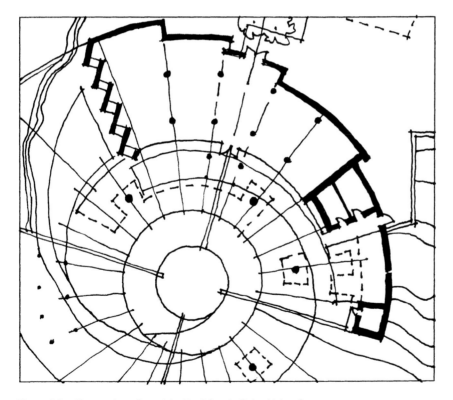

Figure 8.3 Plan and section of the Real Goods Solar Living Center.

cated as the image of the sun crosses the line for true north. The solar prism will be used to create a calendar corresponding with significant solar events and to reveal our seasonal journey around the sun. This installation also creates a solar rainbow which helps visitors to understand the movement of the earth: "If we stand inside this Rainbow, we become the 'Pot of Gold" and see the Earth turning under our feet in a moment of awesome delight. . . . The Solar colors and shapes in Rainbow Sundial Calendar change constantly with the hours and the seasons. Play inside this rainbow and you'll notice you often have three or four color shadows, and they are all colored sunlight. . . ."[24] Another solar calendar in the gardens adjacent to the building is designed to celebrate the equinoxes and solstices.

Exhibits are also used to educate visitors about the building and ecological issues. A demonstration and children's area includes a global-warming display, hydroelectricity demonstration, creative play area, and sighting tower. As sculptor Baile Oakes explains, "The bottom line for all these displays is the whole body is involved in the education process. . . . The children's area will only come alive when the children discover the connection between themselves and the dance of the Sun."[25] The concept of engaging the body is an important aspect of ecological education. It is through our physical encounters with the building—modifying, tuning, and adjusting it for the seasons and time of day—that we begin to make connections with the environment, that we begin to experience being part of a larger cosmic and ecological whole. (See Figures 8.1 to 8.3.)

ECOLOGICAL EXPERIENCES

Michael Hough explains in *Out of Place* that our common everyday experiences provide the seeds of ecological understanding and compassion: "True understanding and commitment to the environment begins with the emotional and the intellectual experience of ordinary events and phenomena one finds every day in familiar but often ignored surroundings. . . . An emotional investment in one's own place may also be the stepping-stone to an investment in someone else's."[26] Movement through the built and natural environments is one such ordinary experience that can reveal subtle yet meaningful lessons about places, sites, and even ecological processes. Movement is a way of connecting the external and internal environments—whether it is the movement of the sun through a window, the wind through a room, or the journey of the body through a building and landscape. This final discussion will consider how the Finnish Forest Museum by Kaira-Lahdelma-Mahlamäki and the Rio Grande Nature Center by Antoine Predock use movement and light to educate people about the buildings and surrounding ecosystem. As Michael Hough suggests, if we engage these types of simple everyday events, we might begin to learn from and about the world in which we live.

A Forest Ecosystem

The Finnish Forest Museum and Information Center by Kaira-Lahdelma-Mahlamäki is sited on a 40-acre arboretum in Punkaharju, Finland. The project is also known as *Lusto,* which in Finnish refers to the annual growth ring of a tree. Mature pine

Figure 8.4 North entry and bridge to the Finnish Forest Museum.

(Jussi Tiainen)

forest, a gently rolling topography, and numerous lakes provide a
stunning ecological context for the museum. Metaphorical references and physical connections to the forest ecosystem are made
through the experience of light in both the landscape and architectural designs. The museum is the first stop along a hiking path

Figure 8.6 Northern exhibition area at the Finnish Forest Museum.

(Jussi Tiainen)

that guides visitors through the museum to outdoor exhibits. The hiking path proceeds along two small lakes and through the arboretum to Lake Saimaa. The building comprises an overlapping circular and rectilinear form. The two-story circular portion of the museum contains public spaces, such as the exhibition area, reception area, museum shop, offices, and archives; the one-story rectilinear portion contains support spaces, such as the conservation area, workshops, and storage.

Sited on a sloping hillside, the two-story museum is approached along a path in the woods. The path leads to a delicate pedestrian bridge spanning the hillside and a rooftop entry terrace located above the support spaces. The trellised cage of the bridge creates a dappled quality of light and shadow reminiscent of the forest. After crossing the bridge, space opens to create a sun-filled clearing on the entry terrace. A tall canopy supported by thin, hemp-wrapped columns that are reminiscent of vertical tree trunks marks the entry of the building. Once inside, visitors cross a second bridge that spans the entry terrace and the circular exhibition spaces. The museum is an internally focused building that is primarily illuminated by toplighting; sidelighting is used selectively to provide views and borrowed light. Visitors begin their journey through the building by starting at the shadowy center of the drum, which contains the reception area, museum shop, and auditorium. Wooden screens spatially separate activities while providing glimpses of the exhibitions below. After

Figure 8.7 Exhibition area and entry to auditorium at the Finnish Forest Museum.

(Timo Kilpeläinen)

passing through the heart of the building, visitors move along a switchback ramp that radiates from the center to the exterior of the building. The midpoint of the switchback extends beyond the envelope of the solid circular concrete drum to provide stunning views of the arboretum and Lake Saimaa. After experiencing the site, visitors turn 180° to follow the ramp to the lower-level exhibitions. Partition walls along the ramp obscure views of the exhibitions until this 180° transition is completed. The lower level is organized as a series of concentric layers, with the auditorium at the center, wrapped by the exhibition spaces and a bermed gallery at the outer edge of the northern boundary.

The two-story exhibition space is illuminated on the north and east by a semicircular skylight. The depth of the skylight well and the generally low sun altitude create a soft, indirect wallwashing along the upper perimeter of the exhibition space. (Located at 62°

Figure 8.8 View of south facade and adjacent lake at the Finnish Forest Museum.

(Jussi Tiainen)

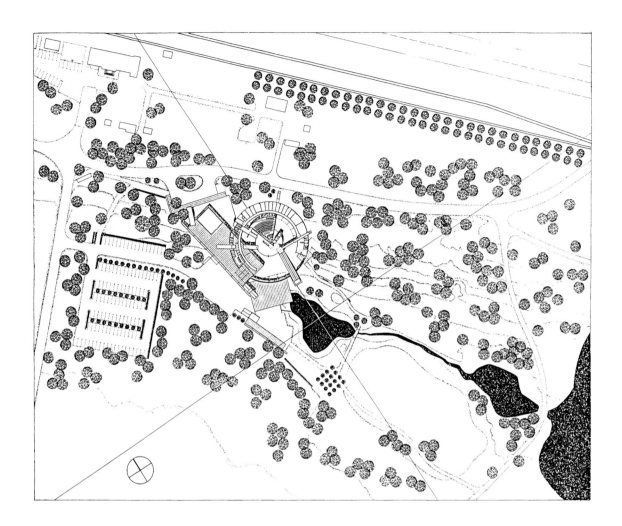

Figure 8.9 Site plan of the Finnish Forest Museum.

(Kaira-Lahdelma-Mahlamäki)

north latitude, the solar altitude at noon varies from 4.5° in winter to 51.5° in summer.) Reminiscent of the rings of a tree, horizontal wood cladding wraps the walls of the concrete structure and reflects a warm hue throughout the space. During the summer months, direct sunlight moves along the upper portion of the walls to mark the diurnal and seasonal movements of the sun. A luminous glow along the solid north wall draws people to the exhibition space and provides orientation. In contrast, direct sunlight is admitted to the south side of the exhibition space through a clerestory and sidelighting. The high south-facing clerestory monitor brings sunlight deep within the drum while also providing a view of the sky and sun. Sidelighting provides site connections to the adjacent terrace and small lake as well as glimpses of Lake Saimaa in the distance. A variety of forms and sizes of windows puncture the solidity of the circular concrete drum. Three-dimensional windows periodically slice through the drum to create small rooms of light at important thresholds and transition points. Other windows are two-dimensional horizontal and vertical bands, which capture sunlight and frame particular views. Several windows are wrapped with tamarack siding on the exterior to provide privacy, shading, and a filtered connection to the site. Other windows are placed low to connect with the earth or high to connect with the sky. The varied window forms and place-

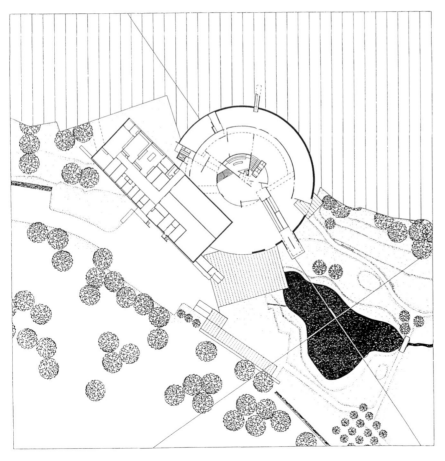

Figure 8.10 Upper-level plan of the Finnish Forest Museum.

(Kaira-Lahdelma-Mahlamäki)

Figure 8.11 Lower-level
plan of the Finnish
Forest Museum.

(Kaira-Lahdelma-Mahlamäki)

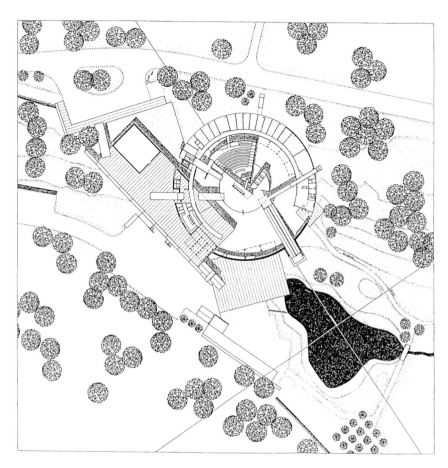

ments are designed to create contrasting qualities of light and varied physical and visual relationships with the site and forest ecosystems of the arboretum.

Two distinct qualities of light are provided within the exhibition space. Artifacts and materials that require protection from sunlight can be exhibited under the indirect daylight on the north. Three-dimensional objects and materials that are not sensitive to daylight can be exhibited to the south (which has adjustable interior blinds that can be used to control sunlight). The experience and mood of the exhibition space, which wraps the outer layer of the drum, is dramatically different on the north and south sides. Filtered toplighting along the northern exhibition space evokes the quality of light found deep within the forest. There is a sense of enclosure and vertical orientation that is reminiscent of the soft

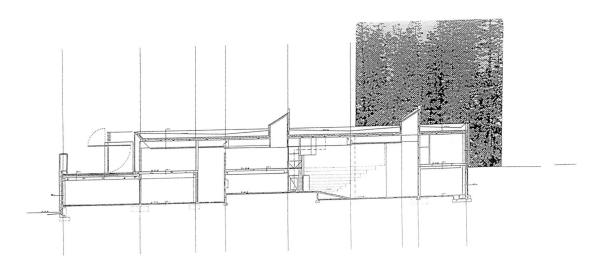

light filtered through a canopy of leaves. The southern gallery is reminiscent of a forest clearing, with direct sunlight and dramatic patterns of light and shadow contrasting with the soft illumination to the north. Distinct daylighting strategies are used to organize the building, to illuminate different types of exhibitions, and to provide orientation to the site. The varied luminous qualities, views, and connections to the site are intended to prepare the visitors physically and metaphorically as they move into the forest ecosystem. (See Figures 8.4 to 8.12.)

Figure 8.12 Section of the Finnish Forest Museum.

(Kaira-Lahdelma-Mahlamäki)

A Wetland Ecosystem

The Rio Grande Nature Center in Albuquerque, New Mexico, was designed by Antoine Predock to provide insight into wetland ecosystems and ecological processes. This educational facility is sited on a 170-acre preserve located on the Rio Grande Flyway for migratory waterfowl. The unique site and its ecological features shaped the design, as Antoine Predock explains, "The Nature Center Building acts as a 'blind,' affording visitors panoramic views over these wildfowl areas without intrusion. . . . The Rio Grande Nature Center site is a symbol of a profoundly important, but rapidly diminishing, New Mexico ecosystem. . . . The natural wetlands ecosystem harbors a diverse set of processes that contrast magnificently with the upland semi-arid mesas. . . ."[27] The daylighting design plays a primary role in capturing and revealing the ecology of the site.

Figure 8.13   View of
south entry at the Rio
Grande Nature Center.

(Marietta Millet)

Similar to the Finnish Forest Museum, the Rio Grande Nature Center is the first stop along a hiking path that moves visitors through the wetlands. Visitors enter the preserve through what Predock describes as "a tunnel of trees" which leads to the building entry on the bermed south facade (recessed into the hillside and planted with native grasses). The entry is created by a metal culvert that slices through the earth to lead visitors to the interior of the building. Views of the wetlands are withheld until after the building has been entered. The transition from the dappled light of the trees into the darkness of the culvert marks a threshold from the forest into the wetlands on the north side of the building. The contrast between the south facade, which disappears into the earth, and the north facade, which appears to emerge from the wetlands, further enhances the distinction between the forest and wetlands.

Two distinct zones are distinguished inside the building. A trapezoidal upper level contains the entry, lobby, library, discovery room, and support spaces, while a circular portion of the building on the north contains the exhibits. The two zones are divided by a row of water-filled fiberglass columns that arc along the outer edge of the circular exhibition area. The dark lobby is punctured by light from irregularly shaped skylights above and adjacent to the water wall. In addition to providing borrowed light, the water wall allows visitors to glimpse the exhibitions and wetlands beyond through a shimmering wall of light. A ramp moves to the lower level, which contains educational exhibits and carefully framed views of the landscape. The windows in the exhibition space were carefully choreographed to connect with the surrounding ecosystem, as Peter Papademetriou explains: "Its center flares out to 'view rays' and is organized as a progression to both specific and directed views, and to facilitate a ramp that literally and symbolically takes the visitor 'through' layers of the site: from high views of the *bosque* canopy, to the mountains, to a specific cottonwood tree, to the fields and wetlands, and a reverse periscope for an underwater view."[28] In contrast to the dark shadows and toplighting in the upper level, the circular exhibition

Figure 8.14 View of north facade at the Rio Grande Nature Center.

(Tim Hursley)

space is sidelit with deeply splayed windows of varying heights, forms, and sizes. The windows, concrete wall, and exhibits are detailed to incorporate carefully framed views. Visitors shift from textual and graphic exhibits to windows that provide glimpses of the real ecosystem. The windows also create a dynamic rhythm of light and shadow which animates the exhibition space. In contrast to the punctured windows and framed views in the exhibition space, floor-to-ceiling windows in the library minimize the boundary between inside and outside to provide expansive views of the landscape and wetland ecosystem. Flooded with the changing qualities of light from outside, the library creates a visual connection to the life of the wetlands. A glazed partition wall in the library provides borrowed light to the

Figure 8.15 Interior view of water wall and exhibition area at the Rio Grande Nature Center.

(Tim Hursley)

Figure 8.16   View of the
wetlands from the library.
(Marietta Millet)

exhibition area and creates an acoustic separation. The discovery
room, located adjacent to the library and near the exit to the
arboretum paths, contains workstations and additional educational materials. In contrast to the openness of the north, small,
high windows in the discovery room reveal that the south side of
the building is partially bermed underground. The contrasting
luminous experiences in the building are choreographed to reveal
contrasting aspects of the preserve. Visitors move through the forest and into the earth to arrive within the building lobby. This
dark, enclosed entry, punctured by toplighting, slowly transitions
through a sequence of framed views of the marsh and ecosystem.
Views from the library expand and open onto the wetlands, providing visitors with a visual transition from inside to outside just
before they leave the building. The path continues through the
building to the hiking trails that encircle the wetlands. (See Figures 8.13 to 8.19.)

Kaira-Lahdelma-Mahlamäki and Antoine Predock use daylighting to create narrative journeys that frame various aspects of the
ecosystem. The buildings and exhibits educate visitors and prepare them to better understand the ecosystems that they enter
after leaving the buildings. The experience of the buildings,

exhibits, and daylighting is not intended to replicate the ecosystem, but rather to reveal an ecological story that draws from and is compatible with the particular ecosystem. These two projects have explicit ecological and daylighting agendas; however, all buildings can tell an ecological story, whether it is one of neglect, indifference, or stewardship. Each designer makes a choice, consciously or unconsciously, to respond to or ignore the processes of

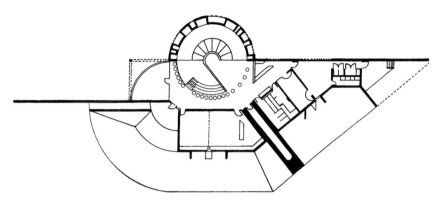

Figure 8.18   Plan of the Rio Grande Nature Center.

(Joe Ford)

nature and the ecosystems of which we are a part. Ecological design and its movement toward a more sustainable future are inherently experimental, exploratory, and perhaps even revolutionary. As Sim Van der Ryn explains, "Ecological design reflects new dreams that can be embodied in new kinds of environments. . . . We can create an Ecological Revolution every bit as profound as the preceding Industrial Revolution. The pieces are well understood, from energy efficiency and sustainable agriculture to ecological water treatment and bioregional design. We pos-

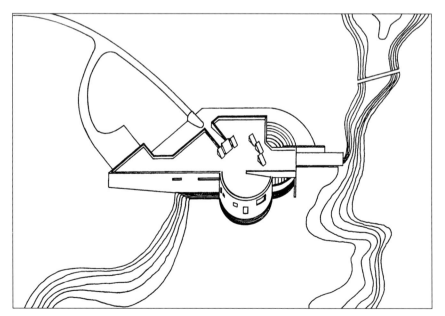

Figure 8.19   Axonometric drawing of the Rio Grande Nature Center.

(Joe Ford)

sess the collective potential to create environments that nurture both the human spirit and the more-than-human living world. The work awaits us."[29]

David Orr reminds us, "If literacy is driven by the search for knowledge, ecological literacy is driven by the sense of wonder, the sheer delight of being alive in a beautiful, mysterious, bountiful world."[30] The seeds of change are found in the process of awakening the human spirit and in our sense of wonder and delight in the world. Architectural, technological, and scientific advances will do little to resolve pressing ecological problems unless we have the desire, willingness, and passion to apply our knowledge for the benefit of life. Despite progress, we still have much to learn about ecological design. We can sense the magnitude of our task when we recall that daylighting is just one of many ecological design issues. The principles discussed in this book are an attempt to provide a framework for reconsidering daylighting from a broader ecological perspective. The principles are but stepping-stones for reconsidering and advancing daylighting design. They should be viewed as malleable, adaptable, and capable of change and evolution. The principles discussed in this book are only a beginning. Yet the words of Louis Kahn suggest that there may be no better place to be: "I love beginnings. I marvel at beginnings. I think it is beginning that confirms continuation. If it did not—nothing could be or would be. I revere learning because it is a fundamental inspiration. It isn't just something which has to do with duty; it is born into us. The will to learn, the desire to learn, is one of the greatest inspirations."[31] Whether we are at the beginning or somewhere along the path, the sun itself can be a constant source of inspiration and wisdom. May we learn from the sun, the source of light, and the giver of all life. Circle back.

ENDNOTES

1. David Orr, *Ecological Literacy: Education and the Transition to a Postmodern World* (Albany: State University of New York Press, 1992), 155.
2. The greatest challenge to realizing a sustainable future may reside not in greater innovations and technological advances, but rather in how we perceive and interpret the world in

which we live. For a compelling discussion on ecological living, see Duane Elgin, *Voluntary Simplicity: Toward a Way of Life That Is Outwardly Simple, Inwardly Rich,* rev ed. (New York: William Morrow & Co., 1993), 138.

3. Ibid., 137–139.
4. Robert Thayer, *Gray World, Green Heart: Technology, Nature, and the Sustainable Landscape* (New York: John Wiley & Sons, 1994), 310–311. For an additional discussion of the concept of "visual ecology," see Sim Van der Ryn and Stuart Cowan, *Ecological Design* (Washington, D.C.: Island Press, 1996), 160–172.
5. Leonard Shlain, *Arts & Physics: Parallel Visions in Space, Time, & Light* (New York: William Morrow & Co., 1991), 59.
6. For a concise history of influential individuals in the development of ecological design thinking, see Doug Aberley, ed., *Futures by Design: The Practice of Ecological Planning* (Philadelphia, Pa.: New Society Publishers, 1994), 6.
7. William R. Catton Jr., *Overshoot: The Ecological Basis of Revolutionary Change* (Urbana: University of Illinois Press, 1982), 95.
8. Ibid., 95–96.
9. Sim Van der Ryn and Stuart Cowen, 104.
10. The author gratefully thanks Malcolm Wells for the gentle awaking his book provided during the ecological vacuum of the early 1980s. See Malcolm Wells, *Gentle Architecture* (New York: McGraw-Hill, Inc., 1981).
11. David Bower with Steve Chapple, *Let the Mountains Talk, Let the Rivers Run: A Call to Those Who Would Save the Earth* (New York: HarperCollins Publishers, 1995), 134.
12. Malcolm Wells, 29.
13. Malcolm Wells, 38–40.
14. Nancy Jack Todd and John Todd, *Bioshelters, Ocean Arks, City Farming: Ecology as the Basis of Design* (San Francisco: Sierra Club Books, 1984), 19–92.
15. William McDonough, Hannover Principles, http://repont.tcc .virginia.edu/classes/tcc315/Resources/ALM/Environment/ hannover.html, Internet.
16. Ibid.
17. John Tillman Lyle, *Regenerative Design for Sustainable Development* (New York: John Wiley & Sons, 1994), 10.
18. Ibid., 38–45.

19. Sim Van der Ryn and Stuart Cowan, 18.
20. Ibid., 31.
21. Ecological Design Institute, "EDI's Solar Living Center Project Team," Real Goods Trading Corp., http://www.realgoods .com/slc/design/building.htm., Internet.
22. Sim Van der Ryn and Stuart Cowan, 57–171.
23. David Arkin, "Passive Solar & Ecological Features of the Real Goods' Retail Showroom," Real Goods Trading Corp., http:// www.realgods.com/slc/design/building.htm., Internet, 1.
24. Peter Erskine, "Rainbow Sundial Calendar," Real Goods Trading Corp., http://www.realgods.com/slc/design/building .htm., Internet, 1.
25. Ibid., 3
26. Michael Hough, *Out of Place: Restoring Identity to the Regional Landscape* (New Haven: Yale University Press, 1990), 167.
27. Antoine Predock, "Rio Grande Nature Center," *Places* 4, no. 4 (1987): 24–25.
28. Peter C. Papademetriou, "Blind Trust," *Progressive Architecture,* March 1984, 88.
29. Sim Van der Ryn and Stuart Cowan, 171.
30. David Orr, 86.
31. Alexandra Tyng, *Beginnings: Louis I. Kahn's Philosophy of Architecture* (New York: John Wiley & Sons, 1984), 177.

Bibliography

Aberley, Doug, editor. *Futures by Design: The Practice of Ecological Planning.* Philadelphia, Pa.: New Society Publishers, 1994.

Ackerman, Diane. *A Natural History of the Senses.* New York: Vintage Books, 1990.

Aitken, Donald. "Frank Lloyd Wright's Solar Hemicycle Revisited: Measured Performance Following Thermal Upgrading." In *Proceedings of the 17th National Passive Solar Conference.* Boulder, Colo.: American Solar Energy Society, 1992.

Albers, Josef. *Interaction of Color.* New Haven: Yale University Press, 1963.

Alberts, Anton. "Dialogue: Anton Alberts." *Design Book Review,* no. 20 (spring 1991): 12–14.

Alexander, Christopher. *Notes on the Synthesis of Form.* Cambridge, Mass: Harvard University Press, 1967.

———. *The Timeless Way of Building.* New York: Oxford University Press, 1979.

American Institute of Architects (AIA). *Environmental Resource Guide.* New York: John Wiley & Sons, 1996.

American Solar Energy Society (ASES). Internet: Available from http://www/sni/net/solar/.

Amourgis, Spyros, editor. *Critical Regionalism: The Pomona Meeting Proceedings.* Pomona, Calif.: College of Environmental Design, California Polytechnic University, 1991.

Ander, Gregg D. *Daylighting: Performance and Design.* New York: Van Nostrand Reinhold, 1995.

Anshel, Dr. Jeffrey. "Computer Vision Syndrome: Causes & Cures." *Managing Office Technology,* July 1997. Internet. Available from http://www.meadhatcher.com.

Aschoff, Jurgen. "Naps as Integral Parts of the Wake Time within the Human Sleep-Wake Cycle." *Journal of Biological Rhythms* 9 (1994): 145–155.

Banham, Reyner. *The Architecture of the Well-Tempered Environment.* Chicago: The University of Chicago Press, 1969.

Barnett, Dianna Lopez, and William D. Browning. *A Primer on Sustainable Building.* Colorado: The Rocky Mountain Institute, 1995.

Bateson, Gregory. *Mind and Nature: A Necessary Unity.* New York: E. P. Dutton, 1979.

Bayes, Kenneth. *Living Architecture.* New York: Anthroposophic Press, 1994.

Beckett, H. E., and J. A. Godfrey. *Windows.* London: Crosby Lockwood Staple, 1974.

Behnisch, Günter. "Plenary Chamber Complex in Bonn," Firm literature from Behnisch & Partners (October 1994): 3.

Berry, Thomas. *The Dream of the Earth.* San Francisco: Sierra Club Books, 1988.

Bookchin, Murray. "An Outline for an Ecological Politics." In *Futures by Design,* edited by Doug Aberley, 43–49. Philadelphia: New Society Publishers, 1994.

Bower, David, and Steve Chapple. *Let the Mountains Talk, Let the Rivers Run: A Call to Those Who Would Save the Earth.* New York: HarperCollins Publishers, 1995.

Brainard, George C. "The Future Is Now: Implications of the Effect of Light on Hormones, Brain & Behavior." *Journal of Healthcare Design* 7. Internet. Available from http://www.healthdesign.org/library/jounal/journal1/j77.htm.

Brainard, George, et al. "Architectural Lighting: Balancing Biological Effects with Utility Costs." In *The Biologic Effects of Light,* edited by M. R. Holick and E. G. Jung, 169–185. New York: Walter de Gruyter & Co., 1994.

Brand, Stuart. *How Buildings Learn.* New York: Penguin Books, 1994.

Breeding, David. *Surveying Office Illumination.* Internet. Available from http://www.meadhatcher.com.

Brown, Lester R., editor. *State of the World.* New York: W.W. Norton & Co., 1996.

Brown, Lester R., Hal Kane, and Ed Ayres, editors. *Vital Signs 1993.* New York: W.W. Norton & Co., 1993.

Browning, William. "Knock on Brick." *Progressive Architecture* 74, no. 3 (February 1993): 80–81.

Bruenig, John. *See the Light: Good Lighting Balances Sources.* Internet. Available from http://www.meadhatcher.com.

Burroughs, John. *Complete Writings of John Burroughs,* edited by Wake-Robin. New York: W. H. Wise, 1924.

———. In *The Soul of the World,* edited by Phil Cousineau. San Francisco: HarperCollins, 1993.

———. *Light of Day: Religious Discussions and Criticisms from the Naturalists Point of View.* Boston: Houghton Mifflin & Co., 1900.

Button, David, and Brian Pye, editors. *Glass in Building.* Oxford: Butterworth Architecture, 1993.

Campbell, S. S., et al. "Light Treatment for Sleep Disorders, Consensus Report, III. Alerting and Activating Effects." *Journal of Biological Rhythms* 10, no. 2 (June 1995): 129–132.

Capra, Fritjof. *The Turning Point: Science, Society, and the Rising Culture.* New York: Simon & Schuster, 1982.

Carlgren, Frans. *Rudolph Steiner and Anthroposophy,* translated by Joan Rudel and Siegfried Rudel. London: Rudolf Steiner Press, 1979.

Carmody, John. *Residential Windows: A Guide to New Technologies and Energy Performance.* New York: W.W. Norton, 1996.

Catton, William R. Jr. *Overshoot: The Ecological Basis of Revolutionary Change.* Urbana: University of Illinois Press, 1982.

Clark, Roger H., and Michael Pause. *Precedents in Architecture.* New York: Van Nostrand Reinhold, 1985.

Clery, Val, et al. *Windows.* New York: Penguin Books, 1979.

Coates, Gary J. *Erik Asmussen, Architect.* Stockholm: Byggförlaget, 1997.

Coates, Gary J., and Susanne Siepl-Coates. "New Design Technologies: Healing Architecture—A Case Study of the Vidarkliniken." *Journal of Healthcare Design* 7. Internet. Available from http://www.healthdesign.org/library/journal/journal8/j817.htm.

Coffin, Christine Johnson. "Thick Buildings." *Places* 9, no. 3 (winter 1995): 70–75.

Cole, Ray, and Nils Larsson. *GBC '98 Assessment Manual,* vol. 2, *Office Buildings.* Vancouver, B.C.: School of Architecture at the University of British Columbia and CANMET Energy Technology Centre at the Natural Resources Canada, 1998.

Cook, Jeffrey. "A Post-industrial Culture of Regionalism." In *Critical Regionalism: The Pomona Meetings Proceedings,* edited by Spyros Amourgis, 164–180. Pomona, Calif.: College of Environmental Design, California Polytechnic University, 1991.

Cottom-Winslow, Margaret. *Environmental Design: Architecture and Technology.* Glen Cove, N.Y.: PBC International, 1995.

Cousineau, Phil. Introduction to *The Soul of the World,* edited by Phil Cousineau. New York: HarperCollins Publishers, 1993.

Crosbie, Michael. "Desert Shield." *Architecture* 80, no. 5 (May 1991): 76–81, 142.

Dawson, Layla. "Light Spirited." *Design Review* 197, no. 1175 (January 1995): 20–21.

Day, Christopher. *Places of the Soul.* Northamptonshire, England: Thorsons Publishing Group, 1990.

Dillard, Annie. *Teaching a Stone to Talk.* New York: Harper & Row, 1982.

Dillon, David. "Drama of Nature and Form." *Architecture* 77, no. 5 (May 1988): 148–153.

Eastman, C. I. et al. "Light Treatment for Sleep Disorders: Consensus Report, VI. Shift Work." *Journal of Biological Rhythms* 10, no. 2 (June 1995): 157–164.

Ecological Design Institute. "EDI's Solar Living Center Project Team." Real Goods Trading Corp. Internet. Available from http://www.realgoods.com/slc/design/building.htm.

Elgin, Duane. *Voluntary Simplicity: Toward a Way of Life That Is Outwardly Simple, Inwardly Rich,* rev. ed. New York: William Morrow & Co., 1993.

Energy Efficient and Renewable Energy Division (EERE), U.S. Department of Energy, 1997. 1998 Budget Briefing. Internet. Available from SEIA homepage at http://www.ecn.nl/eii/homepgnl/eii_138.html.

Erwine, Barbara. "A View to the Future." *Lighting Design + Application* 26, no. 2 (February 1996): 34–38.

Ewen, Stewart. "Waste a Lot, Want a Lot." In *Learning to Listen to the Land,* edited by Bill Willers, 183–194. Washington, D.C.: Island Press, 1991.

Faedda, G. L., et al. "Seasonal Mood Disorders: Patterns of Seasonal Recurrence in Mania and Depression." *Archives of General Psychiatry* 50 (1993): 17–23.

Gallin, P. F. et al. "Ophthalmologic Examination of Patients with Seasonal Affective Disorder, Before and After Bright Light Therapy." *American Journal of Ophthalmology* 119, no. 2 (1995): 202–210.

Gardner, Carl, and Barry Hannaford. *Lighting Design.* N.Y.: John Wiley & Sons, 1993.

Gendler, Ruth. *Changing Light: The Eternal Cycle of Night and Day.* New York: HarperCollins Publishers, 1991.

Giorgi, Manolo de. "Glenn Murcutt: House at Moruya (NSW), Australia." *Domus,* no. 691 (February 1988): 68–75.

Giurgola, Romaldo, and Jaimini Mehta. *Louis I. Kahn.* Boulder, Colo.: Westview Press, 1975.

Goethe, Johann Wolfgang von. *Theory of Colours,* translated by Charles Lock Eastlake. Cambridge, Mass: MIT Press, 1990.

Gradwohl, Judith. *Saving the Tropical Rain Forest.* London: Earthscan Publications Ltd., 1988.

Griffin, Fritz, and Marietta Millet. "Shady Aesthetics." *Journal of Architectural Education* 37, no. 3 (spring–summer 1984): 43–60.

Grudin, Robert. *Time and the Art of Living.* New York: Ticknor & Fields, 1982.

Gutman, Robert. "The Social Function of the Built Environment." In *The Mutual Interaction of People and Their Built Environment,* edited by Amos Rapoport, 37–49. Paris: Mouton Publishers, 1976.

Gyatso, Tenzin. In *The Soul of the World,* edited by Phil Cousineau. San Francisco: HarperCollins, 1993.

Haeckel, Ernst Heinrich Philipp August. *Wonders of Life: A Popular Study of Biological Philosophy.* New York and London: Harper & Brothers, 1905.

Hanh, Thich Nhat. "Love in Action." In *The Soul of Nature,* edited by M. Tobias and Georgianne Cowan, 123–136. New York: Penguin Books, 1996.

———. *The Sun My Heart.* Berkeley: Parallax Press, 1988.

Hathaway, Hargreaves, Thompson, and Novitsky. *A Study into the Effects of Light on Children of Elementary School Age—A case of daylight robbery.* Policy and Planning Branch, Planning and Information Services Division, Alberta Education, January 1992.

Hawken, Paul. *The Ecology of Commerce: A Declaration of Sustainability.* New York: HarperCollins, 1993.

Hawkes, Dean. *Environmental Tradition: Studies in the Architecture of Environment.* London: E & FN Spon, 1996.

Hedge, Alan. *Indoor Air Quality and "Sick" Building Syndrome in Offices.* Internet. Available from http://www.meadhatcher.com.

Hertzberger, Herman. *Lessons for Students in Architecture.* Rotterdam: Utgeverji 010, 1991.

Herzog, Thomas. *Thomas Herzog: Bauten 1978–1992, Buildings.* Stuttgart: Hatje Verlag, 1993.

Hill, Laura Newland. "Problem Definition: Sick Building Syndrome." *Seminar in Risk Communications.* Internet. Available from http://funnelweb.utcc.utk.edu.

Hix, John. *The Glass House.* London, England: Phaidon Press Ltd., 1974.

Holthaus, Gary H. *Circling Back.* Salt Lake City: Gibbs M. Smith, Inc., 1984.

Hough, Michael. *Out of Place: Restoring Identity to the Regional Landscape.* New Haven: Yale University Press, 1990.

Humm, Othmar, and Peter Toggweiler. *Photovoltaics in Architecture.* Basel: Birkhäuser Verlag, 1993.

Jackaway, Adam, and David Greene. "PowerGen in the Light of Day." *The Architects' Journal* (14 March 1996): 46–47.

———. "Shedding Light on Ionica." *The Architects' Journal* (28 March 1996): 51–53.

Jackson, John Brinckerhoff. *A Sense of Place, a Sense of Time.* New Haven: Yale University Press, 1994.

Jackson, Wes. *Becoming Native to This Place.* Lexington: University Press of Kentucky, 1994.

Jahn, Graham. *Contemporary Australian Architecture.* Australia: Gordon and Breach Arts International, 1994.

Jahrbuch für Licht und Architektur. Berlin: Ernst & Sohn, 1992.

Joffe, R. T. et al. "Light Visor Treatment for Seasonal Affective Disorder: A Multicenter Study." *Psychiatry Research* 46, no. 1 (1993): 29–39.

Kahn, Louis I. *Light Is the Theme: Louis I. Kahn and the Kimbell Art Museum: Comments on Architecture,* compiled by Nell E. Johnson. Fort Worth, Tex.: Kimbell Art Foundation, 1975.

———. *Louis I. Kahn: Talks with Students.* Houston, Tex., 1969.

Kawneer Company, Inc. 1600 PowerWall Product Literature, Form No. 96-1268, Kawneer Company, Inc., 1996.

Knowles, Ralph. "For Those Who Spend Time in a Place." *Places* 8, no. 2 (fall 1992): 42–43.

Kohlmaier, Georg, and Barna von Sartory. *Houses of Glass.* Cambridge, Mass.: MIT Press, 1981.

Lam, Dr. Raymond. Department of Psychiatry, Vancouver Hospital and Health Sciences Center. "Seasonal Affective Disorder." *Current Opinion in Psychiatry,* January 1994. Internet. Available from http://www.mentalhealt . . . k/p4Osad.html#Head_10.

Lam, William M. C. *Sunlighting as Formgivers for Architecture.* New York: Van Nostrand Reinhold, 1986.

Lamarre, L. "Lighting the Office Environment." *Electric Power Research Journal* (October 1996): 16–39.

Lawrence Berkeley National Laboratory, Environmental Energy Technologies Division. "Aerogel: Energy-Efficient Material for Buildings." Internet. Available from http://cande.lbl.gov/CBS/NEWSLETTER/NL8/Aerogel.html, Internet.

Le Corbusier. *Le Corbusier Talks with Students from the Schools of Architecture,* translated by Pierre Chase. New York: Orion Press, 1961.

———. *Le Corbusier: As Artist, as Writer,* translated by Haakon Chevalier. Neuchâtel, Switzerland: Editions du Griffon, 1970.

Leslie, Russell. "Listening to Lighting's Music." *Lighting Design and Applications* 31, no. 3 (March 1991): 8–12.

Lewy, A. J., et al. "Light Suppresses Melatonin Secretion in Humans." *Science* 21 (1980): 1267–1269.

Lindheim, Roslyn. "New Design Parameters for Healthy Places." *Places* 2, no. 4 (1985): 17–27.

Linn, Charles. "Jewel Box." *Architectural Record* 182, no. 9 (September 1994): 62–67.

Logsdon, Robert M. "The Human Side: Understanding the Application of Lazure Painting Techniques." *Journal of Healthcare Design* 7. Internet. Available from http://www.healthdesign.org/library/journal/journal7/j728.html.

Lopez, Barry. *Arctic Dreams: Imagination and Desire in a Northern Landscape.* Toronto: Bantam Books, 1986.

Lovins, Amory, and Hunter Lovins. *Brittle Power.* Andover, Mass.: Brick House Publishing Co., 1982.

Lyle, John Tillman. *Regenerative Design for Sustainable Development.* New York: John Wiley & Sons, 1994

Lynch, Kevin. *Site Design.* Cambridge, Mass.: MIT Press, 1984.

———. "The Waste of Place." *Places* 6, no. 2 (winter 1990): 10–23.

Mark, Robert. *Light, Wind, and Structure.* Boston: Massachusetts Institute of Technology, 1990.

McCleary, Peter. "Some Characteristics of a New Concept of Technology." *Journal of Architectural Education* 42, no. 1 (February 1988): 4–9.

McDonough, William. *Hannover Principles.* Internet. Available from http://repont.tcc.virginia.edu/classes/tcc315/Resources/ALM/Environment/hannover.html.

McLuhan, T. C. *The Way of the Earth*. New York: Simon & Schuster, 1994.

Meyer, Scherer & Rockcastle. Firm literature on Sahara West Library and Art Museum, Minneapolis, Minn.

Milbrath, Lester. *Envisioning a Sustainable Society: Learning Our Way Out*. Albany: State University of New York Press, 1989.

Millet, Marietta. *Light Revealing Architecture*. New York: Van Nostrand Reinhold, 1996.

Mitler, Merrill, et al. "Catastrophes, Sleep, and Public Policy: Consensus Report." *Sleep* 11 (1988): 100–109.

Moore, Fuller. *Concepts and Practice of Architectural Daylighting*. New York: Van Nostrand Reinhold, 1985.

Moore, Thomas. "Ecology: Sacred Homemaking." In *The Soul of Nature: Celebrating the Spirit of the Earth,* edited by Michael Tobias, 137–144. New York: Penguin Books, 1996.

Mumford, Lewis. *Art and Technics*. New York: Columbia University Press, 1952.

———. *The Myth of the Machine*. New York: Harcourt, Brace & World, Inc., 1967.

———. *Architecture as a Home for Man*. New York: Architectural Record Books, 1975.

NASA Clean Air Study—Sick Building Syndrome. "Hydroculture: The Cure for Sick Building Syndrome. Internet. Available from http://.interurban.com/hydroponics/articles/tap.html.

———. "What Is Sick Building Syndrome?" Internet. Available from http://www.zone10.com/Tech/NASA/SICK_BLD.htm.

National Science Foundation Center for Biological Timing. Internet. Available from http://www.cbt.virginia.edu/tutorial/REFERENCES.html.

Neumann, Tali. "Design Trends: Creating a Healing Healthcare Environment." *Journal of Healthcare Design* 7. Internet. Available from http://www.healthdesign.org/library/journal/journal7/j712.htm.

Nicklas, Michael H., and Gary B. Bailey. "Analysis of the Performance of Students in Daylit Schools." In *Proceedings of the 22st National Passive Solar Conference*. Boulder, Colo.: American Solar Energy Society, 1996.

Norberg-Schulz, Christian. *Intentions in Architecture*. Oslo: Universitetsforlaget, 1963.

———. *Genius Loci*. New York: Rizzoli, 1980.

———. *The Concept of Dwelling: On the Way to Figurative Architecture*. New York: Rizzoli, 1985.

Odum, Eugene Pleasants. *Fundamentals of Ecology.* Philadelphia: Saunders, 1953.

———. *Ecology and Our Endangered Life-Support Systems.* Sunderland, Mass.: Sinauer Associates, 1989.

Orr, David. *Ecological Literacy: Education and the Transition to a Postmodern World.* Albany: State University of New York Press, 1992.

Osteoporosis and Related Bone Diseases National Resource Center, National Osteoporosis Foundation. Washington, D.C. Internet. Available from http:www.osteo.org.

Owen, Graham, editor. *Architecture Canada: The Governor General's Awards for Architecture.* Ottawa: Royal Architectural Institute of Canada, 1994.

Papademetriou, Peter C. "Blind Trust." *Progressive Architecture* 65, no. 3 (March 1984): 86–90.

Paradis, Alan, and Daniel S. Shugar. "Photovoltaic Building Materials." *Solar Today* 8, no. 3 (May–June 1994): 34–37.

Pepchinski, Mary. "RWE AG Hochhaus Essen, Germany." *Architectural Record* 185, no. 6 (June 1997): 144–151.

Photo Therapeutics References. Internet. Available from http://www.phothera.com/ptref.htm.

Physician's Desk Reference: Family Guide Encyclopedia of Medical Care. Internet. Available from http://www.healthsquare.com/hspage2.htm.

Postel, Sandra. "Carrying Capacity: Earth's Bottom Line" In *State of the World 1994,* edited by Lester Brown, et al., 13–19. New York: W.W. Norton & Co., 1994.

Predock, Antoine. "Rio Grande Nature Center." *Places* 4, no. 4 (1987): 24–25.

Quantrill, Malcolm. *Alvar Aalto, a Critical Study.* New York: Schocken Books, 1983.

Rae, Mark S., editor. *Lighting Handbook,* 8th edition. New York: Illuminating Engineering Society of North America, 1995.

Rapoport, Amos. *House Form and Culture.* Englewood Cliffs, N.J.: Prentice-Hall, 1969.

Rapoport, Amos, editor. *The Mutual Interaction of People and Their Built Environment.* Paris: Mouton Publishers, 1976.

Rea, Mark S., editor. *Lighting Handbook.* New York: Illuminating Engineering Society of North America, 1995.

Reynolds, John. Panel discussion at the "Window Technology Session," *20th National Passive Solar Conference,* American Solar Energy Society, Minneapolis, Minn., July 1995.

Riley, Terence, exhibit organizer. *Light Construction.* New York: Museum of Modern Art, 1995.

Roeder, Craig. "Environmental Design Technology: Using Color & Light as Medicine." *Journal of Healthcare Design* 8. Internet. Available from http://www.healthdesign.org/library/journal/journal8/j821.htm.

Rosenking, Mark R., et al. "Crew Factors in Flight Operations IX: Effects of Planned Cockpit Rest on Crew Performance and Alertness in Long-Haul Operations." In *NASA Technical Memorandum No. 108839:* Moffett Field, Calif.: Ames Research Center, 1994.

Rosenthal, N. E., et al. "A Multicenter Study of the Light Visor for Seasonal Affective Disorder: No Difference in Efficacy Found Between Two Different Intensities." *Neuropsychopharmacology* 8, no. 2 (1993): 151–60.

Rosenthal, N. E., et al. "Seasonal Affective Disorder: A Description of the Syndrome and Preliminary Findings with Light Therapy." *Archives of General Psychiatry* 41 (1984): 72–80.

Rothenberg, David. *Hand's End: Technology and the Limits of Nature.* Berkeley, Calif.: University of California Press, 1993.

Royal Architectural Institute of Canada. "Seabird Island School, Patkau Architects." In *Architecture Canada: The Governor General's Awards for Architecture,* 59–63. Ottawa: Royal Architectural Institute of Canada, 1992.

Ruusuvuori, Aarno, editor. *Alvar Aalto, 1898–1976.* Helsinki: Museum of Finnish Architecture, 1978.

Scherer, Jeff. *Changing Workplace: Flexible for the Mobile Worker.* Meyer, Scherer & Rockcastle firm literature, Minneapolis, Minn.

Schildt, Göran. *Alvar Aalto: The Mature Years.* New York: Rizzoli International Publications, 1989.

Schumacher, E. F. *Small Is Beautiful.* New York: Harper & Row, 1973.

Scully, Vincent Joseph. *Frank Lloyd Wright.* New York: G. Braziller, 1960.

———. *Louis I. Kahn.* New York: G. Braziller, 1962.

———. *Architecture: The Natural and the Manmade.* New York: St. Martin's Press, 1991.

Shepard, Paul. *Man in the Landscape: A Historic View of the Esthetics of Nature.* New York: Knopf, 1967.

Shlain, Leonard. *Arts & Physics: Parallel Visions in Space, Time, & Light.* New York: William Morrow & Co., 1991.

Siegel, Bernie S. "Healthcare Design in the Next Century." *Journal of Healthcare Design* 7. Internet. Available from http://www .healthdesign.org/library/journal/journal7/jj72.htm.

Skolimowski, Henryk. *A Sacred Place to Dwell: Living with Reverence upon the Earth.* Rockport Mass: Element Books Ltd., 1993.

Slessor, Catherine. *Eco-tech: Sustainable Architecture and High Technology.* New York: Thames and Hudson, 1997.

Smith, Richard. "Light and Health: A Broad Overview." *Lighting Design + Application* 26, no. 2 (February 1986): 32–40.

Solar Energy Industries (SEIA) Fact Sheets. Internet. SEIA Homepage, 1995. Available from http://www.ecn.nl/eii/homepgnl/ eii_138.html.

Spence, Rory. "At Bingie Point." *Architectural Review* 179, no. 1068 (February 1986): 70–75.

————. "Nature in the City." *Architectural Review* 189, no. 1134 (August 1991): 43–48.

Stephen Holl Architects. Firm literature on the Chapel of St. Ignatius, New York, New York.

Stonehouse, Roger. "Dwelling with the Environment." Paper presented at the *Architecture + Environment Conference,* California State University Polytechnic, Pomona, October 1994.

Suzuki, David, and Peter Knudtsun. *Wisdom of the Elders: Sacred Native Stories of Nature.* New York: Bantam Books, 1993.

Tanizaki, Jun'ichirō . *In Praise of Shadows.* New Haven: Leete's Island Books, 1977.

Terman, et al. "Seasonal Symptom Patterns in New York: Patients and Population." In *Seasonal Affective Disorder,* edited by C. Thompson and T. Silverstone, 77–95. London: Clinical Neuroscience Publishers, 1989.

Thayer, Burke Miller. "A Passive Solar University Center." *Solar Today* 10, no. 2 (March–April 1996): 37.

Thayer, Robert. *Gray World, Green Heart: Technology, Nature, and the Sustainable Landscape.* New York: John Wiley & Sons, 1994.

Thomas, Reandall. *Environmental Design: An Introduction for Architects and Engineers.* London: E & FN Spon, 1996.

Thoreau, Henry David. *In Wildness Is the Preservation of the World,* selections and photographs by Eliot Porter. San Francisco: Sierra Club, 1962.

————. *The Selected Works of Thoreau,* revised by Walter Harding. Boston: Houghton Mifflin, 1975.

———. *Clear Sky, Pure Light: Encounters with Henry David Thoreau,* compiled and edited by Christopher Childs. Lincoln, Mass: Penmaen Press, 1978.

Tobias, Michael, and Georgianne Cowan, editors. *The Soul of Nature.* New York: Penguin Books, 1996.

Todd, John, and Nancy Jack Todd. *Tomorrow Is Our Permanent Address.* New York: Harper & Row, 1980.

Todd, John. *Living Machines for Pure Water: Sewage as Resource.* Internet. Ocean Arks International Homepage, 1995. Available from http://www.earthbase.org/guests/oai/oailivmachjt.html.

Todd, Nancy Jack, and John Todd. *Bioshelters, Ocean Arks, City Farming: Ecology as the Basis of Design.* San Francisco: Sierra Club Books, 1984.

Tuan, Yi-Fu. *Topophilia.* New York: Columbia University Press, 1974.

———. *Passing Strange and Wonderful: Aesthetics, Nature, and Culture.* Washington, D.C.: Island Press, 1993.

Tyng, Alexandra. *Beginnings: Louis I. Kahn's Philosophy of Architecture.* New York: John Wiley & Sons, 1984.

United States Environmental Protection Agency, Office of Air and Radiation, Indoor Environments Division. *An Office Building Occupant's Guide to Indoor Air Quality.* EPA-402-K-97-003. Washington, D.C.: EPA Office of Air and Radiation, October 1997.

———. *Indoor Air Facts No. 4* (revised). Washington, D.C.: EPA Office of Air and Radiation, April 1991.

———. *Targeting Indoor Air Pollution.* EPA Document #400-R-92-012, Washington, D.C.: EPA Office of Air and Radiation, March 1993.

University of British Columbia/Vancouver Hospital and Health Sciences Center Mood Disorders Clinic. Information about Seasonal Affective Disorder (SAD). Internet. Available from http://www.psychiatry.ubc.ca/mood/md_sad.html.

Updike, John. "The Music Room." In *The Great American Short Story.* New York, 1997. Quoted by Gary Holthaus, 178. Salt Lake City: Gibbs M. Smith, Inc., 1984.

Vale, Brenda and Robert. *Green Architecture: Design for an Energy-Conscious Future.* Boston: Little, Brown & Company, 1991.

Van der Ryn, Sim, and Stuart Cowan. *Ecological Design.* Washington, D.C.: Island Press, 1996.

Venolia, Carol. *Healing Environments*. Berkeley, Calif.: Celestial Arts, 1988.

Vischer, Jacqueline. "The Psychology of Daylighting." *Architecture* 76, no. 1 (June 1987): 109–111.

Vitruvius, Pollio. *Vitruvius: The Ten Books on Architecture*. Translated by Morris Hicky Morgan. New York: Dover Publications, 1960.

Wells, Malcolm. *Gentle Architecture*. New York: McGraw-Hill, Inc., 1981.

Willers, Bill, editor. *Learning to Listen to the Land*. Washington, D.C.: Island Press, 1991.

Wirth, Timothy. *Second Conference of the Parties Framework Convention on Climate Change*. Geneva, Switzerland, July 17, 1996. Internet. Solar Energy Industries Association (SEIA) Homepage. Available from http://www.ecn.nl/eii/homepgnl/ eii_138.html.

Wordsworth, William. *The Complete Poetical Works of William Wordsworth*. New York: Thomas Y. Crowell & Co., 1892.

World Commission on Environment and Development. *Our Common Future*. New York: Oxford University Press, 1987.

World Conservation Union. *The Botanic Garden Conservation Report*. Switzerland: World Wide Fund for Nature, 1989.

Wright, Frank Lloyd. *The Natural House*. New York: Horizon Press, 1954.

———. *Frank Lloyd Wright, Collected Writings,* edited by Bruce Brooks Pfeiffer. New York: Rizzoli, 1992.

Wurman, Richard Saul. *What Will Be Has Always Been: The Words of Louis I. Kahn*. New York: Rizzoli International Publications, Inc., 1986.

Wyon, D. P. "The Ergonomics of Healthy Buildings: Overcoming Barriers to Productivity." In *IAQ '91,* 449–452. Washington, D.C.: ASHRAE, 1991.

Yannas, Simos. *Solar Energy and Housing Design,* vol. 2. London: Architectural Association, 1994.

Yeang, Ken. *Designing with Nature: The Ecological Basis for Architectural Design*. New York: McGraw-Hill, 1995.

Zeiher, Laura C. *The Ecology of Architecture: A Complete Guide to Creating the Environmentally Conscious Building*. New York: Whitney Library of Design, 1996.

Index

437

About the Author

MARY GUZOWSKI is an associate professor of architecture at the University of Minnesota and the director of the university's Daylighting Lab. She is interested in emerging theories and practices of ecologically responsive design and their significance for architecture and human experience.